Secularism, Islam and public intellectuals in contemporary France

Manchester University Press

Secularism, Islam and public intellectuals in contemporary France

NADIA KIWAN

Manchester University Press

Copyright © Nadia Kiwan 2020

The right of Nadia Kiwan to be identified as the author of this work has been asserted by her in accordance with the Copyright, Designs and Patents Act 1988.

Published by Manchester University Press
Oxford Road, Manchester M13 9PL
www.manchesteruniversitypress.co.uk

British Library Cataloguing- in- Publication Data
A catalogue record for this book is available from the British Library

ISBN 978 1 7849 9412 9 hardback
ISBN 978 1 5261 6079 9 paperback

First published 2020
Published in paperback in 2022

The publisher has no responsibility for the persistence or accuracy of URLs for any external or third- party internet websites referred to in this book, and does not guarantee that any content on such websites is, or will remain, accurate or appropriate.

Typeset by Newgen Publishing UK

Contents

Notes on the text	vii
Acknowledgements	viii
Introduction	1
1 Abdelwahab Meddeb: post-foundational Islam	20
2 Malek Chebel: Enlightenment Islam	52
3 Leïla Babès: spirituality, affect and women	85
4 Dounia Bouzar: public intellectuals as policy experts in times of crisis	107
5 Abdennour Bidar: existentialist Islam as intercultural translation	129
Conclusion	162
Bibliography	171
Index	181

Notes on the text

All citations from French published sources have been translated from French to English and are provided alongside the French original. The reference details for the French original appear in parentheses before the English translation. These translations are my own unless otherwise stated.

Acknowledgements

This book bears the fruit of a long-term project which has involved me in discussions with many colleagues, both here in Aberdeen and at a range of institutions across the UK, Ireland and France. I would like to thank those colleagues and students who responded so carefully to the various conference, departmental and seminar papers which all fed into this book. Their questions, comments and remarks were invaluable to me as I focused on refining my thinking and approach. In particular, I would like to thank my colleagues at the University of Aberdeen for their encouragement as I developed my ideas at an early stage of the project. I am also grateful to the Research Committee of the School of Language, Literature, Music and Visual Culture at the University of Aberdeen for the two periods of research leave which I was granted in order to develop the book proposal and complete the first draft of the manuscript. The team at Manchester University Press has been immensely supportive and helpful throughout and I am very grateful to them for their enthusiasm, guidance and professionalism from the outset. My thanks also go to the anonymous readers for their extremely useful suggestions on how to improve the proposal and manuscript. Finally, I would like to express my gratitude to my family for their unconditional support, faith and abiding patience throughout the duration of this project. I dedicate this book to them.

Introduction

Challenging the narrative of French Islam as 'controversy'

Islam in France is generally regarded as a political 'issue'. Indeed, most of the scholarly and public debates about Islam in contemporary France over the last thirty years have concentrated on the supposedly 'antagonistic' relationship between France, Islam and its Muslims, with a tendency to focus either on the headscarf or on the growth of radical Islamist ideologies since the late 1980s. Whilst the headscarf debates have centred on Muslim women, the debates about Islamist violence have mainly focused on men. The academic literature on the headscarf polemic is vast and includes well-known titles such as Bowen's *Why the French Don't Like Headscarves* (2007), Gaspard's and Khosrokhavar's *Le Foulard et la République* (1995), Keaton's *Muslim Girls and the Other France* (2006), Kemp's *Voices and Veils* (2010), Laborde's *Critical Republicanism* (2008), Scott's *The Politics of the Veil* (2007) and Winter's *Hijab and the Republic* (2008). The literature on Islamist ideologies and violence is equally extensive, including works such as Burgat's *L'Islamisme à l'heure d'Al-Qaida* (2010), Kepel's *Jihâd, expansion et déclin de l'islamisme* (2000), Khosrokhavar's *Radicalisation* (2014) and Roy's *Généalogie de l'islamisme* (2011), to name a few. Beyond scholarly literature, there has been a lot of coverage in the media and in non-academic publications, more often than not denouncing the veil such as in essayist Chahdortt Djavann's *Bas les voiles!* (2006) or journalist Leila Djitli's *Lettre à ma fille qui veut porter le voile* (2004). The same can be said with regard to violence and Islamism, with titles such as *Pourquoi l'islamisme séduit-il?* (2015) by journalist Mohammed Sifaoui or *Une France Soumise* edited by Georges Bensoussan (2017) becoming widely read 'popular current affairs' interventions on the issue. The ubiquity of both these themes – veil and violence – clearly demonstrate a great sense of anxiety about Islam and Muslims in contemporary France.

Indeed, the 1989 headscarf *affaire*, when three pupils were suspended from a *collège* (middle school) in Creil for refusing to remove their veil, became the first in a series of high-profile polemics about the signification of the headscarf and how it should be 'managed' in a secular state such as France. The issue was temporarily resolved in 1989 when the then socialist *Ministre de l'Éducation* Lionel Jospin argued that the headscarf should be dealt with on a case-by-case basis, a position that was backed up by the highest court in the land, the *Conseil d'État*, which argued that headscarves were not, in themselves, contradictory to the principles of *laïcité*. However, the controversy resurfaced in 1994 when the centrist *Ministre de l'Éducation* François Bayrou decreed that 'ostentatious' signs of religious belief would be banned in schools. Then followed the 2003–2004 polemic over the headscarves of the Lévy sisters at a *lycée* (high school) in Aubervilliers, which led to the establishment of the Stasi Commission to examine the application of the principles of *laïcité*. A law was subsequently passed in 2004 explicitly banning the wearing of religious signs or items of clothing which clearly denote a pupil's religious affiliation in middle schools and high schools.[1] The next manifestation of the headscarf debate came in 2010 when a new polemic about the *burqa*, *niqab* or full-face veil came to the fore, once again leading to legislation banning full-face coverings in public spaces.[2] The two latest iterations of the quarrel about Muslim women and their clothing in 2016 and 2017 have taken the form of a heated public discussion over the rights of female university students to wear the veil and the issue of the whether the *burkini* should be allowed on France's beaches. All of these *affaires* demonstrate a deep malaise about the visibility of Islam in contemporary France, a visibility which is focused on Muslim women's bodies. This unease concerns the academic, political, civil, legal and media spheres; in that sense, the veil has become one of the totemic issues through which contemporary French society thinks about its national identity in the late twentieth and early twenty-first centuries.

The other totemic issue underpinning how French society thinks about its relationship with itself and with Islam, namely Islamist violence, can be attributed to the fact that France has been the target of repeated waves of terrorist attacks, perpetrated in the name of Islam and extending back to the mid-1990s when, most notably, the Algerian *Groupe Islamique Armé* carried out attacks in Paris, Lyon and Lille. The most recent mass terrorist attacks perpetrated by Al-Qaida and ISIS, which targeted *Charlie Hebdo*'s journalists and illustrators in January 2015 and the general public in the November 2015 Paris and July 2016 *Fête Nationale* Nice atrocities have further fed into a broader narrative which suggests that the issue of Islam in contemporary France is first and foremost a highly sensitive and conflictual one. The collective trauma of the attacks themselves, the establishment of a state of emergency in November 2015 and a parliamentary bill in 2016 to strip dual nationals of their French nationality if convicted of terror charges have, to a significant extent, reflected a sombre and tense socio-political climate in France.[3]

Against such a troubled backdrop, however, this book looks at the ways in which certain prominent French Muslims seek to articulate a vision of multi-faith co-existence via a universalist notion of *le vivre ensemble*. The expression *le vivre ensemble* became a major watchword during the Hollande presidency (2012–2017). It was initially regarded as Hollande's attempt to mark a distinction from President Sarkozy's hostile approach to immigration and diversity (Tissot 2014). However, it has been in widespread political usage since at least the 1990s, as public policies have attempted to address growing problems of urban segregation and violence. More recently, *le vivre ensemble* has taken on a more explicitly inter-faith signification, illustrated by a speech given by President Hollande in February 2015, shortly after the *Charlie Hebdo* attacks, in which he stated that 'La laïcité n'est pas négociable car elle nous permet de vivre ensemble' (Hollande 2015) (Secularism is not negotiable since it allows us to live together). It could be argued that given the twin shadows cast by the repeated headscarf debates and Islamist terrorism incidents, scholarly research on the theme of Islam in France has paid scant attention to those Muslim voices which consistently argue that Islam should not be regarded as being in conflict with the Republic, and that Islam and *laïcité* are and should be reconciled since *laïcité* guarantees not only the separation of the State and religion but also the freedom of religious conscience. I refer to these voices as 'secular Muslim voices' and they emanate from a small number of prolific and engaged intellectuals who actively seek, via their publications, public interventions and media appearances, to reconcile *islamité* and *laïcité* in twenty-first century France. It should be noted that although many of the figures who feature in this book engage with the Quran and Islamic thought, my approach is based on a contextualised examination of what *they* claim about Islam and Muslims. As such, I do not approach Islamic writings and thought as an Islamic Studies scholar might do. Rather, my study should be considered as a Francophone Studies analysis of the intellectual and political discourses about Islam and Muslims which structure the contemporary French public sphere.

Shifting understandings of *laïcité*

The French word *laïcité* is often translated into English as secularism, but as political scientist Olivier Roy points out, there is a key difference between secularism or secularisation and *laïcité*, since whereas secularisation refers to a process whereby society emancipates itself from the notion of the sacred, without necessarily rejecting religion per se, *laïcité* implies the 'expulsion' of religion from the public sphere by the State as a result of specific legislation (Roy 2005: pp. 29–30). In France, this specific legislation was the 1905 law, which instituted the official separation between the Church(es) and the State.[4] Article 1 of the 1905 law states that the Republic guarantees liberty of conscience and ensures the free practice of religion in accordance with certain restrictions relating to public order. Article 2 of the 1905 law clearly states that the Republic neither recognises nor funds any religion. However, historian and sociologist Jean Baubérot points out that Article 4 of the 1905 law stipulates that the State will respect the internal regulations of all religions in the Republic (Baubérot 2012: pp. 52–53). Indeed, for Baubérot, *laïcité*, as set out in the 1905 law, was primarily about removing the Catholic Church's political power whilst at the same time promoting the freedom of religious conscience:

> La loi de 1905 est la dernière des grandes lois politiquement libérales de la IIIe République … Oui, la laïcité historique a été conflictuelle, et elle a supprimé tout aspect officiel du catholicisme (article 2 de la loi de 1905), mais c'était pour pouvoir assurer la liberté des citoyens, établir les libertés laïques qui comprennent la liberté de conscience et de culte (article 1). (Baubérot 2012: pp. 51–53)

> (The law of 1905 is the last of the great politically liberal laws of the Third Republic … Yes, historical secularism was conflictual, and it abolished all official aspects of Catholicism (article 2 of the 1905 law), but this was so as to ensure the liberty of the citizens, and to establish secular liberties which included freedom of conscience and religion (article 1).)

Despite the liberal stance of the 1905 law with regard to religious conscience, Baubérot argues that *laïcité* has been 'falsifiée', i.e. distorted and hijacked by the right and extreme right in France, as evidenced by the Islam-hostile UMP debate on *laïcité* in 2011 and the adoption of *laïcité* as a political football by Marine Le Pen's *Front National* party. For Baubérot, this 'nouvelle laïcité' has become shorthand for anti-Muslim scapegoating whereby it has been argued by politicians such as Le Pen and Sarkozy that Muslims pose a threat to the 'one and indivisible' Republic through their *communautariste* demands to wear headscarves, eat halal school meals and to build new mosques. Baubérot describes a context whereby calls to defend *laïcité* have become synonymous with what Cécile Laborde ironically calls 'le communautarisme national' (Laborde 2016) (national communitarianism). The latter is a deeply polarising political discourse which stigmatises whole swathes of the French population in its rallying cry to defend a mythical idea of a culturally, ethnically and religiously homogenous French nation. By focusing on 'secular Muslim intellectuals' in France, then, this book challenges such polarising accounts of Islam and Muslims in France, which have been ubiquitous in political and media debates for the last thirty years. The book departs from the 'clash of civilisations' approach which was revived in the aftermath of the September 11 terrorist attacks and was premised on the idea that, post-1989, the main external threat to Western societies was no longer communism but Islam, and that 'Islamic culture' was somehow inherently at odds with the supposed shared cultural and political norms of Western liberal democracies (Huntington 1998; Lewis 2002; Pipes 2003). Equally, this book departs from an approach which argues that European 'multiculturalism' has failed in the face of recent European migration patterns whereby Islam and Muslims are constructed as constituting a threat to European democratic principles and values (Joppke 2004, 2015).

Islam in Europe

Indeed, beyond France, the notion that Islam and Muslims present a challenge to European social and cultural cohesion has gained currency across a number of European countries including France, the UK, the Netherlands and Germany in the wake of 9/11, the Madrid 2004 and London 2005 bombings, the 2012 Mohammed Merah affair in France, the rise of so-called Islamic State or ISIS, the *Charlie Hebdo* massacre, followed more recently by atrocities in Paris, Brussels, Nice and Germany in 2016 and the Manchester and London attacks of 2017. As a consequence, we have witnessed in Europe a shift away from discourses and policies constructed around the accommodation of cultural and religious difference (albeit to differing degrees across EU member states) towards a consensus about the need for more assimilationist-oriented positions and policies. This is a context where, on the one hand, we see the mainstream political parties place ever greater emphasis on the importance of shared European values which are invoked through reiterative claims for liberal democracy, freedom of speech and gender equality, and on the other hand, we see the rise of nationalist and xenophobic political parties and grassroots movements such as the *Front National* in France, UKIP in the UK or *Alternative für Deutschland* and the Pegida movement in Germany.[5] The notion that it is imperative to foster shared British, French and European values is premised on a sense of threat or fear that permeates many postcolonial governments and societies with regard to their Muslim populations (Todorov 2010; Alexander 2013). This sense of threat regarding European Muslims and Islam straddles both the left and the right of the political spectrum and has been particularly heightened in the context of the global refugee crisis. The generalised anxiety about immigration and cultural diversity was also central to the debates around the UK's place in the EU and the consequent Brexit referendum in June 2016. The French presidential election in France was similarly illustrative of the growing appeal of populist, anti-Islam, anti-immigration rhetoric when the *Front National* achieved its best ever result in the presidential and legislative elections, with Marine Le Pen winning 10.6 million votes, a 33.9 per cent share of the votes in the second round of the presidential race, and the *Front National* obtaining eight seats in the *Assemblée Nationale*.[6]

Against this backdrop, my research takes as its starting point the notion of cultural complexity (Hannerz 1992; Beck 2006; Beck and Grande 2007;

Robins 2014) whereby Islam is not conceptualised as a monolithic socio-cultural system which defines the lives of Muslims (Marranci 2010). Rather, this book is concerned with how Muslim individuals define Islam in varied ways, and how they embrace a critical secularism in multi-faith and no-faith contexts, i.e. how they are active in developing new forms of civic engagement which simultaneously draw on religious and secular humanist traditions. The study of individual 'Muslim secular intellectuals' in contemporary France thus takes seriously the claim that the categories of religion and the secular are more closely intertwined than we might assume (Asad 2003; Triandafyllidou *et al.* 2011). Indeed, Asad underscores the need to recognise that the secular is 'neither singular in origin nor stable in its historical identity' (Asad 2003: p. 25). This gesture towards the notion of multiplicity leads Asad to consider how in a modern democratic polity 'everyone may live as a minority among minorities' (Asad 2003: p. 180). The 'minorities among minorities' principle resonates with this book since it foregrounds an approach which moves beyond a same–other paradigm (Watkin 2007) and which simultaneously draws on the notion of a 'cosmopolitics', as developed by Etienne Balibar (2011).

The changing figure of the French public intellectual

Intellectuals have traditionally played a major part in French public life and, as Christophe Charle argues, it is generally accepted that the idea of the public intellectual emerged around the time of the Dreyfus affair, when engaged thinkers and writers rallied round in defence of the integrity of the Jewish army captain, as exemplified by Émile Zola's *J'Accuse* open letter to the President of the Republic in January 1898 (Charle 1990). In their seminal study, historians Pascal Ory and Jean-François Sirinelli define the French intellectual as:

> *un homme du culturel, créateur ou médiateur, mis en situation d'homme du politique, producteur ou consommateur d'idéologie.* Ni une simple catégorie socioprofessionnelle, ni un simple personnage, irréductible. Il s'agira d'un *statut*, comme dans la définition sociologique, mais transcendé par une *volonté* individuelle, comme dans la définition éthique, et tourné vers un *usage* collectif. (Ory and Sirinelli 2004: p. 15; emphasis in the original)

> (*a cultural individual, a creator or mediator, a politically situated individual, a producer or consumer of ideology.* Neither simple socio-professional category, nor simply an indomitable personality. It is a *status*, as in the sociological definition, but is also transcended by individual *will*, as in the ethical sense, and geared towards a collective *purpose*.)

For Ory and Sirinelli, the individual intellectual is motivated, then, by an ethical desire to have an impact on collective issues. Indeed, as Imogen Long points out, the notion of '*engagement* of public figures in cases of injustice in the public sphere' (Long 2013: p. 1) is also central to understandings of what public intellectuals do. Shlomo Sand also argues that efforts to understand the specificity of the French public intellectual must acknowledge that 'the public sphere here is more homogenous and more centralised than in any other liberal democracy' (Sand 2018: p. 5).

However, our current era is markedly different to that of the universal, albeit left-wing intellectual, as embodied by figures such as Jean-Paul Sartre and Simone de Beauvoir (Reader 1987). Ory and Sirinelli write about the long and steady decline of the intellectual in the period following the fall of the Berlin Wall and the discrediting of communism, the rise of post-modernism and the rejection of the notion of master narrative, leading to what they refer to as 'les paradigmes perdus' (Ory and Sirinelli 2004: p. 400) (lost paradigms). So the voice of the left-wing intellectual may not be as audible as it once was; indeed, Ory and Sirinelli (and others such as Chabal 2010 and Sand 2018) discuss the emergence of a 'nouvelle droite' (new right) in the intellectual field from the 1980s onwards, as exemplified by the success of Alain Finkielkraut's *La Défaite de la pensée* in 1987 (Ory and Sirinelli 2004: pp. 400–401), whose works focus mainly on the 'decline' and fragmentation of French society, due to the 'challenges' of cultural pluralism.[7] And yet, it can also be argued that in the post-9/11 context we have witnessed the renewal of *another* type of public intellectual, whose interventions are increasingly and more optimistically focused on urgent cultural and religious divisions and how they might be overcome. Whilst in one sense the emergence of intellectuals who are motivated by cultural and identity politics simply reflects the paradigm shifts of our contemporary era, in another sense we could argue that those intellectuals who are interested in cultural struggles have *deliberately* surfaced in an attempt to actively develop an engaged response to some of the major injustices of today's world. Those injustices operate as mechanisms of exclusion when culture or religion-understood-as-culture is used to stigmatise and discriminate against certain populations, whether through increasingly restrictive global migration – the *physical* border-control regime – which in some ways is akin to a mass form of cultural apartheid, or within the fetishised and fantasised *cultural* borders of the nation state (van Houtum 2010). The intellectuals who feature in this book can therefore all be seen to intervene in ways which attempt to resist the cultural forms of exclusion in contemporary France, through their consistent demonstration that Islam has its place in a secular modern Republic.

The book will focus on a discursive and contextualised analysis of the published works and public interventions of Abdelwahab Meddeb, Malek Chebel, Leïla Babès, Dounia Bouzar and Abdennour Bidar – intellectuals who have received little scholarly attention despite being well-known figures in France. One possible explanation for the lack of scholarly attention to these individuals is the recent emergence of their work. The very existence of what we might call a 'secular Muslim intellectual field' is a relatively new phenomenon which has only emerged in the last fifteen to twenty years. In addition, the post-9/11 context has meant that most scholarship has focused on issues connected to so-called Muslim revivalism, whether in the form of the increased public visibility of the veil and burqa or in the form of 'radicalisation' and Islamism (revivalism is a misnomer since often what has taken place is the invention of new modes of religiosity and religious allegiance, rather than a revival of former practices and beliefs). Furthermore, it is possible to argue that these authors have not always all benefitted from the public acceptance and consecration that one has come to expect of the figure of the French public intellectual. Of these five thinkers, Bidar, Bouzar and Chebel have perhaps been the most visible in the French mainstream media and public policy circles. Meddeb has also had significant exposure via the highbrow radio station Radio France Culture. Babès is less well known than the other four thinkers and corresponds more closely to the figure of the university academic. However, none of these authors has the same level of visibility as the most mediatised public intellectuals such as Alain Finkielkraut, Luc Ferry or Michel Onfray. The fact that, with the exception of Bidar, none of the above intellectuals are philosophers may also have something to do with the fact that their work is not universally well known (Chebel was primarily an anthropologist and psychoanalyst, although he was also sometimes referred to as a *philosophe*). The academic discipline of Philosophy and the academic profession of *le philosophe* still enjoy a significant degree of cultural capital in contemporary France, as attested to by the myriad of programmes on radio and television which are presented and dedicated to philosophy (*Philosophies* on ARTE, *Les Nouveaux chemins de la connaissance* on Radio France Culture and *Philosophies* magazine are just a few examples of the esteem for philosophy in contemporary mainstream cultural print and broadcast media). A further reason why these individuals have not been written about extensively may be related to the fact that some of them have been regarded as being too close to the structures of power, another element which can lead to the social disqualification or relegation of the public intellectual, who as Ahearne points out, has historically been expected to speak 'truth to power' (Ahearne 2006: p. 335), that is, to be a critic of governments and status quo power structures. Bidar, for instance, is a member of the *Observatoire de la laïcité* and a *chargé de mission sur la laïcité* for the *Ministère de l'Éducation nationale*. The *Observatoire de la laïcité*, set up in 2013, is a publicly funded consultative commission which advises the French government on how to ensure the respect of the principle of *laïcité* in public life.[8] Furthermore, between 1991 and 2009, Bouzar was a researcher based at the *Ministère de la Justice* and formerly a member of the *Conseil français du culte musulman*. She is also a member of the *Observatoire de la laïcité* and worked in partnership with the *Ministère de l'Intérieur* on a 'deradicalisation' project.

In spite of the lack of scholarly attention that these authors have collectively received, this monograph argues that their work is significant because it expresses, in diverse ways, an 'internal' or, in Gramscian terms, 'organic' vision of Islam which demonstrates how Islam, Muslim identification and Islamic practices can successfully engage with and be part of a culture of secularism (*laïcité*) (Gramsci 2007). Indeed, the major point of convergence amongst these thinkers is their attachment to an individual and critical approach to Islamic beliefs and practices. Meddeb (who died in November 2014) was a poet and comparative literature scholar. He emphasised the need to historicise the Quran in order to move away from a literal interpretation. Chebel (who passed away in November 2016) was an anthropologist and psychoanalyst and published widely on the topic of *l'islam des Lumières* (Enlightenment Islam) through which he argued in favour of reason above all forms of belief. Babès is a sociologist of religions who consistently foregrounds a spiritual approach to Islamic belief and practice. Bouzar is an anthropologist who can also be described as an activist-intellectual and is engaged in how the political debates concerning women, the veil, religious diversity in the workplace and de-radicalisation affect the lives of individual Muslims. Finally, Bidar is a philosopher who sketches out the contours of what he calls existentialist Islam, whereby principles such as freedom of conscience, expression and dissent are central.

Chapter 1 focuses on the Franco-Tunisian poet Abdelwahab Meddeb. During his lifetime Meddeb taught comparative literature at Paris Nanterre University (and previously at Yale and Geneva universities), was the director of the international literary journal *Dédale* and hosted the Radio France Culture programme *Cultures d'islam*. One of the main ideas developed by Meddeb since 2001 is the notion that Islam is an 'ailing' religion and that its 'cure' can be achieved via a process of historicising Quranic scripture in order to move away from essentialist interpretations. Meddeb consistently posited himself in his media interventions and publications as a secular or even atheist Muslim and regularly appeared in the French media as the intellectual antithesis of Tariq Ramadan, who has been widely regarded in France as embodying a radical stance on Islam which is incompatible with a secular French state (see for example Fourest 2004; Landau 2005; Zemouri, 2005; Hamel 2007; Berman 2011). The texts to be discussed in this chapter were all published in the aftermath of the 9/11 attacks when Meddeb began his cycle of essays on what he regarded as the so-called *maladie* of Islam, namely fundamentalism. In order for Islam to 'heal' itself, Meddeb argues that it is incumbent on Muslims to foster public debate and discussion as well as to promote the notion of 'différence' and 'polyphonie' as opposed to 'unanisme' (Meddeb 2002). Indeed, Meddeb's intellectual activity was underpinned by a desire to sketch out a post-theological stance with regard to Islam (Watkin 2011; Qadiri 2013). His focus on the notion of a 'created Quran' is of particular significance, because it allows him to argue that the Quran is 'contingent' and, although inspired by God, it is nevertheless expressed in human language (Meddeb 2008). Chapter 1 will also problematise some key aspects of Meddeb's approach to the question of Islam in France and Europe. In particular, Meddeb's emphasis on an Islam which is ailing, a Quranic text which he argues is above all a literary, created text, his performative stances as a secular and atheist Muslim intervening in the French public sphere and his dismissal of the practices of many ordinary Muslims both within and beyond Europe (e.g. veiling, prayers, belief in the Quran as foundational divine text) could be seen to have a disenfranchising effect on Muslims.

Chapter 2 focuses on the anthropologist and psychoanalyst Malek Chebel, who taught at a diverse range of universities including the Sorbonne, the Université libre de Bruxelles, the University of Marrakesh, the University of Chicago and the University of California, Los Angeles (UCLA). It will provide a critical assessment of his work on the relationship between Islam and the Enlightenment. Chebel coined the term 'un islam des Lumières' in his text *Manifeste pour un islam des Lumières* (2004). In this manifesto, Chebel outlines a range of proposals to reform Islam and he positions himself as the inheritor of earlier Islamic reform movements such as the nineteenth-century *nahda* (awakening or renaissance) and other thinkers ranging from the twelfth to the twenty-first centuries such as Averroës, Mohammed Iqbal, Mohamed Talbi, Mohammed Arkoun, Bichara Khader, Mohammad Said al-Ashmawy, Nassar Abu Zayd and Mohammed Abed Al-Jabri. The chapter will also discuss Chebel's historical examination of the notions of subjectivity and reason in Islam, as well as his stance on the notion of *le vivre ensemble* in a diverse society such as contemporary France. Finally, it will examine Chebel's books on the notion of sin and transgression in the Quran and the life of the Prophet Mohammed. Chapter 2 will focus specific attention on Chebel's commitment to an *islam des Lumières* as a strategic intervention in a French public sphere which has become increasingly preoccupied with the potential challenges that certain forms of Islam present to the Republican principle of *laïcité*. By foregrounding the notions of reason, subjectivity and freedom of thought, Chebel's work explores not only the relationship between *laïcité* and Islam but seeks to demonstrate how the two principles can mutually reinforce each other from within.

Chapter 3 will examine the work of Leïla Babès, Professor of Sociology of Religions at the Université catholique de Lille. Her ideas about *lived* Islam, which she observes through ethnographic research, in addition to her concern for women's equality within Islam are key features of her work (Babès 2000; Babès and Oubrou 2002). Babès is sympathetic to what she calls 'une intériorisation de la foi' (Babès 1996: p. 129) (an internalisation of faith) and has been a fierce critic of the so-called *voile islamique* and *voile intégral*. Yet unlike other critics of the headscarf, such as the 'ex-Muslim' Chahdortt Djavann, author of *Bas les voiles!* (Djavann 2006), Babès nevertheless maintains a position as a secular Muslim public intellectual who argues that Islam can be a progressive and positive phenomenon, if its reactionary and conservative spokespersons are marginalised. Her weekly radio editorials on Medi1 Radio (*Points de vue*) and her blog provide a critical commentary on current affairs, with the expressed aim of deconstructing discourses and mechanisms of domination at work in the fields of politics, religion and culture. Chapter 3 will demonstrate why Babès' contributions are significant in the sense that they go well beyond the recurrent public debates regarding so-called 'Islamic dress', i.e. the 'external' face of Islam, in order to contemplate the 'banality' of everyday Islam, a narrative which runs counter to social and political constructions of Islam as a monolithic entity in contemporary France.

Chapter 4 will engage with the work of Dounia Bouzar and how her engagement in the political debates about Islam and Muslims in France raises significant questions concerning the themes of religious identities and the experiences of women. Bouzar has an academic background as an anthropologist of religions, but she can also be described as an activist and a public policy 'expert' at national and European levels (Council of Europe). In addition to being a member of the *Observatoire de la laïcité*, she has published widely on the topic of Islam, religious diversity and *laïcité* and is founding director of *Bouzar Expertises: Cultes et Cultures* – a consultancy organisation which advises French private and public sector employers on how to positively engage with religious diversity in the workplace, within the parameters of *laïcité*. More recently, Bouzar has made several public interventions regarding processes of Islamist radicalisation, particularly those concerning women, and in 2014 she set up the *Centre de prévention contre les dérives sectaires liées à l'islam*. Bouzar's work takes as its starting point the notion that Muslim French and secular feminist identities can and do mutually reinforce each other, but also how a greater degree of multi-faith and no-faith co-existence can be facilitated in the public arena in contemporary France. The particular focus of this chapter will be an analysis of the process by which specific experts become the legitimised interlocutors of the French government and media establishments and what effects such 'expertise communities' can produce in particularly fraught discursive and political contexts.

Chapter 5 explores the work of Abdennour Bidar, philosopher, member of the *Observatoire de la laïcité* and *chargé de mission sur la laïcité* for the *Ministère de l'Éducation nationale*. Through his publications, scholarly articles and radio programmes on Radio France Inter and Radio France Culture, Bidar attempts to sketch out the contours of what he calls a Muslim existentialism in post-secular societies (Bidar 2008/2012a). Muslim existentialism emerges from what Bidar calls 'un islam sans soumission' (Islam without submission). Islam or Islamic belief without submission is premised on a profound desire for freedom of conscience, expression and dissent. Bidar argues that the roots of such an understanding of freedom can be located in the Quran itself, which he describes as an 'instrument of liberation' (Bidar 2008/2012a: p. 17) through which human beings can become conscious of their abilities. Prior to his work on Islam without submission, Bidar also developed the concept of 'self Islam' to describe the process by which Muslims and those with Muslim heritage may choose to define their diverse relationships with Islam on their own terms. Self Islam should not, according to Bidar, be understood as a selfish or individualist undertaking, but rather as one which is premised on the notion of autonomy and personal responsibility. Bidar can be seen as a cultural intermediary or translator, whose multi-faceted work serves to foreground a particular vision of Islam as being characterised by spirituality rather than submission to religious laws and dogma. His work, which places him at the intersections of the academic world, the media and the political arena, makes him a particularly relevant figure through which to investigate further the notion of intercultural translation as well as the circulation of narratives concerning French Muslims and their diverse relationships to *laïcité*.

Any process of selection is bound to be open to critique, but the choice of these five intellectuals is based on the fact that they all share a common interest in the relationship between secularism, humanism and Islam, making a meaningful comparison of their interventions possible. They are all near-contemporaries of each other (with Bidar being the youngest and in spite of the untimely deaths of Meddeb and Chebel) and all share a universalist and individualist outlook. Indeed, the language which all of these intellectuals use is highly significant, since terms such as *la raison* (Meddeb), *l'islam des Lumières* (Chebel), *l'islam positif/intérieur* (Babès), *les libertés individuelles et le vivre ensemble* (Bouzar) and *l'existentialisme musulman* (Bidar) all have particular resonance in a public sphere which has been chronically preoccupied with the potential challenges that Islam and French Muslims pose to the principles of *laïcité* and *le vivre ensemble*.

Language, Orientalism and symbolic power

Pierre Bourdieu's research on language and symbolic power is of great relevance to my examination of the five figures discussed in this book. Indeed, in his work on language, Bourdieu constructs a critique of both Saussure and Chomsky for what he sees as their failure to sufficiently take into account the social nature of language. So, for Bourdieu, language should not be regarded as an object but 'as an instrument of action and power' (Bourdieu 1991: p. 37). According to Bourdieu, language is also

> an economic exchange which is established within a particular symbolic relation of power between a producer, endowed with a certain linguistic capital, and a consumer (or a market), and which is capable of producing a certain material or symbolic profit. (Bourdieu 1991: p. 66)

In other words, Bourdieu argues that language is not only a means of communication but also a means by which power is asserted and performed. Power not only derives from words or utterances but from the social institutions that house those utterances. Indeed, Bourdieu evokes the 'mystery of ministry' (Bourdieu 1991: p. 209) whereby individuals who represent certain social institutions command an audience because they are endowed with sufficient linguistic capital and symbolic power. They may be part of recognised social institutions, for example, the Church, the judiciary, the media or academia. It is to such individuals who are part of such social institutions that ordinary citizens delegate their power; these individuals become their spokespersons who are expected to represent their interests and voices. However, Bourdieu is wary of such promises of democratic representation through the language of the spokesperson. He sees representation as a process of substitution where the elected spokesperson ultimately ends up controlling the group it is supposedly meant to represent. Bourdieu calls this the 'oracle effect', through which 'the spokesperson gives voice to the group in whose name he speaks, thereby speaking with all the authority of that elusive, absent phenomenon' (Bourdieu 1991: p. 211).[9] A further perverse effect of the process of delegation and representation of groups via a spokesperson that speaks on their behalf is that it is the existence of 'the spokesperson who creates the group' (Bourdieu 1991: p. 204). According to Bourdieu, this creates symbolic violence because of the 'limiting form of performativity' (Bourdieu 1991: p. 212), which means that the oracle or spokesperson constrains the actions of the members of the group. Bourdieu argues that this constraining effect is most pronounced during moments of crisis. During periods of crisis, the group spokesperson exercises violence over the group on whose behalf s/he speaks because of 'the quasi-physical impossibility of producing a divergent, dissident speech against the *enforced* unanimity which is produced by the monopoly of speech' (Bourdieu 1991: p. 213).

The issue of discourse and power is central also to the work of Edward Said on Orientalism. Indeed, Said draws on Michel Foucault's concept of discourse in *The Archaeology of Knowledge* and *Discipline and Punish* and defines Orientalism as both a discourse and 'a style of thought based upon an ontological and epistemological distinction between "the Orient" and (most of the time) "the Occident"' (Said 1978: p. 2). At the heart of Said's discussion of Orientalism lies the question of power and (mis)representation: 'Orientalism is more particularly valuable as a sign of European-Atlantic power over the Orient than it is a veridic discourse about the Orient (which is what, in its academic or scholarly form, it claims to be)' (Said 1978: p. 6). Said distinguishes between different types of power at work within Orientalist discourse and refers to it as existing

> in an uneven exchange with various kinds of power, shaped to a degree by the exchange with power political (as with the colonial or imperial establishment),

power intellectual (as with reigning sciences like comparative linguistics or anatomy, or any of the modern policy sciences), power cultural (as with orthodoxies and canons of taste, texts, values), power moral (as with ideas about what 'we' do and what 'they' cannot do or understand as 'we' do). (Said 1978: p. 12)

Of particular significance to this study are the notions of intellectual, cultural and moral power. Secular Muslim public intellectuals who become spokespersons for the Muslim population in general tend to assert what Said refers to as 'a kind of intellectual *authority* over the Orient within Western culture' (Said 1978: p. 19). For Meddeb, for instance (Chapter 1), an intellectual who repeatedly positioned himself as being from the 'Orient', i.e. from Tunisia but located and educated in the West, i.e. France, this authority is presented as being all the more tangible and convincing because of his dual cultural affiliations. Said's methodology for studying authority is premised on the notion of strategic location (Said 1978: p. 20) and, indeed, not only Meddeb but also Chebel, Bouzar and Bidar (see Chapters 2, 4 and 5) can be described as having strategically placed themselves as individuals who have the intellectual, cultural and moral authority (power) to talk about Islam and Muslims.

Self-orientalisation?[10]

Whilst Said insists that 'Orientalism is premised upon exteriority' (Said 1978: p. 20), i.e. that it is based upon the Orientalist scholar making the Orient comprehensible to those *exterior* to it, I would suggest that in the case of secular Muslim intellectuals in contemporary France, we are, at times, dealing with a process of *self-orientalisation*. The term self-orientalisation refers to a process by which individual scholars claim some sort of affiliation to the 'Orient' (Islam/Muslim cultures), i.e. they strategically situate themselves as being *inside* the Orient, whilst simultaneously strategically situating themselves as *exterior* to the Orient, often by virtue of living, working, or having been educated in the West (e.g. France). Crucially then, Said's claim that 'all of Orientalism stands forth and away from the Orient' (Said 1978: pp. 21–22) resonates with the positions adopted by some of the intellectuals discussed in this book, in particular Meddeb, Chebel and Bidar (see Chapters 1, 2 and 5) who, whilst being based in France, have been concerned with describing, delimiting and making intelligible the Orient via their publications and media interventions about Islam and Muslims.

Ideology, discourse and performance

It is pertinent to explore the phenomenon of secular Muslim intellectual discourses and critically analyse them as attempted performances of 'exemplarity' or 'exceptional' citizenship (Fernando 2009) in a context whereby certain 'mots d'ordre' (disciplinary norms) (Foucault 1972) regulate our disciplinary societies (Deleuze and Guatarri 2004), i.e. *laïcité, la raison, l'universalisme* (secularism, reason, universalism) in the French case. Indeed, Religious Studies scholar Ruth Mas queries to what extent the 'public performativity' of the secular Muslim or cultural Muslim can be 'an act of discursive agency for the emergence of Muslim subjectivities' (Mas 2006: p. 589). The basis for her questioning of the public performativity of secular Islam is an exploration of France's colonial legacy and ongoing forms of colonial-style political discourse in contemporary postcolonial France. Drawing on Louis Althusser's work on ideology and interpellation in *Lenin and Philosophy*, Mas states that 'the interpellation of a "secular Muslim" certainly bears colonial weight' (Mas 2006: p. 593). This is because such a term resonates with the how some Muslims in Algeria, Tunisia and Morocco were secularly governed, whilst the term 'French Muslim' was devised by the Algerian *bureaux arabes* to regulate mixed marriages. Furthermore, Mas argues that the identifier 'secular Muslim' must be seen as part of a wider discursive context whereby Muslims in contemporary France are often associated with Islamism (extremism). So, in this sense, the Althusserian theory of interpellation is useful in so far as it invites us to think about the subject formation of French Muslims in a context where the hegemonic discourse about Muslims is bound up in questions about secularism, social cohesion and political Islam or Islamism. As sociologist Sarah Bracke also points out in relation to her work on Dutch Muslim women and debates about gender equality and emancipation in the Netherlands, using Althusser's work on interpellation is productive because it can shed light on how 'the subject comes into being through an initial submission to power, as it depends on hegemonic discourse and emerges within its terms' (Bracke 2011: p. 37). Interpellation and ideology are closely related to each other in Althusser's work on everyday social practices, as illustrated by the following situation:

> There are individuals walking along. Somewhere (usually behind them) the hail rings out: 'Hey you'. One individual (nine times out of ten it is the right one) turns around, believing/suspecting/knowing that it is for him, i.e. recognising that 'it really is he' who is meant by the hailing. (Althusser 1971: p. 163)

In the above scenario, ideology is represented within the institution of the law (one of the Ideological State Apparatuses, or ISAs; others are the family, the education system, the media, the church and culture) and it leads to the formation of the subject, because as the subject is *hailed* or *interpellated* and turns, s/he enters into a relationship with that institution or hegemonic discourse. As commented on by Steve Smith, this is not a free, autonomous subject, but one that exists in a subordinate position vis-à-vis the law and other ISAs (Smith 2004). Robert Birdwell's discussion of Althusser's theory of ideology and interpellation is similarly useful in so far as it reminds us of how the process of subject formation is bound up with an imagined relationship with the world and with others. Birdwell argues:

> Interpellation is the process of a subject being caught up in an 'imaginary' relation to other people and to the social whole. This relation is imaginary because it is the stage on which a subject assumes an illusory freedom; in fact its actions are determined by the ISAs. (Birdwell 2017: p. 315 cites Althusser 1971: p. 182)

It is also significant that in his examination of the concept of the French intellectual, Shlomo Sand argues that 'the term "intellectual" did not initially appear as a neutral professional category, but rather as an *ideological* expression par excellence' (Sand 2018: p. 10; emphasis added). Indeed, in relation to the authors discussed in this book, one of the central questions informing my approach to their work is to what extent their various public interventions can be regarded as fully autonomous discussions about Islam and Muslims in contemporary France, and to what extent they should be seen as being hemmed in (interpellated) by a hegemonic discourse in the French political, education, legal systems and media, which consistently posits Islam as France's 'problematic Other'. As such, whilst recognising the immense value of the work of the authors under discussion in this book, this study is also particularly attentive to the difficult and constraining conditions under which their work has emerged.

Part of this attentiveness to the fraught context invites us to think more broadly about readership, or rather intended readership. For it seems that one cannot fully approach these public intellectuals without also considering who they *think* they are addressing, i.e. who they imagine they are in dialogue with. In considering the dialogic aspects of their works, Mikhail Bakhtin's notion of the 'superaddressee' in his essay on communication and speech genres is particularly pertinent, as we shall see in Chapters 3, 4 and 5 in particular (on Babès, Bouzar and Bidar, respectively). Indeed, Bakhtin argues that

> any utterance always has an addressee ... whose responsive understanding the author of the speech work seeks and surpasses ... But in addition to this addressee (the second party), the author of the utterance, with a greater or lesser awareness, presupposes a higher superaddressee (third), whose absolutely just responsive understanding is presumed, either in some metaphysical distance or in distant historical time ... In various ages and with various understandings of the world, this superaddressee and his ideally true responsive understanding assume various ideological expressions (God, absolute truth, the court of dispassionate human conscience, the people, the court of history, science, and so forth). (Bakhtin 2006: p. 126)[11]

If we consider the published works and public appearances (broadcasts, open letters etc.) of the five intellectual figures who feature in this book as *utterances* in the Bakhtinian sense, we can approach them as efforts to communicate with various *third parties* or *superaddressees*, which are often ideological in nature. Bakhtin's terms 'the people', 'the court of history' and 'science' could also be understood in the present context as wider French society: the intellectual, political and media classes. Furthermore, the concern of Bakhtin for the notion of ideology connects to the discussion of Althusser's work on ideology whereby the idea of a free or autonomous individual agent is not a given. These writers write in a specific context – their work takes on a specific significance in post-9/11 and post-*Charlie Hebdo* contexts. As high-profile Muslims, they are engaging in performative discursive practices.

It is therefore also possible to evoke Erving Goffman's ideas in *The Presentation of Self in Everyday Life* (1959) whereby positing oneself as a *secular* (or atheist in the case of Meddeb) Muslim can be seen as relating to the dynamics of 'social performance'. Hence according to Mas, the emergence of secular Muslim groups and public intellectuals in contemporary France should be understood in reference to Judith Butler's interpretation of Foucault, 'where the subject is understood as being compelled to act from within a set of norms through which it negotiates its sense of self' (Mas 2006: p. 602). The 'set of norms' or normative values attached to the terms *musulman/islam and 'laïque'* within the French public sphere in post-9/11, post-*Charlie Hebdo*, post-Paris and post-Nice contexts are closely related to the notion of an (internal) threat or enemy on the one hand and the weapon of containment on the other. So, viewed from this perspective, Mas concludes that the public posturing of *musulmans laïques* is both limited and self-limiting, since it emerges from what she refers to as postcolonial (discursive) 'violence' towards French Muslims.[12]

Sand (2018) writes about the risk of idealisation of intellectuals as autonomous critical thinkers, when history shows us that sometimes public intellectuals have been politically ambiguous figures, to say the least (variously defending colonialism, Stalinism, Maoism and Nazism). However, rather than such an observation becoming an incitement to anti-intellectualism, he argues that any serious study of intellectual life should therefore take into account 'the complex relationships that exist between intellectuals and power' (Sand 2018: p. 24). My own study attempts to do just that, by being mindful of the broader cultural, political and social contexts in which these thinkers are working. Thus the critical engagement with the works of Meddeb, Chebel, Babès, Bouzar and Bidar takes into account the relationship between these intellectuals and power, understood in the broadest terms – that is, in the literal politico-administrative or institutional sense but also in its less tangible manifestations, such as via hegemonic discourse or, to use Foucault's term, 'discursive structures' regarding Islam, Muslims and *laïcité* in contemporary France (Mills 2004). Although the work of the five intellectuals in this book throws up certain ambiguities and blind spots, it would be excessive to consider their work as only 'self-limiting', since they all defend fairly audacious positions in many ways, as we shall see in the chapters that follow. However, we will return to the assessment of the impact and the legacy of their work in the concluding chapter of the book. In particular, we will ask to what extent their ideas and approaches are likely to be accepted, revised or rejected by the next 'millennial' generation of French Muslim voices to emerge in the twenty-first century public sphere.

Notes

1 LOI n° 2004-228 du 15 mars 2004 encadrant, en application du principe de laïcité, le port de signes ou de tenues manifestant une appartenance religieuse dans les écoles, collèges et lycées publics. Available at www.legifrance.gouv.fr/affichTexte.do?cidTexte=JORFTEXT000000417977&categorieLien=id; accessed 28 June 2017.
2 LOI n° 2010-1192 du 11 octobre 2010 interdisant la dissimulation du visage dans l'espace public. Available at www.legifrance.gouv.fr/affichTexte.do?cidTexte=JORFTEXT000022911670; accessed 28 June 2017.
3 In 2018, there were three further notable Islamist terror attacks in Carcassonne and Trèbes, Paris, and Strasbourg.
4 Loi du 9 décembre 1905 concernant la séparation des Eglises et de l'État. Available at www.legifrance.gouv.fr/affichTexte.do?cidTexte=LEGITEXT000006070169&dateTexte=20080306; accessed 20 June 2019.
5 In the UK, whilst UKIP has lost much of its momentum since the 2016 Brexit referendum, it is arguable that its discourse has impacted political, public and media debates about immigration and national sovereignty and that the Conservative Party has now adopted much of the UKIP rhetoric about national borders and 'taking back control' from the EU. The *Front National* changed its name to *Rassemblement National* in June 2018.
6 See www.interieur.gouv.fr/Elections/Les-resultats/Presidentielles/elecresult__presidentielle-2017/(path)/presidentielle-2017/FE.html; accessed 28 June 2017.
7 Publications such as Renaud Camus' *Le Grand remplacment* (2011), Eric Zemmour's *Le suïdice francais* (2014) or Michel Houellebecq's *Soumission* (2015) have also been illustrative of the recent climate.
8 See www.gouvernement.fr/missions-de-l-observatoire-de-la-laicite. The *Observatoire* has a strong pedagogic function, and has, for example, produced various guides on how best to apply the principle of *laïcité* across a range of settings (schools, hospitals, local authorities), including gradually bringing Alsace-Moselle more into line with the rest of France in the application of secularism.
9 The 'oracle effect' is similar to what Shlomo Sand describes as 'charismatic authority' held by certain public intellectuals in France (see Sand 2018: p. 14).

10 Other researchers have used the term 'self-orientalisation' to refer to related but distinct processes in South East Europe or in Cuba. See, for example, Georgiev (2012) and López-Calvo (2008).
11 For further discussion and analysis of Bakhtin in relation to cultural translation, see Buden *et al.* (2009).
12 Mas's argument clearly resonates with the analyses offered by French scholars such as Guénif Souilamas (2006), Guénif Souilamas and Macé (2004), Blanchard *et al.* (2005) and Silverstein 2004. Some elements of the present discussion about the performance of secular Muslim identities appear in Kiwan 2013.

1

Abdelwahab Meddeb: post-foundational Islam

This chapter examines the published works of Abdelwahab Meddeb.[1] Of specific significance is Meddeb's foregrounding of a *language* of Islamic secularism, which I argue can be interpreted as an attempt to transform perceptions of Islam and thus to intervene into the *symbolic* power relations between the Republican state and France's Muslim citizens. This chapter also poses questions about the consequences of deploying certain forms of discursive agency for secular Muslim intellectuals. What are the outcomes of their interventions in the public arena? What are the possible *effets pervers* (unintended consequences) of their interventions, if any? It is arguable that the work of Abdelwahab Meddeb embodies most explicitly some of the tensions or paradoxes which can emerge when intellectuals speak for and on behalf of a 'minority community' or, if we do not want to adopt that problematic term due to its suggestion of a hermetic and homogenous group, on behalf of a religious–cultural minority population.

Language, Orientalism and symbolic power

Pierre Bourdieu's research on language and symbolic power, as discussed in the Introduction, is, I argue, pertinent to an analysis of the work of Meddeb as a Muslim public intellectual, in particular the problems associated with speaking on behalf of others, which Bourdieu (1991) examines as particularly relevant. Bourdieu is suspicious of claims to democratic representation through the language of the spokesperson. He sees representation as a process of substitution where ultimately the spokesperson manipulates the group s/he is supposedly meant to represent. In addition to the so-called oracle effect (Bourdieu 1991: p. 211), a further risk associated with the representation of groups via a spokesperson who speaks on their behalf is that it is the existence of 'the spokesperson who creates the group' (Bourdieu 1991: p. 204). According to Bourdieu, this creates symbolic violence because of the 'limiting form of performativity' (Bourdieu 1991: p. 212), which means that the 'oracle' limits the agency of the members of the group, particularly during periods of crisis (Bourdieu 1991: p. 213).

It would seem that Meddeb appointed himself as a sort of spokesperson for Muslims, and indeed he writes in his introduction to *La Maladie de l'islam* that 'je tiens, comme on dit, à commencer par balayer devant ma porte' (Meddeb 2002: p. 10) (I am keen, as they say, to start by sweeping up in front of my own door). However, in writing about his own religious and cultural experiences as a secular, or even atheist Muslim, it is arguable that Meddeb's oeuvre generates symbolic violence which affects Muslims in general, and practising (i.e. non-secular/non-atheist) Muslims in particular. Furthermore, Bourdieu's three key concepts of habitus, field and capital are useful when thinking about Meddeb's ideas and interventions in the public arena as an intellectual. Meddeb's self-proclaimed habitus as a writer who has a responsibility to expose the causes of Islamic fundamentalism that are internal to it (Meddeb 2002: p. 10) is certainly illustrative of his symbolic capital in a field made up of the mainstream and high-brow media and the French political class. At the start of his 2002 essay, *La Maladie de l'islam*, Meddeb opines: 'Il est du rôle de l'écrivain de pointer la dérive des siens et d'aider à leur ouvrir les yeux sur ce qui les aveugle' (Meddeb 2002: p. 10) (It is the role of the writer to highlight the downward spiral of his own people and to help them to open their eyes to what is blinding them).

It is curious that Meddeb's work does not appear to be directed at the academic field as such, but rather at French society more generally, and in this sense he conformed to a certain definition of the public intellectual as someone with a scholarly background, employed by or associated with a higher education institution but who is not necessarily an academic in the traditional sense of the term. Bourdieu's work on intellectual language and authority is particularly useful here. With regard to social science, Bourdieu writes that 'social science must include in its theory of the social world a theory of the theory effect which, by helping to impose a more or less authorised way of seeing the social world, helps to construct the reality of that world' (Bourdieu 1991: p. 106). Whilst Meddeb was not a social scientist, but rather a literary scholar, Bourdieu's 'theory effect' could also be referred to as the 'knowledge effect' since the construction and dissemination of public knowledge about Muslims arguably creates the parameters of the debates about Islam and affects how Muslims engage in and with the public sphere. Indeed, as discussed in the Introduction, Ruth Mas argues that secular Muslim groups in contemporary France should be understood in light of Judith Butler's reading of Michel Foucault (Mas 2006). If we accept Mas's assessment of secular Muslims and the context of discursive violence in which they are supposed to have emerged, then it is possible to argue that by extension there comes a point when discursive violence can be turned against the self. This discursive violence can result from the symbolic power and symbolic violence of specific utterances and ideas which are disseminated by, amongst others, public intellectuals such as Meddeb. As Bourdieu states, symbolic power is

> a power of constituting the given through utterances, of making people see and believe, of conforming or transforming the vision of the world, and thereby, action on the world and thus the world itself, an almost magical power which enables one to obtain the equivalent of what is obtained through force (whether physical or economic). (Bourdieu 1991: p. 170)

When applied to the field of intellectual discourse, it is possible to argue that the interventions of a public intellectual such as Meddeb may be intended to transform representations of Islam for the better but, as we shall see below, this process of transformation may not always be so positive for Muslims – certainly not for those who do not conform to the secular, cultural or even atheist Islam laid out by Meddeb.

The relationship between knowledge and power in the context of Orientalist intellectual discourse is also fundamental to the exploration of Meddeb's work that follows, in so far as the public scholar is endowed with a cultural, intellectual and moral authority or power over the 'community' of ordinary Muslims which s/he has decided to describe and, to a certain extent, represent. Representation is only partial since the detached secular Muslim scholar is keen to distance him/herself from what are constructed as problematic beliefs and cultural practices. This desire to detach oneself from the population that one's work is about seems to arise in a broader context of what Said calls 'cultural domination' (Said 1978: p. 25). The extraordinary prevalence of that cultural domination is such that postcolonial subjects risk 'employing this structure upon themselves or upon others' (Said 1978: p. 25). What Said describes here is suggestive of the process of *self-orientalisation* – a concept which I develop throughout the book as a whole (see the Introduction). We see this in Meddeb's work, especially in his tendency to associate the Islamic Orient with 'sensuality, its tendency to despotism, its aberrant mentality…' (Said 1978: p. 205). Yet what is paradoxical about Meddeb and hence why we may argue that his stance is one of self-orientalisation is that he makes it his mission to explain the *maladie de l'islam* to his intended French readership (the 'superaddressee' in the Bakhtinian sense) and thus posits himself as a sort of essential or *incontournable* cultural translator or intermediary, in a similar manner to Abdennour Bidar who perpetuates this type of project (see Chapter 5).[2] Once again, this resonates with Said's description of the modern Orientalist: 'without his mediating, interpretative role the place [the Middle East] would not be understood, partly because what little there is to understand is fairly peculiar, and partly because only the Orientalist can interpret the Orient, the Orient being radically incapable of interpreting itself' (Said 1978: p. 289). We shall see below how Meddeb's writings in the post-2001 period appear to be principally motivated by a desire to educate his French readership about Islam in addition to enlightening the Muslim masses about the richness of a cultural history of which, according to Meddeb, the vast majority of them are unaware.

Meddeb, who died in November 2014 after a short illness, was a French-Tunisian writer, essayist and poet who taught comparative literature at the Paris Nanterre University (and previously at Yale and Geneva universities). He was the director of the international literary journal *Dédale*, commissioning editor at Éditions Sindbad between 1974 and 1987, which brought the work of a range of Sufi thinkers to the French public's attention, and the host of the Radio France Culture programme *Cultures d'islam*. Meddeb was born in Tunis in 1946 and came to Paris to study History of Art, followed by a Masters in *Lettres* at the Sorbonne in 1967. Via a corpus of about thirty published works (novels, poetry, essays and monographs)[3] Meddeb claimed to be motivated by a dual concern:

> lever, d'une part, la méconnaissance des occidentaux qui souvent assimilent l'islam à l'islamisme; afin de réparer, d'autre part, l'oubli des musulmans de la densité et de la complexité de leur legs culturel; oubli qui les prédisposent à accueillir le message islamiste qui propose une vision réductrice de l'islam, devenu une idéologie des pulsions où le principe de mort terrasse le principe de vie.[4]
>
> (to remove Western ignorance which often associates Islam with Islamism; and on the other hand in order to rectify Muslim amnesia about the richness and complexity of their cultural legacy; amnesia which makes them more likely to accept the Islamist message which offers a reductive vision of Islam, and which has become an impulsive ideology whereby the principle of death overrides the principle of life.)

In particular, one of the main ideas developed by Meddeb since 2001 is the notion that Islam is an ailing religion and that its 'cure' can be achieved via a process of historicising Quranic scripture in order to move away from essentialist interpretations and towards a post-theological engagement with regard to Islam. Meddeb consistently presented himself in his media interventions and publications as a secular or even atheist Muslim and regularly appeared in the French media as the adversary of Tariq Ramadan, who is widely regarded in France as embodying a radical stance on Islam which is incompatible with a secular French state (see, for example, Fourest 2004 and Zemouri 2005). Meddeb and Ramadan famously had a pointed debate on Frédéric Tadeï's current affairs television programme, *Ce soir ou jamais*, on France 3 in January 2008.[5] The texts to be discussed in this chapter were all published in the aftermath of the September 11 terrorist attacks in 2001 and include *La Maladie de l'islam* (2002), *Face à l'islam* (2004), *Contre-prêches* (2006), *Sortir de la malédiction: l'islam entre civilisation et barbarie* (2008), *Pari de civilisation* (2009), *Printemps de Tunis: métamorphose de l'Histoire* (2011) and *Le Temps des inconciliables: contre-prêches 2* (2017).

Pathologising Islam

In *La Maladie de l'islam*, published in 2002, Meddeb argues that *islamisme*, i.e. fundamentalism of the Wahhabi–Saudi Arabian variety in particular (Meddeb 2002: p. 12), is the *maladie* of Islam. He argues that the *maladie* comes from within and therefore decides to focus on the internal reasons which explain such an 'affliction'. In his attempt to draw up a genealogy of fundamentalism that created the conditions that produced the 9/11 attacks, Meddeb argues that one of the main internal reasons that explains the fundamentalism affecting Islam stems from a situation whereby too many people with limited cultural or educational capital have been given the opportunity to interpret the Quran:

> avec les effets de la démographie et de la démocratisation, les semi-lettrés ont proliféré et les candidats qui s'autorisent à toucher à la lettre sont devenus plus nombreux; et le nombre renforce leur férocité. La lettre coranique, soumise à une lecture littérale, peut résonner dans l'espace balisé par le projet intégriste. (Meddeb 2002: pp. 12–13)

> (due to demography and democratisation, the semi-literate have proliferated and those who believe they have the authority to interpret the scripture have become more numerous; and their increasing number reinforces their zeal. The Quranic text, when subjected to a literal reading, can reverberate around the space circumscribed by the fundamentalist project.)

The term *semi-lettré* frequently arises in Meddeb's writing and is regarded as a consequence of processes of democratisation devoid of democracy, processes which have particularly affected postcolonial Muslim societies. However, this could arguably be seen as Meddeb asserting an element of symbolic power through his status and adopted language of an erudite *homme de lettres*. Indeed, the essay gives a historical account of how certain Islamic leaders have promoted literal Quranic interpretations and fundamentalist forms of Islam, and his analysis discusses the influence of the eighth century Ibn Hanbal, the medieval Syrian theologian Ibn Taymiyya and the eighteenth century Saudi Arabian Ibn Abd al-Wahhab, from whose name derives the currently dominant form of Islam in Saudi Arabia (Wahhabi Islam). Meddeb is highly critical of Wahhabi Islam (Meddeb 2002: p. 71), arguing that it is this form of Islam which has led to the emergence of violence in the name of Islam because of literalist interpretations of Quranic scripture regarding combat and *jihad*. In his interview with essayist and journalist Philippe Petit, published as the book-length *Face à l'islam* in 2004, Meddeb disqualifies the very notion of *jihad*, arguing that 'les deux notions de *jihâd* et de *shahîd* (martyr), qui sont au fondement de l'idéologie intégriste, ne disposent d'aucune légitimité scripturaire; leur construction est post-coranique' (Meddeb 2004: p. 147) (the two notions of *jihad and shahid* [martyr] which are the basis of the fundamentalist ideology, do not have any scriptural legitimacy; their construction is post-Quranic).

Clearly, the title of Meddeb's 2002 essay *La Maladie de l'islam* indicates that his central thesis is constructed around the dual tropes of illness and cure. One of the main 'afflictions' that characterises contemporary Islamic societies and Muslim populations, according to him, is the resentment and hatred that fundamentalist Muslims feel towards the West. However, Meddeb does not tackle the fundamentally political question of colonialism and postcolonialism and the ways in which colonial expansion and, in some cases, bitter processes of decolonisation are also part of the broader context. For example, in relation to the non-application of Enlightenment thought and ideals in France's colonies and protectorates, notably in the education system in North Africa, Meddeb is fairly muted: 'Mais ce n'est pas le lieu de faire le procès du colonialisme ou de l'aporie et du paradoxe dans lesquels s'épuisait le message de Jules Ferry lorsqu'il parvenait aux colonies' (Meddeb 2004: p. 31) (But this is neither the place to interrogate colonialism, nor the internal contradiction and paradox in which Jules Ferry's message faltered when he arrived in the colonies). He simply refers to this as '"l'aporie occidentale" ou "l'épreuve de l'universel"' (Meddeb 2004: p. 34 cites Meddeb 1986) ('the Western aporia' or 'the challenge of the universal'). This somewhat truncated discussion of colonial and postcolonial politics is all the more surprising given that Meddeb was based in France (Paris) where there is a large postcolonial population of North African origin.

One of the very few references to links between Islamism, educational segregation and social exclusion in contemporary postcolonial Europe is made by Meddeb in *Face à l'islam*, where he argues that Islam should not become a religion with which only the socially excluded identify (Meddeb 2004: p. 192). Whilst Meddeb agrees with Edward Said that Islam should be regarded as internal to Europe ('D'abord l'islam comme civilisation nous appartient à tous; il constitue un bien commun qui participe à la mouvante formation de l'identité collective'; Meddeb 2004: p. 195 (First and foremost Islam as civilisation belongs to us all; it is a common good which contributes to the fluid formation of collective identity), he does not go as far as Said in his critique of Western portrayals of Islam, particularly via the media. Indeed, when he does broach the topic of the media, it is generally to deplore the ways in which Islamist fundamentalists and terrorists make use of the image and the media to propagate their message to as broad an audience as possible. Only at the very end of his 2002 essay and in very brief terms is the notion that the West may also be part of the *maladie* of Islam evoked when Meddeb mentions the historical non-recognition of Islam, coupled with conscious as well as unconscious Islamophobia.

In his 2004 text, *Face à l'islam*, Meddeb almost seems to avoid actually employing the term Islamophobia when arguing that anti-Islam sentiment surely arises out of frustration and anger that certain values which are taken for granted in democracies are readily contested by some elements of that society: 'La diminution de l'islam, son dénigrement, le statut inférieur qu'on lui accorde est probablement dû à la contrariété qu'instaure la contestation de valeurs qu'on croyait définitivement acquises' (Meddeb 2004: p. 100) (The belittlement of Islam, its denigration, the inferior status that it is accorded is probably due to the frustration caused by the contestation of values which were held to be definitively established). Meddeb argues that it is up to schools to reinforce such values. For example, he asserts that schools should be the place where Islamism is tackled in Muslim majority societies: 'Il faudrait que les manuels scolaires rendent assimilables l'habeas corpus, 1789; qu'ils se fassent conjoindre les œuvres occidentales fondatrices des Lumières et les œuvres critiques émergeant en Islam' (Meddeb 2004: pp. 67–68) (School textbooks should make the notion of *habeas corpus* and 1789 understandable; they should link the foundational Western works of the Enlightenment and the critical works which emerge within Islam).

Four years after the publication of *La Maladie de l'islam*, Meddeb reflects on the outrage caused by his 2002 essay in *Contre-prêches* (2006), pointing out that his thesis was in fact supported by an Egyptian-Australian mufti, Taj ad-Din al-Hilali, writing in *The Australian* in response to the 2005 London terror attacks.[6] Meddeb thus argues that even 'un homme de religion' can use the same metaphor as him. This defensive stance allows Meddeb to refine his approach adopted in *La Maladie de l'islam* by claiming that: 'l'islamisme est la maladie engendrée par l'islam' (Meddeb 2006: p. 399) (Islamism is the malady engendered by Islam). However, it is not really clear whether such a statement is more nuanced than the thesis outlined in *La Maladie*. We are still, after all, in a lexical field which is characterised by the use of pathological metaphors. Indeed, in this passage of *Contre-prêches*, Meddeb cites the Egyptian-Australian mufti's claims that *islamistes* should be in clinics rather than prisons in order to prevent the 'contagion' of their ideas (al-Hilali's term). This does not in any way take into account the social or meta-political aspects of Islamism, except in some vague acknowledgement by Meddeb of 'des troubles de l'identité propres à des corps en croissance et à des esprits en manque de repères' (Meddeb 2006: p. 401) (identity problems peculiar to growing bodies and to individuals lacking in reference points). Yet it is possible to argue that Meddeb potentially ends up contradicting himself and his pathologising model of Islamism by claiming that it was somehow the political model of tolerance in the UK which led to the visibility of radical preachers such as Abu Qatada. This claim would seem to suggest, then, that Meddeb does, perhaps reluctantly or unwittingly, identify some of the broader socio-political conditions which can lead to the development of radical Islamist ideologies.

The pathologising trope of illness and cure in *La Maladie de l'islam* is fairly consistent throughout Meddeb's work and re-emerges in *Sortir de la malédiction: l'islam entre civilisation et barbarie* (2008). Not only does the very title of *La malédiction* already indicate that Meddeb classifies Islam into two binary categories, the 'acceptable' and the 'problematic', but it also suggests that Islam's challenges are inherent to it. One of the key issues that Meddeb identifies as problematic in Islam and Islamic thought is the question of the separation of the religious and political spheres. Meddeb's secular stance is reiterated in this 2008 text where he makes an explicit case for the need to separate the religious and political spheres:

> L'islam ne parviendra pas à trouver une solution acceptable à ses problèmes tant qu'il persistera à vouloir situer la question du politique, c'est-à-dire du droit de l'État, dans le lieu de l'Absolu, car il renvoie alors cette question à un impossible. (Meddeb 2008: p. 27)

> (Islam will not manage to find an acceptable solution to its problems as long as it persists in wanting to situate the question of the political, that is, the law of the State, in the realm of the Absolute, since it thereby shifts this question into the realm of the impossible.)

In making this secular claim, Meddeb offers up the West as an example of how this process of separation can and should be achieved:

> Tout le processus de la pensée et de l'histoire occidentale a en effet consisté – et réussi – à détacher la Loi de cet impossible, grâce à la séparation du politique et de religieux: le premier terme est assumé par des constructions provisoires, qui sont appelées au perfectionnement parce qu'on reconnaît leur inachèvement; le second pôle, en revanche, a été neutralisé par la critique radicale de l'opération mythique qui voudrait donner statut d'absolu à une vérité relative. (Meddeb 2008: p. 27)

> (The whole process of Western thought and history effectively consisted of the successful detachment of the law from this realm of the impossible, thanks to the separation of the political and the religious spheres. The first sphere is taken up by temporary structures, which, due to their unfinished nature, are expected to enhance themselves; the second sphere, on the contrary, was neutralised by the radical critique of the mythical endeavour which would attempt to grant absolute status to a relative truth.)

Meddeb thereby argues that it is via the historicisation of religious texts that Western thought and Western societies have been able to embark on a path of secularisation, whereby religion and politics are separated from each other. Whilst Meddeb does not seem to dwell on post-secular critiques of this process of Western secularisation, or the way in which political secularism is regarded by some commentators as a public religion in itself (see, for example, Baubérot 2012), his use of the West as a model fits neatly with his post-theological approach to Islamic scripture.[7]

In Meddeb's *Pari de civilisation* (2009) he adopts an equally essentialising and pathologising stance to what he refers to as 'Islamic civilisation' and the manner in which 'la barbarie' has always potentially lurked within it, except when political authorities had the presence of mind to contain it (Meddeb 2009: p. 113). A particular risk in Meddeb's view is the temptation to focus on a mythic purity of Islam's origins and scripture and an ensuing suspicion of cultural mixing and foreign (i.e. non-Islamic) intellectual and cultural influences. Meddeb then discusses the eighteenth-century theologian Ibn Taymiyya, widely regarded as a founding father of Wahhabi Islam, and his claims that Greek philosophy, Sufism, the cult of saints and cross-referencing between the Quran and the Bible in scriptural interpretation were all threats to the so-called purity of Islam due to the Greek, Indian, Iranian, Christian, Pagan, Mesopotamian and Egyptian mixed heritages associated with all these values and beliefs. Meddeb's criticism of Ibn Taymiyya's drive for cultural purity is pertinent to his broader claims, but it is something of an analytical leap from that point to one which warns against a sort of axiomatic tendency for 'la négation de la civilisation' (Meddeb 2009: p. 113) (negation of civilisation), which is how Meddeb defines 'la barbarie'.

Meddeb further develops a deterministic approach in relation to the question of violence in Islam in *Le Temps des inconciliables: contre-prêches 2*, and here his position is similar to that articulated by Leïla Babès, whose book *L'Utopie de l'islam* (see Chapter 3 in this volume) he cites in so far as he argues that violence is most likely to emerge when unitary or monolithic positions are adopted and held on to. Meddeb somehow sees violence or violent Islamism as inevitable if there is strict adherence to 'l'idéal islamique' (Islamic ideal) because, according to him, such an ideal destroys 'le politique même de l'État' (Meddeb 2017: p. 61) (State politics itself). Against both the 'idéal islamique' and the Wahhabi current of Islam, Meddeb argues that it is imperative to demonstrate that historically Islam had provided a forum for debate and discussion amongst its interpreters and followers and that in order for Islam to 'heal' itself, it is incumbent on Muslims to return to public debate and discussion, to promote the notion of 'différence' (difference) and 'polyphonie' (polyphony) as opposed to 'unanisme' (group consciousness) (Meddeb 2002: p. 13).

Despite repeated calls for the recognition and valorisation of pluralism within Islam throughout Meddeb's work, the overriding impression is one whereby Meddeb's pathologising approach to Islam remains reasonably intact across his publications between 2002 and his death. Indeed, via his posthumously published anthology of *chroniques* (op-ed pieces) in *Le temps des inconciliables: contre-prêches 2*, Meddeb refers to the Nigerian extremist group Boko Haram as '*contaminés* par le *virus* de l'identité exclusive' (Meddeb 2017: p. 48; emphasis added) (*contaminated* by the *virus* of exclusive identity) and to the development of fundamentalist Islam in Tunisia via the Ennahdha movement as 'le *cancer* salafiste' (Meddeb 2017: p. 73; emphasis added) (the Salafist *cancer*).

The importance of Sufi Islam

Perhaps this can be seen as one of the major paradoxes and tensions in Meddeb's work. On the one hand, we see a tendency towards reductivism via his pathologising tropes, yet on the other hand it is possible to identify a deep interest in pluralism within Islam. It is thus arguable that Meddeb's claim to promote a pluralist approach to Islam which is not based on literalist and narrow interpretations of the Quran explains his focus on Sufi Islam as a model of pluralism, tolerance and cultural openness.[8] In *Contre-prêches* (2006) he speaks favourably of 'nos islams vernaculaires' (Meddeb 2006: p. 20) (our vernacular Islams). In *Les Temps des inconciliables: contre-prêches 2*, he writes positively about the Sufi veneration of the saints as an important vernacular Islamic tradition because of both its cathartic and aesthetic qualities. In one of his *chroniques*, he even goes so far as to claim that 'nul doute: la solution, c'est le soufisme' (Meddeb 2017: p. 223) (without a doubt, the solution is Sufism). The problem to which Sufism is the solution in Meddeb's view is Islamist extremism and its associated rigorist, hegemonic and nihilist approach to scripture. Meddeb argues that it is via Sufism that we will be able to re-articulate modernity and tradition and to reject monolithic or hegemonic Islamism via a positive engagement with the notion of alterity within 'la mêlée humaine' (humanity): 'l'esprit du soufisme prédispose à honorer l'altérité en son accueil et sa célébration dans le respect de sa différence' (Meddeb 2017: p. 225) (the spirit of Sufism predisposes believers to honour and celebrate alterity within humanity, in respect of difference). It is curious and perhaps even paradoxical that a claim or call for the acceptance of pluralism locates the solution in only one place and via only one solution. It would seem therefore that Meddeb's valorisation and call for pluralism brings with it a risk of *pensée unique* (monolithic thinking). Despite such a risk – which he never acknowledges in his own writing – Meddeb clearly sees the potential for political dynamism within Sufi Islam and, indeed, he argues that the principles underpinning Sufism are somehow connected with the Tunisian Revolution, or at least its spirit (Meddeb 2011: p. 11).

Post-foundational Islam

This move away from essentialism links his work to those French philosophers who adopt post-foundational approaches to ontology and ethics. Indeed, Meddeb's intellectual activity is underpinned by a desire to sketch out a post-theological stance with regard to Islam (Watkin 2011; Qadiri 2013). Qadiri argues that the term post-theological, as deployed by Watkin in his study of French atheistic thought in Alain Badiou, Jean-Luc Nancy and Quentin Meillassoux, can be applied to Meddeb's work in that it implies 'a new intellectual move that sets aside traditional theological considerations when engaging with sacred scripture' (Qadiri 2013: p. 50). Indeed, Meddeb is keen to describe himself as 'un mauvais musulman' (a bad Muslim) and in so doing compares himself to Leo Strauss's assessment of Spinoza as 'un mauvais juif' (a bad Jew) (Meddeb 2004: p. 208). What allows Meddeb to be a 'bad Muslim' is the fact that he strategically locates himself in what he calls 'la demeure post-islamique du musulman athée' (Meddeb 2004: p. 208) (the post-Islamic dwelling of the Muslim atheist). Such a post-Islamic location or stance develops, in turn, as a consequence of the process of detachment from religion. Meddeb emphasises this point at the end of his discussion with Petit in *Face à l'islam*: 'je dis que l'islam n'a jamais été aussi intelligent et aimable depuis que je le perçois comme trace, dans la distance de la séparation, à partir de la scène du dépassement' (Meddeb 2004: p. 210) (I am saying that Islam has never been as intelligent and agreeable as when I perceive it as a trace, in the distance of separation, from beyond). So Meddeb's self-identifying as a Muslim atheist reflects his engagement with the Quran and in particular with its more literary and mystical verses (as opposed to the legislative verses) rather than his rejection of it. Indeed, in *Les Temps des inconciliables*, Meddeb foregrounds the Quran as an aesthetic project whereby language is fundamental: 'la célébration de la parole inspirée par la psalmodie et la calligraphie' (the celebration of the word inspired by chants and calligraphy) is what seems to underpin what Meddeb refers to as 'la spécificité de la créativité islamique' (Meddeb 2017: p. 18) (the specificity of Islamic creativity). We may also qualify Meddeb's approach as post-foundational in that he is keen to argue against a 'foundational moment of Islam', thus denying 'the notion that the revelation of the Quran heralds an originary moment' (Qadiri 2013: pp. 57, 56).

His focus on the notion of a 'created Quran', after the Mu'tazilite movement of ninth-century Baghdad, is of particular significance because it allows him to argue that the Quran is 'contingent' (Meddeb 2008: p. 17), and although inspired by God it is nevertheless expressed in human language: 'Ce qu'on entend des versets coraniques ne peut pas être la parole même de Dieu, mais celle du prophète inspiré par Dieu' (Meddeb 2008: p. 18) (What we hear in the Quranic verses cannot be the precise word of God but that of the prophet inspired by God). Meddeb thus evokes the necessity of historicising sacred texts such as the Quran in order to move away from literal and essentialist interpretations. In the earlier *Face à l'islam*, Meddeb argues against the principles of sharia law and criticises Tariq Ramadan for his stance on sharia. Meddeb's broader critique of essentialist interpretations of the Quran is premised on a rejection of legalistic approaches to religiosity and a preference for what he calls the civilisational aspects of Islam, in a similar manner to Leïla Babès (see Chapter 3 and Babès 2008). It is this foregrounding of the 'civilisation' as opposed to 'law' which, Meddeb argues, places him in direct opposition to Tariq Ramadan:

> Il [Ramadan] continue de percevoir dans l'islam l'amour de la Loi alors que je n'en privilégie que les faits de civilisation qui ont contourné la loi, ou qui l'ont transgressée, ayant apporté une densité qui l'a neutralisée, sinon absorbée ou abolie. (Meddeb 2004: p. 207)
>
> (He [Ramadan] continues to perceive within Islam the love of the law whereas I only emphasise those civilisational aspects which have bypassed the law, or which have transgressed it, thereby having brought with them a density which has neutralised it, not to mention absorbed or abolished it.)

Meddeb's rejection of literalist or foundational approaches to the Quran is not always entirely convincing, however, since it could be argued that he himself engages in such modes of reading when it comes to the veil, as we shall see in more detail below. For example, in *Pari de civilisation*, Meddeb argues that there should be no doubt that the word *hijab* in suras 33, v. 53 and 42, v. 51 of the Quran refers to creating a civil code which simply separates the public and private spheres and to 'une draperie, un rideau, un voile qui sépare deux espaces' (Meddeb 2009: p. 179) (drapery, a curtain, a veil which separates two spaces). Meddeb is unable to envisage *any* alternative signification, stating with regard to sura 33, v. 53 that 'le texte est explicite: il ne peut être lu autrement' (Meddeb 2009: p. 179) (the text is explicit: it cannot be read any other way) and with reference to sura 42, v. 51 that 'jamais ici le mot ne peut être compris dans le sens limitatif du voile porté par les femmes' (Meddeb 2009: p. 179) (here the word can never be understood in the limiting sense of the veil worn by women). It seems that here Meddeb is at risk of reproducing what he criticises in other Muslims' approaches to the Quranic text – namely a rigidity which does not acknowledge a non-neutral subject position and which attributes a sense of absolute truth to the text – an essentialist move which he dismisses amongst those whom he regards as fundamentalist or *intégriste*.

Self-orientalisation

Certainly, the extent to which Meddeb consistently maintains his announced commitment to 'polyphonie' and pluralism is questionable. For example, in his 2002 essay *La Maladie de l'islam*, he seeks to develop the argument that the most attractive form of Islam is in fact that which is most closely associated with what he calls 'occidentalisation' (westernisation). He takes this argument further in *Face à l'islam* (2004) where he uses the broader term 'occidentalisation', which is to be distinguished from 'américanisation'. For Meddeb 'occidentalistion' is a positive process whereas 'l'américanisation' is something which he critiques and rejects because 'l'américanisation vous propose la Technique et n'exige pas de vous la réforme de l'âme' (Meddeb 2004: p. 30) (Americanisation proposes Technology without reform of the soul). Occidentalisation, on the other hand, is described by Meddeb in the following terms:

> Avoir les bons côtés de l'occidentalisation, cela veut dire aller au cœur de la culture occidentale, atteindre cette culture de l'esprit dont parlait Valéry. J'aurais aimé que les Tunisiens soient des gens éclairés par la lumière de Diderot, de Montesquieu, de Rousseau, de Voltaire, de Volney, de Condorcet. (Meddeb 2004: p. 58)

> (Having the positive aspects of westernisation means going right to the heart of Western culture, reaching this culture of the mind which Valéry spoke of. I would have liked for Tunisians to be illuminated by the light of Diderot, Montesquieu, Rousseau, Voltaire, Volney and Condorcet.)

Meddeb adds here that the growth of Islamism or *intégrisme* is the consequence of a superficial degree of 'occidentalisation': 'les réformistes échouent dans leur entreprise d'endiguer le phénomène intégriste parce qu'ils sont, d'une part, dans une vision tronquée de leur propre tradition, et, d'autre part, dans une occidentalisation superficielle' (Meddeb 2004: p. 41) (reformists fail in their attempt to contain the fundamentalist phenomenon because, they are, on the one hand, caught up in a truncated vision of their own tradition, and, on the other hand, only superficially westernised). For Meddeb, 'occidentalisation' is synonymous with the post-Enlightenment domination of reason which is cited, in turn, as the most effective remedy to Islam's *maladie*: 'la meilleure façon de guérir cette maladie mortelle est de soumettre le plus grand nombre à l'usage de la raison' (Meddeb 2002: p. 11) (the best way to cure this mortal malady is to submit the greatest number to the use of reason). Reason is not in itself problematised or deconstructed by Meddeb in this claim.

Against the supposed negation of Western values, it is significant that, as a public intellectual, Meddeb consistently positions himself as someone with a dual Western and Eastern (Islamic) heritage (see Meddeb 2002). In his later 2006 *Contre-prêches*, he broadens this claim of 'double généalogie' (dual heritage) to encompass the other Maghreb countries in general, stating that Maghrebis are simultaneously Western and Eastern, highlighting the fact that in Arabic, Maghreb actually means 'West' (Meddeb 2006: p. 18). He goes even further by arguing that Western colonialism in the Maghreb assisted Maghrebis in acceding to modernity and, in an echo of the controversial 2005 law on the teaching of colonial history in France, Meddeb claims that it is important to 'apprécier positivement' (positively appreciate) the colonial period by going beyond 'la blessure infligée par cette séquence de l'histoire' (the wound inflicted by this sequence of history) (Meddeb 2006: p. 19). So, in a move which unfortunately resonates with a triumphalist attitude regarding Western and French colonialism in North Africa and its aftermath, Meddeb argues that it is the adoption of the French language as an official language that fostered the development of modernity, and that the presence of French alongside Arabic and Berber should be seen as a way to combat a 'crisis of civilisation' which affects societies which are structured by Islamic belief. This is presumably because, for Meddeb, a recognition of the positive influence of French colonialism in North Africa allows him to develop his 'double généalogie' narrative as well as to refute Huntington's 'clash of civilisations' thesis. However, whilst it could be argued that refuting the 'clash of civilisations' thesis is a worthwhile effort (this volume is also partially informed by such a stance), Meddeb's subsequent silence around the extreme violence of French colonialism and the toxic legacies of colonialism in the postcolonial period is highly problematic. Such a silencing arguably contributes to the undermining of his own project for the wider recognition of the cultural complexity within Islam, via a process of what I call 'self-orientalisation'. This process becomes particularly visible in *Pari de civilisation* (2009) when Meddeb appears to subscribe to a deterministic approach to civilisational or cultural development, whereby he argues that since the main locus of 'civilisation' (understood in terms of intellectual, scientific and philosophical 'progress') is located in the West, Muslims should embrace their 'Westernness' in order to be in step with such progress. Quite simply, Meddeb calls on his readers in a direct fashion: 'Et maintenant que la civilisation est occidentale, à mon tour, je dis à ceux avec qui j'ai l'origine en partage: "Occidentalisez-vous!"' (Meddeb 2009: p. 119) (And now that civilisation is Western, I in turn say to those with whom I share my heritage: "westernise yourselves!").

Whilst Meddeb argues that the westernisation of the non-Western subject should not mean a fixed understanding of Westernness, but one founded on its own malleability and unending 'perfectability' (Meddeb 2009: p. 119) and indeed on what Meddeb ambiguously names the 'occidentalité intrinsèque' (Meddeb 2009: p. 111) (intrinsic Westernness) of Muslim subjects, it is nevertheless disconcerting to note that Meddeb is not seemingly aware of the West's own shortcomings and limitations with regard to civilisational progress. Perhaps the fact that Meddeb was writing this volume well before the current wave of exclusionary populism and nationalism began sweeping through Europe and the United States explains his stance. However, given that he himself recognises that so-called modern civilisation produced the horrors of the Nazi era, it is surprising that he so wholeheartedly places his faith in a Western model of progress and civilisation. Meddeb's approach could be regarded as a process of self-orientalisation because it is premised on the binary between East and West about which Edward Said wrote. It further perpetuates a hierarchy of civilisational achievement. Even if Meddeb does dedicate a large proportion of his work to discussing the intellectual, scientific and architectural achievements of Muslim scholars throughout history, the notion that Western civilisation has progressed and left the East/

Islam 'behind' is predicated on an idealised and hence mythical vision of the West, which causes symbolic violence to non-Western, i.e. Muslim subjects.

On 'Arab decline'

Such symbolic or intellectual violence is particularly visible when Meddeb goes on to claim in *Pari de civilisation* (2009) that contemporary Arab cultural or intellectual achievements are more likely to occur outside of the Arab world. In his chapter entitled 'Du déclin arabe' (Arab decline), Meddeb argues that although to be Arab today is an enormous source of pride, it is also the cause of deep disappointment and uneasiness when faced with what he calls today's 'cultural desert' (Meddeb 2009: p. 59). The evidence of Arab 'decline' for Meddeb is apparent in statistics that reveal that only 50 per cent of women in Arab nation states are literate and that only 330 books are translated every year in that part of the world. He then argues that Arabs tend to thrive outside of their country of origin: 'Très souvent, l'excellence arabe s'exerce dans l'expatriation' (Meddeb 2009: p. 60) (Very often, Arab excellence is realised via expatriation). He previously claimed, in his *chronique* entitled 'Arabité de Séville', published in *Contre-prêches* (2006), that every time he returns to Seville he is overcome with sadness at the sense of loss in terms of civilisational achievement (Meddeb 2006: p. 96). Such a damning assessment of the contemporary Arab world is all the more disenchanting if we take into account the contemporary global migration regime (akin to a global form of border apartheid) which is not one that favours south–north/east–west mobility or expatriation (i.e. permanent settlement). But Meddeb does not mention these sorts of obstacles. Rather, he argues that the decline is the consequence of the various despotic regimes across the Arab world as well as the influence of Wahhabi orthopraxis which, according to him, results in the negation of civilisation. For Meddeb, Wahhabi Islam or Islamism is part of an anti-Western sentiment which can also be located within pan-Arabism. Indeed, he argues that Islamism and pan-Arabism are two sides of the same coin, despite the fact that pan-Arabism is traditionally considered to be a secular political movement. However, where Meddeb sees their bond is in the common rejection of Western ideals, their anti-democratic credentials and their rejection of pluralism. Meddeb's model is problematic in light of the so-called Arab Spring, which began less than two years after the publication of *Pari de civilisation*, in so far as the Ennahdha party – an Islamist party – emerged from the democratic elections. This outcome also jars with his claim in his essay entitled *Printemps de Tunis* (2011) that the Tunisian revolution was somehow the result of an openness to Western ideals, which he refers to in terms of a 'don occidental' (Meddeb 2011: p. 100) (Western gift).

Beyond the post-revolutionary electoral dynamics in Tunisia, Meddeb's alignment of Islamism and pan-Arabism is problematic because it appears to be based on the premise that somehow democracy is the sole domain of the West.

We are once again within the self-orientalisation paradigm, because the association of democracy with the West de-historicises Meddeb's discussion in so far as Western imperial history is concerned. This is particularly apparent when Meddeb minimises the impact and legacy of colonisation of the Arab and Islamic world. He does concede that 'bourgeois imperialism' and colonisation are part of the reason for failed modernisation since the start of the nineteenth century and discusses the example of the British protectorate in Egypt, whereby the efforts of Egyptian educators to translate scientific works into Arabic were rejected by the British authorities, thus leading to the disassociation of the Arabic language and scientific modernity (Meddeb 2009: p. 67). However, he also admiringly alludes to how Napoléon Bonaparte's 'expédition en Egypte' in 1798 was responsible for the dissemination of Enlightenment ideas and an Arab awakening (Meddeb 2009: p. 130) which had followed a period of intellectual and scientific lethargy between the fourteenth and nineteenth centuries. He argues that such an awakening led to a 'désir d'Europe' and a 'mouvement occidentaliste' which spread across a number of Muslim societies in the nineteenth century, such as in the Ottoman Empire (under Sultan Mahmut II, or Abdulmacid) or in Egypt (under Mehmet Ali).[9]

Meddeb thus regrets that the European Enlightenment philosophies were not more influential on Islam, for this could perhaps have averted the growth of anti-Western sentiment within fundamentalist movements of Islam, associated from the 1920s onwards with Ibn Taymiyya (Meddeb 2009: pp. 131, 137). Furthermore, Meddeb's discussion of the impact of colonialism is arguably quite muted in comparison to his claims about the intellectual potential of the Arab world. Indeed, he ends his chapter entitled 'Du déclin arabe' with a discussion of how the vast 'potential' of the Arab world could be fulfilled if it chose westernisation over and above any temptation to indulge in melancholy or nostalgia. Meddeb seems unaware of the parallels between his analysis of the intellectual context of the contemporary Arab world and old colonial narratives about the primary resources in colonised lands and their *mise en valeur* by their colonial masters. That Meddeb posits such a process of 'occidentalisation' as being part of a new *cosmopolitan* era, defined by a *common* Western-Arab project, may reduce its symbolic violence, but it is nevertheless clear that for Meddeb the future of the Arab world is dependent on an acknowledgement of its own 'double-généalogie'. Meddeb thereby seems to assume that he can transfer his own dual heritage as 'arabe-islamique' and 'laïque-européenne' (Meddeb 2009: p. 68) on to the Arab world, as a whole, in a frictionless process.

Indeed, Meddeb arguably seeks to do this in relation to the Tunisian Revolution. He attributes much of the momentum behind the Revolution to young people, from both the working and middle classes, with those hailing from the middle classes being described by Meddeb as similar to their European counterparts in their mistrust of the political class, a status which he describes as 'postpolitical' (Meddeb 2011: p. 122). In addition to the link Meddeb draws between the Tunisian Revolution and Western ideals, he does not seem to see any paradox in claiming that the youth behind the Tunisian Revolution were postpolitical, given that a revolution or overthrow of the existing order is arguably the most *political* act available to citizens of any polity. Furthermore, he also does not seem to recognise that his earlier work on 'Arab decline' would seem to be in need of some revision, given that political change in the Tunisian case emerged from *within* the Arab world.

Elitism, erudition and a post-Western cosmopolitics?

Such a tendency to assume that his own personal experience and worldview (i.e. his 'double généaologie') can somehow serve as a basis for generalisation is particularly apparent in Meddeb's elitist tendencies. In his 2006 *Contre-prêches*, Meddeb writes about how erudition of the spirit can serve as an antidote to a 'clash of civilisations' discourse. In his piece entitled 'Aristocrates du goût' which discusses a recent visit he made to the *Festival d'Avignon*, Meddeb argues that: 'Quiconque possède la distinction de l'esprit et de l'être est aristocrate … Un miséreux peut être aristocrate' (Meddeb 2006: p. 93) (Whoever possesses distinction in spirit and being is an aristocrat … The destitute can be aristocrats). Seemingly unaware of Bourdieu's work on the relationship between taste, social class and distinction, Meddeb opines about how a gathering of 'taste aristocrats' such as that which unfolds before him at the Avignon Festival can serve as a basis to go beyond any notion that East and West, Europe and Islam are enemies (Meddeb 2006: pp. 93–95).

Beyond the spectacular or performative aspects of cultural erudition, Meddeb does make a more modest argument in favour of literature and the specific role that world literature or literature in translation can play in overcoming nationalism and cultural essentialism, which in turn fuels a 'clash of civilisations' narrative. In *Contre-prêches*, Meddeb discusses Goethe's *West–östlicher Divan* (1814–1816) (translated into French as *Divan Occidental–Oriental*) and Goethe's translation into German of a number of Muslim poets such as Hafez. Indeed, Meddeb reinforces this point about the role of world literature in combating nationalism by citing Goethe's quatrain from *Divan* as follows:

> *Celui qui se connaît lui-même et les autres*
> *Reconnaît aussi ceci:*
> *L'Orient et l'Occident*
> *Ne peuvent plus être séparés.* (Meddeb 2006: p. 262)
>
> (He who knows himself and others
> Also recognises this:
> The East and the West
> Can no longer be separated.)

Meddeb's commitment to an ethics of *Weltliteratur* (world literature), as developed by Goethe, is part of a broader engagement with a cultural politics which could be described as a politics of 'dépassement de son origine' (Meddeb 2006: p.226) (going beyond one's origins) or, as Amina and Hind Meddeb describe it in their preface to *Les Temps des inconciliables*, 'une éthique de l'ouverture' (Meddeb 2017: p. 7) (an ethics of openness). In his *chronique* entitled 'Entre Islam et Europe', Meddeb criticises the Middle East historian Bernard Lewis's thesis about the supposed demographic threat that Islam poses to the West and appears to agree with Edward Said's description of Lewis as Islamophobic, in so far as such a thesis reinforces the concept of a clash of irreconcilable civilisations. In response to such a claim, Meddeb offers an alternative vision, which is based on the dual 'dépassement de son origine et le refus d'assimilation' (Meddeb 2006: p. 226) (going beyond one's origins and the rejection of assimilation). Meddeb regards this as a dialectic or a productive tension which will characterise the development of democracy and universalist Enlightenment ideals in *both* Islamic and European contexts.

Meddeb's understanding of universalism and the Enlightenment appears to develop in his writings, from one which in his earlier texts, such as *La Maladie de l'islam* and *Sortir de la malédiction*, may appear at the outset to be constructed as a European 'import' which he calls on Muslims to embrace, to one which in his later writings, such as *Pari de civilisation* (2009), *Printemps de Tunis* (2011) and *Le Temps des inconciliables* (2017), becomes more nuanced. In *Le Temps des inconciliables*, for example, Meddeb's *chronique* entitled 'La Trahison des Occidentaux' (The Betrayal of the Westerners) makes the case for a renewed universalism in order to revitalise a crisis in humanist ideals (Meddeb 2017: p. 136). He also calls on 'l'homme européen' to finally revive a discredited universalism via an exemplary coherence between European principles and European actions (Meddeb 2009: p. 138). Meddeb calls this 'une cosmopolitique post-occidentale' (Meddeb 2009: p. 177) (a post-Western cosmopolitics) and in so doing draws on the legacy of Immanuel Kant and his concept of perpetual peace, as well as Meddeb's and others' own work on the *convivencia* period of Muslim Spain whereby the three monotheisms co-existed peacefully. Meddeb gives the example of the Turkey–EU accession negotiations as an indicator that Europe itself is willing to admit its own triple Judeo-Christian-Muslim cultural heritage in a move beyond (*dépassement*) purely Eurocentric identity narratives (Meddeb 2006: p. 71). Furthermore, in *Les Temps des inconciliables*, Meddeb makes reference to Edouard Glissant's concept of 'mondialité' (wordliness)[10] and 'la nouvelle universalité' (new universality) (Meddeb 2017, p. 229) in a move that links him not only to Abdennour Bidar's concept of 'l'universel partagé' (the shared universal), discussed later in this volume (see Chapter 5) but also to Etienne Balibar's cosmopolitics (Balibar 2011).

Meddeb's gesture towards a cosmopolitics is also bound up with his ideas on worldliness or world citizenship, and this in turn became increasingly linked to his growing environmentalist awareness. In some sense, we may even speak of an eco-critical Islamic perspective developed by Meddeb in his later interventions. In his *chronique* entitled 'Le gouvernement mondial' (world government), Meddeb argues that whilst a Western model of technical progress and individualism should be available to all, the accompanying consumerist model needs to be revised via a new ecological awareness. He proposes an ethical charter which, reflecting 'l'horizon de la cosmopolitique' (Meddeb 2017: p. 235) (the horizon of cosmpolitics), would promote public transport to reduce air pollution, encourage the reduction in the use of plastics and promote recycling. It is interesting that towards the end of his life (the *chronique* was broadcast in September 2013; he passed away 14 months later) Meddeb simultaneously developed a grounded and higher level perspective within his cosmopolitical perspective, whereby he claimed that by honouring 'le pacte cosmopolitique' (the cosmopolitical pact), we can become 'citizens of the world' (Meddeb 2017: p. 237).

The notion that cultural, artistic or literary erudition can serve as a sort of pluralist defence against identitarian essentialism or Islamist extremism is a consistent claim in Meddeb's works, and he develops this theme in his 2009 *Pari de civilisation* whereby he discusses the legal status of the *dhimmi*, which was historically accorded to non-Muslims, i.e. Jews and Christians, and which provided them with some protection in Muslim-majority societies such as Muslim Spain and the Ottoman Empire. Meddeb quotes eighteenth century European visitors to Turkey, such as the British Ambassador's wife Lady Montagu, who wrote that she was impressed by the spirit of religious tolerance amongst the Istanbul elite when she resided there between 1717 and 1718 (Meddeb 2009: p. 38 cites Montagu 1991).

For Meddeb, this apparent tendency for religious tolerance and openness to religious pluralism characterises an elite which was influenced by a spiritual tradition in Islam, known as 'akbarism', associated with the Ibn Arabi and Sufi Islam. However, he laments that this spiritual tradition, which is based on the notion of acknowledging the religion of the Other, remains largely unknown to the masses and that it is a tradition that became obsolete following the democratic invention of civic equality (Meddeb 2009: p. 48). It is hard, then, not to sense an almost latent suspicion of the concept of democratic citizenship, which when added to Meddeb's apparent nostalgia for the *dhimmi* status of fourteenth-century Al-Andalus seems to reinforce the notion that Meddeb is elitist in his approach and focus. Indeed, he ends *Pari de civilisation* with an epilogue discussing President Obama's speech at Cairo University in June 2009. Meddeb welcomes Obama's public recognition of the Islamic contribution to the West in terms of science, architecture, mathematics, astronomy and medicine, because it confirms his own rejection of the 'clash of civilisations' narrative and goes in the direction of a new phase of global inclusion of the Islamic world as an equal partner rather than as the West's enemy. He then somehow makes a link back to the colonial period and argues that even if the West and East were clearly enemies at that point in time, when, for example, Abd-el-Kader lost to the French, there was no sense of resentment. This lack of *rancune* (resentment) was due to the prevalence of a 'morale aristocratique, mue par l'esprit chevalresque et les lois de l'hospitalité accordant statut d'hôte à l'étranger, même lorsque celui-ci se présentait en agresseur ou en envahisseur' (Meddeb 2009: p. 206) (an aristocratic moral code, driven by the chivalric spirit and the laws of hospitality which accorded the status of guest to the foreigner, even when the latter presented themselves as aggressor or invader). Meddeb argues that this aristocratic code of honour was still active during the colonial period and that it was only from the 1920s onwards that a new moral code, which he calls 'la morale du ressentiment' (the ethics of resentment), developed alongside the emergence of 'des semi-lettrés' (the semi-literate, i.e. the uneducated) on the political scene via the Islamist movement, characterised by groups such as the Muslim Brotherhood in Egypt. Meddeb associates the ethics of resentment with humiliation and violence. This claim suggests two things. First, it reconfirms Meddeb's elitist tendencies whereby for him the political agency or engagement of the 'semi-lettrés' is suspect. Second, it once again demonstrates a colonial apologetics which glosses over the violence and imbalance of power between East and West – coloniser and colonised. It could thus be argued that Meddeb's high-brow ('oracle') approach causes further symbolic violence to the ordinary Muslims and Arabs who are left out of his model. He thus reproduces the colonial narrative of the 'évolué' about which Fanon wrote so eloquently in *Peau noire, masques blancs* (Fanon 1952). In fact, Meddeb's prose would sometimes appear to recall Fanon's 'évolué', especially in his analysis of European sources of knowledge and the French language, which elsewhere he claims to be 'inhabited by'.

It is of course possible to draw a distinction between the concepts of erudition and elitism. Erudition stems from precise yet broad intellectual and cultural knowledge, whereas elitism is arguably bound up with a political manoeuvre which seeks to exclude others (the non-elite). Meddeb's wife and daughter certainly describe Meddeb's approach as 'une approche érudite de l'islam et de sa civilisation' (Meddeb 2017: p. 9) (an erudite approach to Islam and its civilisation) in their preface to *Les Temps des inconciliables: contre-prêches 2*. They observe how Abdelwahab Meddeb had made it his mission to counteract the toxic influence of the 'fanatic preachers' on young people (hence his use of the term *contre-prêches* or counter-sermons) who, he argued, spread discourse which could only be described as 'faussement érudit[s]' (Meddeb 2017: p. 8) (falsely erudite).[11] It is arguable, then, that this is at the heart of how Meddeb saw his role as a public intellectual – to use his knowledge in a very public process of Sartrean *engagement* in the service of a broader cause. However, even within his own oeuvre, Meddeb sometimes slips between a vocabulary of erudition and one of elitism. This is most apparent when he creates categories such as the 'semi-lettrés' and in his admiration for aristocratic ethics and the political elites of the Ottoman Empire and Muslim Spain. It is also arguable that Meddeb's project slides from erudition to elitism in so far as it is political or rather politically exclusive. By politically exclusive I am referring to the process by which Meddeb excludes from his benevolent purview those French-born or European Muslims who are part of the contemporary subaltern classes. Whilst he claims to wish to 'save' them from the 'prêcheurs fanatiques' (fanatic preachers), he nevertheless seems to be talking *over* them, rather than *to* them. So whilst we have a very detailed and nuanced historical account of learned and inspirational Muslim scholars in Meddeb's work, we do not really have any sense of who contemporary Muslims are – apart from those who embody the spectre of Islamist extremism.

So it can be argued that Meddeb develops a negative portrayal of what he paradoxically calls 'le sujet islamique' (the Islamic subject), since the way in which he describes vastly heterogeneous populations in monolithic terms, i.e. as *potentially* fundamentalist, seems to have the inverse and ultimate effect of stereotyping them. This certainly appears to be the case in the following assertion, in which he further develops his thesis regarding processes of democratisation without democracy in postcolonial Muslim societies whereby '[les] semi-lettrés [qui] sont désormais légion' (Meddeb 2002: p. 22) (the semi-literate [who] are now the multitude) and 'le sujet islamique devient peu à peu l'homme du ressentiment, cet homme frustré, insatisfait, se pensant au-dessus des conditions qui lui sont faites; comme tout semi-intellectuel … candidat à la vengeance, prédisposé à l'action insurrectionnelle' (Meddeb 2002: p. 22) (the Islamic subject gradually became a resentful individual, a frustrated, unsatisfied person, thinking him/herself above their circumstances; like all pseudo-intellectuals … poised to take revenge, predisposed to insurrection). As Vincent Geisser has noted, it is striking that in his denunciation of democratisaton without democracy, Meddeb is silent about the dictatorship of Ben Ali in Tunisia, suggesting his alleged preference for dictatorship over Islamism, according to some (see, for example, 'Abdelwahab Meddeb intellectuel…' 2011 and Gresh 2011). Thus, according to such responses to Meddeb's work, he would seem to impute the Muslim world's problems to religion rather than acknowledging the profoundly political problems which contribute to the *maladie* of Islam (Islamism):

> Abdelwahab Meddeb décrit dans ses différents ouvrages 'La maladie de l'islam' mais il n'a jamais écrit un seul mot sur 'La maladie de Ben Ali', les centaines de femmes violées dans les commissariats de police, les journalistes agressés, les milliers de jeunes tunisiens poussés à risquer leur vie sur les barques de la mort. Un silence total sur les 'raisons politiques' de la dérive dictatoriale du monde arabe qui parle de lui-même. La dictature, c'est la faute aux musulmans, mais jamais aux dictateurs!
> (Geisser 2008)

(In his different publications, Abdelwahab Meddeb describes 'The malady of Islam' but he has never written a single word about 'The malady of Ben Ali', the hundreds of women raped in police stations, assaulted journalists, the thousands of young Tunisians pushed into risking their lives on the boats of death. Total silence reigns over the 'political reasons' for the dictatorial drift of the Arab world, which speaks for itself. Dictatorship is the fault of Muslims, but never the fault of dictators!)

In his 2011 essay *Printemps de Tunis*, Meddeb seems to adopt a rather apologetic attitude to his former silence regarding the human rights abuses of the Ben Ali regime and claims that he is inspired by the youth movements active in the Tunisian Revolution, whom he sees as embodying hope and renewal. He also attempts to reflect on why he was not more actively critical of the regime until the Tunisian youth began to revolt in 2011, although no real response to this soul-searching is provided:

Je m'interroge aujourd'hui sur ce réveil tardif. Est-il dû à la distance de l'expatriation? Est-ce le fait que pour moi l'horizon de l'être est le monde en son étendue? ... Serais-je victime de la vue d'avion que j'emprunte souvent? (Meddeb 2011: pp. 38–39)

(Today I question myself about this late awakening. Is it the consequence of expatriation? Is it the fact that for me, the horizon of being is the whole world? ... Could I have fallen victim to the birds-eye view of the frequent flyer that I am?)

Meddeb seems to blame his cosmopolitanism for his blindness to the Ben Ali regime's flaws, yet admits that the actions of the youth during the Tunisian Revolution re-instilled in him a new sense of patriotism regarding Tunisia: 'Les événements ont déclenché le dégel d'une origine congelée' (Meddeb 2011: p. 40) (The events have triggered the thawing of a frozen heritage). Interestingly, Meddeb's belated political and patriotic awakening also coincided with a rare critical stance regarding the French established civil sphere (Alexander 2006) and the media in particular, since he criticizes the newspaper *Le Figaro* for refusing to publish his article calling for Ben Ali to step down: 'Là où *Le Figaro* se trompe, c'est que la politique fondée sur le primat sécuritaire est dépassée. Soutenir des dictatures pour empêcher l'islamisme n'est plus efficient. L'alternative entre dictature et islamisme n'est plus opérante.' (Meddeb 2011: p. 52) (Where *Le Figaro* gets it wrong is that politics based on the primacy of security is outmoded. Propping up dictatorships to block Islamism is no longer efficient. The choice between dictatorship and Islamism is not functional anymore.)

The veil, the body and women in Islam

Despite criticisms of Meddeb such as those by Vincent Geisser, it can also be argued that his rather static and apolitical portrayal of Muslims can also emerge from an attempt to project a 'positive' image of Islam. Nevertheless, such attempts are ambiguous in so far as he engages in the self-orientalisation process whereby throughout *La Maladie de l'islam* he praises Islam's historic valorisation of sensuality and 'le culte du corps' (Meddeb 2002: p. 135) (the cult of the body). Meddeb laments how Islamic society (again referred to in the singular recalling the expression 'le sujet islamique' mentioned above) has moved away from 'une tradition hédoniste, fondée sur l'amour de la vie, à une réalité pudibonde, pleine de haine contre la sensualité' (Meddeb 2002: p. 135) (a hedonistic tradition founded on the love of life, towards a prudish reality which exudes a hatred for sensuality).[12] He then makes a statement which seems to suggest his nostalgia for a past era characterised by colonialist travel fantasies: 'Quelle occultation connaît la religion qui a tant fasciné les étrangers par le culte du corps et l'appel à la jouissance qui sont dans ses fondements!' (Meddeb 2002: p. 135) (What process of concealment has affected the religion which has so fascinated foreigners through its cult of the body and call to pleasure which are in its founding principles).[13] This leads Meddeb to bemoan one of the visible manifestations of the decline of the cult of the body in Islam as being the emergence on a massive scale of the veiling practices across the Muslim world and within France as well. In *Face à l'islam*, Meddeb explains that, historically, the veil was part of what he calls 'l'islam vernaculaire' (Meddeb 2004: p. 197) (vernacular Islam), and he compares it to Indian saris and African cotton cover-ups 'qui moule les formes' (Meddeb 2004: p. 198) (that cling to curves). So Meddeb argues that what a priori was concerned with modesty and *la pudeur* was actually also part of a process of seduction:

> Ainsi, dans les sociétés traditionnelles, le signe de la pudeur a été transfiguré en signe de séduction, simplement pour honorer la culture de la beauté dont les attributs circulaient avec aisance dans les venelles de la cité. *Les Mille et Une Nuits* témoignent avec constance de ce phénomène. (Meddeb 2004: p. 198)
>
> (In traditional societies, then, a sign of modesty was transfigured into a sign of seduction, simply to honour the culture of beauty whose attributes circulated with ease in the alleys of the city. The *Arabian Nights* consistently demonstrates this phenomenon.)

However, what has taken its place is the emergence of the *hijab*, *niqab* and *burqa*, which Meddeb describes as 'un uniforme idéologique' (Meddeb 2004: p. 197) (ideological uniform) and which is the consequence and symptom of 'la mort anthropologique' (anthropological death). Meddeb returns frequently to the notion of anthropological death in *Face à l'islam*, which he explains is connected to the loss of 'le dionysiaque':

> La mort anthropologique annule le dionysiaque; elle est advenue après que l'autorité politique a refusé de prendre en compte ce que la tradition théologique de l'islam a appelé la coutume ... Dans les monuments qui commémorent la gloire des saints,

le dionysiaque pouvait s'exercer, en tant que carnavalesque fondée sur l'excès, la démesure, la dépense, la circulation et le partage du don. (Meddeb 2004: p. 36)

(Anthropological death annuls all that is Dionysian; it emerged after the political authorities refused to take into account what Islamic theological tradition called custom ... In monuments which commemorate the glory of saints, Dionysian principles could exist, based on carnivalesque excess, immoderation, consumption and the sharing of gifts.)

It is therefore not surprising that Meddeb was a keen supporter of the 2004 law banning visible religious symbols in French schools. In *Face à l'islam*, he shares his satisfaction at having been able to give evidence to the parliamentary commission led by Jean-Louis Debré, established to discuss the matter:

Je me réjouis de la loi qui est en cours d'élaboration interdisant le port des signes voyants à l'école ... Face aux députés, j'ai soutenu que le voile tel qu'il apparaît de nos jours n'est ni un fait de culture ni un signe religieux, mais un uniforme idéologique. (Meddeb 2004: p. 197)

(I am delighted about the law which is being developed to ban the wearing of visible signs at school ... In front of MPs, I have argued that the veil as it appears today is neither an aspect of culture nor a religious sign, but an ideological uniform.)

Meddeb argues, without any reference to the perspectives of the women concerned, that as far as the veil is concerned, it should be denounced as a practice which is on a par with phenomena like polygamy, corporal punishment and repudiation. His 2009 *Pari de civilisation* includes a transcription of a debate between himself and the scholar of Islam, Christian Jambet that was broadcast on Radio France Culture's *Cultures d'islam* programme, which Meddeb used to present. Once again, Meddeb expresses his approval of the future 2004 law banning religious symbols in schools, arguing that for him it is an expression of female inferiority and inequality amongst the sexes (Meddeb 2009: p. 201). In short, for Meddeb the widespread practice of veiling amongst Muslims and in Muslim societies is symptomatic of the demise of a past 'polyphonie' and diversity in Islam and Islamic societies.

In *Contre-prêches*, Meddeb pursues his rejection of the veil, or at least the form of the veil which he identifies as 'le voile "idéologique"', as opposed to what he calls 'le voile traditionnel' (Meddeb 2006: p. 57). His *chronique* entitled 'Haine du voile' (Hatred of the veil) is categorical. It opens with absolute clarity: 'Je n'aime pas le voile' (Meddeb 2006: p. 56) (I don't like the veil), arguing that it represents a state of 'servitude volontaire' (voluntary servitude) which is 'régressif' (regressive) (Meddeb 2006: p. 56), since it goes against the process of 'dévoilement' (unveiling) which had been developing in Islam since the late nineteenth century. Given that he is keen to liberate Muslim women from such apparent servitude, it is curious that much of the *chronique* is taken up with references to the voices and experiences not of the women concerned but of the sixteenth-century French writer Étienne de La Boétie, whose treaty on oppression in *Discours de la servitude volontaire* argued that no form of oppression could take place without the consent of the oppressed. Whilst Meddeb concedes that La Boétie was writing about political forms of tyranny, he argues that modern psychoanalysts have used La Boétie's work to explain how submission can be unconsciously accepted by those who endure it (Meddeb 2006: p. 56). He goes on to discuss how in 1898 the Egyptian legal scholar Qasim Amin was already arguing against the veil for the ways in which it had the potential to reduce women to objects (Meddeb 2006: p. 560). In citing Amin's pamphlets *The Liberation of Women* and *The New Woman*, published in 1898, Meddeb claims that these were influential texts for the development of Egyptian feminism, for example on Houdha Sha'râwi.

In the same *Contre-prêches* volume, Meddeb's *chronique* entitled 'Musulmans de France' could almost be considered a misnomer given the fact that he uses this piece to decry the 17 January 2004 march against legislation on religious symbols in schools. The demonstration, which took place in Paris, is described by Meddeb as 'shocking' and its participants as 'agitators' (Meddeb 2006: pp. 145–146). He writes that the demonstrators are abusing a context of welcome or 'accueil' (welcome) and dishonouring the 'pact of hospitality'. It is striking that Meddeb considers these 'Musulmans de France' as guests as opposed to French women and men. It is also curious that he conceives of the stance and actions of the demonstrators as comparable to the 'petits blancs' in France's colonies (Meddeb 2006: p. 145). Indeed, Meddeb does not appear to see any irony in his comparison – given that the power dynamics are somewhat inverted when we consider the position of white European settlers in the Maghreb and French Muslims in contemporary France. The acknowledgement of the dynamics of power is often absent in Meddeb's work and this certainly appears to be the case in the discussion of the so-called 'pact of hospitality' with an unnamed Moroccan émigré that is recounted as an anecdote in this *chronique*. According to Meddeb's elderly interlocutor: 'le pacte de l'hospitalité, [lequel] repartit entre deux pôles: celui qui accueille doit vous ouvrir ses portes sans condition, sans savoir qui vous êtes; et celui qui vient et entre doit respecter le code de la loi instaurés par celui qui reçoit' (Meddeb 2006: p. 145) (the pact of hospitality [which] is divided into two roles: he who welcomes must open his doors to you unconditionally, without knowing who you are; and he who comes and enters must respect the code of the law established by the host). It could be argued that, as set out here by Meddeb, this is a pact of *hierarchy* rather than a pact of hospitality, which is out of step with the fact that most of those marchers, or 'agitateurs' as he refers to them, will have been born or brought up in France, so any pact of hospitality will not have applied to them but rather to their parents or grandparents. It is also rather striking that Meddeb's only foray into the empirical realm is an anecdote about a conversation that he had with an elderly Moroccan *émigré* who is as equally scandalised as he is. His emotive reaction to the demands of the marchers (to allow religious symbols, including headscarves, to be worn in public schools) does not acknowledge the perspective of the people in the street. Rather, he is concerned with the symbolism of the march and the visual offensiveness (in his eyes) of seeing veiled women and bearded men in the 'la ville des Lumières' (Meddeb 2006: p. 145).

Meddeb argues that the march and its demands will play into the hands of the *Front National* and xenophobes, but arguably his own rejection of the march could potentially play into the hands of Islamophobes, or at least those groups which are particularly hostile to the heightened visibility and audibility of Muslims in the public sphere. It is significant that in his denunciation of the march, he is concerned about xenophobia rather than Islamophobia. Islamophobia is often rubbished by those on the right of the political spectrum who argue that it does not exist (see Bruckner 2017, for example) and, furthermore, it is questionable to identify those French Muslims as potential victims/catalysts for xenophobia since many of them are not foreigners per se but French citizens. Despite his claims elsewhere about the irrelevance of national borders and the importance of a cosmopolitics which refutes the 'clash of civilisations' narrative, Meddeb does not seem to be willing to move beyond an 'islam *en* France' (Islam as a foreign element) towards an 'islam *de* France' (French Islam) model.

This cultural inertia which foregounds an 'islam en France' perspective on Meddeb's part is incoherent if we consider that, in other ways, Meddeb encourages Western Muslim women to 'burn their veils' in an opinion piece entitled 'Femmes d'islam' (Meddeb 2006: p. 266). He further urges them to disregard those elements of the Quran which reinforce inequality between men and women, since he argues that these elements are obsolete and emerge from what he calls 'la part circonstancielle du Coran et non sa part principielle' (Meddeb 2006: p. 265) (the circumstantial part of the Quran and not its principled part). Meddeb does not seem to be aware of the contradiction between his apparent assumptions that the women (and men) demonstrating against the 2004 legislation on religious symbols in Paris are somehow 'alien' or 'foreign' agitators and his subsequent calls for them to disregard certain aspects of their religious and cultural beliefs in the name of gender equality, as though this were a straightforward and seamless process.

It could be argued, then, that more broadly on the theme of the veil, Meddeb demonstrates a lack of reflexivity. Indeed, he argues in a self-orientalising approach developed in *Pari de civilisation* that what interests him is not the practice of veiling but of *unveiling*: 'En somme, tout voile implique le *kashf*, le "dévoilement". Le terme lui-même est ambivalent, il appartient aussi bien au langage érotique qu'au lexique technique des mystiques' (Meddeb 2009: p. 194) (To sum up, every veil entails the concept of *kashf*, of unveiling). The term itself is ambivalent; it belongs at once to erotic terminology and the technical lexis of mystics.) He then references the first Sufi treatise written in Persian by Hujwiri during the eleventh century, entitled *Kashf al-Mahjub*, which, according to Meddeb, literally means 'the discovery of what is veiled' and thereby calls for the unveiling of that which is hidden – the making visible that which is invisible (Meddeb 2009: p. 195).

Despite Meddeb's rather reductive approach to the veil in much of his writings, as detailed here, it does seem that towards the end of his life he had begun to alter his thinking in this domain. For example, in an opinion piece entitled 'Voile et liberté', broadcast in March 2013 on the radio station Médi 1 and reproduced in the posthumously published *Les temps des inconciliables: contre-prêches 2*, Meddeb concedes, perhaps for the first time, that wearing the veil can be regarded as a matter of personal choice. Even though he returns to his earlier critique of the veil on the grounds that, for him, it constitutes 'une forme d'obéissance correspondant à une servitude volontaire' (a form of obedience akin to voluntary servitude) and 'une forme d'aliénation' (a form of alienation) (Meddeb 2017: p. 175), he nevertheless writes that: 'on doit admettre la légitimité du port du voile comme appartenant au choix personnel' (Meddeb 2017: p. 175) (we must acknowledge the legitimacy of the veil as being down to personal choice).

Responses to Meddeb's work

Whilst Meddeb's stance is an intellectually compelling and complex one, it could be argued that his position is potentially disparaging for French Muslims who do not see the Quran as a created, literary text. The issue of language and power as explored by Bourdieu and Said is particularly salient here, since Meddeb appears to strive to assert a certain intellectual authority by locating himself as part of a scholarly genealogy which goes back to Spinoza, Kant, Nietzsche and Kierkegaard. This assertion of intellectual authority or power leads to multiple consequences and is not devoid of a certain level of symbolic violence which affects those Muslims who do not locate themselves in the 'demeure post-islamique du musulman athée' (Meddeb 2004: p. 208) (the post-Islamic dwelling of the Muslim atheist) to which Meddeb lays claim. This perhaps explains Meddeb's limited audience amongst Muslims in France despite his visible and audible presence in the French media, appearing regularly on television and radio programmes. But more fundamentally, it raises questions regarding the challenge of speaking for others (*le sujet islamique*) and how attempts by an erudite to transform perceptions by adopting secular language is fraught with ethical obstacles and potential *effets pervers*. Many Muslims may not recognise themselves in the self-proclaimed hybridity and interstitial position that Meddeb articulates in his 2004 interview with Petit:

> Mes références orientales et occidentales acquièrent ainsi la dignité de la trace, et c'est en tant que telles qu'elles s'inscrivent, qu'elles risquent de s'effacer ou de se superposer, de se chevaucher ou de s'imprimer l'une sur l'autre jusqu'à leur déformation: bref, elles sont au centre de cette aventure en quête d'une forme à venir qui excède tout autant l'origine orientale que l'acquis occidental. (Meddeb 2004: p. 57)
>
> (My Eastern and Western references thereby acquire the dignity of a trace, that is, it is as such that they make their mark, that they are likely to be effaced or to be superimposed, to overlap or to influence each other until they become deformed: in sum, they are at the heart of this quest for a form yet to come which goes beyond Eastern origins as much as any Western knowledge.)

Beyond the potential irrelevance of Meddeb's self-proclaimed hybridity ('double généalogie') to many of the world's Muslims, Meddeb's stance also raises a further question. Indeed, it would seem that there is an expectation for Muslims to qualify themselves and their beliefs, both religious and political, in order to absolve themselves of suspicion about their allegiances. The social media hashtag #pasenmonnom ('not in my name') which has flooded the Internet following Islamist-perpetrated acts of terrorism would seem to demonstrate an unspoken expectation of France's Muslims. The 'Je suis Charlie' hashtag and slogan which emerged in the wake of the *Charlie Hebdo* massacre has also created debate about the manner in which Muslims and Muslim organisations should publicly condemn such extremist violence perpetrated in the name of Islam, whilst also possibly striving to maintain a critical distance from the satirical magazine's portrayal of religion and the religious. Well before the *Charlie Hebdo* attacks of 2015, Meddeb had made the case in *Contre-prêches* for a public 'not in my name' movement in his response to the 7 July 2005 London attacks:

> N'est-il pas le temps que les foules des pays d'islam sortent dans les rues et manifestent contre le crime de Londres? Quiconque dispose d'une parcelle d'autorité morale politique, de quelque influence dans sa communauté, devrait appeler à de telles protestations publiques pour répondre pacifiquement et par non-violence à ceux qui répandent le mal au nom de l'islam. (Meddeb 2006: p. 392)
>
> (Is it not time for the masses in Muslim countries to come out into the streets and demonstrate against the London crime? Whoever has any shred of political morals, and any influence in their community, should call for such public declarations in order to peacefully and non-violently respond to those who spread evil in the name of Islam.)

Meddeb's tacit and, in the case above, explicit requirement that Muslims condemn such acts is arguably bound up with an expectation that 'good' Muslims in France/the West should be exemplary in their behaviour. It also suggests that there is a Bakhtinian 'superaddressee' – namely French and Western society – which is the intended recipient of such exemplarity.

It could indeed be argued that the theme of Muslim exemplarity is fairly central to Meddeb's work. Such exemplarity is characterised by a propensity to transcend, to distance oneself from one's religion and religious heritage to such an extent that it remains but a trace and becomes suitably neutralised for secular societies such as France. This transcendence of religion and religious origins is what Meddeb refers to as 'l'esprit des Lumières, lequel propose le seul universel practicable, celui du dépassement' (Meddeb 2006: pp. 225–226) (the spirit of the Enlightenment, which offers the only feasible universal, that which is non-essentialist). To adopt Meddeb's own self-ascribed term of 'le mauvais musulman', those 'bad Muslims' seem to be hailed as the 'good Muslims' by the French political, intellectual and media class and are thus allowed to speak in the public sphere. The fact that *La maladie de l'islam* was rewarded with the Prix François Mauriac would suggest that such a process may have been at work (previous laureates include Annie Ernaux, Régis Debray and Kamel Daoud) as would the release of an appreciative documentary film, released in cinemas in March 2017, entitled *Islam pour mémoire* about Abdelwahab Meddeb's life and work, directed by French film-maker Bénédicte Pagnot (Pagnot 2018). However, Meddeb's writings do not necessarily represent the diverse views of ordinary Muslims any more than do the conservative *Conseil français du culte musulman* (CFCM) or the *Union des organisations islamiques de France* (UOIF).[14]

The challenge then becomes how to foster a plurality or a 'polyphonie', to use Meddeb's own term, that allows for a diverse range of Muslim voices to be heard, rather than the current pendulum swing that either gives space to conservative-fundamentalist or secular and atheist Muslim views, leaving little space in between for those who do not recognise themselves in either ideological interpellation. This lack of space for those who are neither conservative-fundamentalist nor fiercely secular nor atheist Muslims could arguably be linked to what Meddeb refers to as the refusal to recognise Islam as part of French society, a refusal which is demonstrated through support for the *Front National* by 20 per cent of the electorate (Meddeb 2004: p. 201). What Meddeb is suggesting here is that a tendency to reject the alterity of practising French Muslims delays or blocks a potential politics of recognition of Islam. It is the absence of such recognition which could be regarded as a contributing factor to the difficulty for those Muslims who are neither conservative-fundamentalist nor secular-atheist, but ordinary practising French citizens and individuals, to be represented. The term representation needs some clarification here. Those ordinary practising Muslims will most likely not seek out any official representation – they are satisfied to practice their faith in the private sphere and do not make specific identity claims based on their religion. However, where there is a lack of representation, or rather an element of (mis)representation, is in more diffuse terms, that is, in the media and political discourse and in everyday life and interactions where ordinary Muslims (i.e. those that are neither conservative-fundamentalist nor secular-atheist) do not generally feature. If they did feature, then there would arguably be no need for the #pasenmonnom campaigns which follow Islamist atrocities in their various forms. Meddeb argues that until a certain number of key reforms are made in France, that process of recognition of Islam will remain non-existent. The two changes which Meddeb suggests are of vital concern are the need to construct mosques which are seen as part of the architectural *patrimoine* of France ('des lieux de culte décents'; Meddeb 2004: p. 196 (decent places of worship)), and, secondly, the need for French-educated imams. Meddeb suggests that mosques could be designed by revered architects such as Jean Nouvel or Christian de Portzamparc, for example, and that a faculty of theology could be established under the Strasbourg concordat framework.

Ultimately, Meddeb argues for the need to accept Islam as constitutive of Europe: 'D'abord l'islam comme civilisation nous appartient à tous; il constitue un bien commun qui participe à la mouvante formation de l'identité collective' Meddeb 2004: p. 195) (First and foremost, Islam as civilisation belongs to us all; it constitutes a common good which contributes to the shifting formation of collective identity). This may well be a useful way of thinking about Islam in contemporary Europe. However, the insistence on Islam as civilisation (*culture* rather than *culte* (religion)) once again passes over those Muslims who do not recognise themselves in either secular-atheist or conservative-fundamentalist Muslim identities. For them Islam is not *just* a culture, civilisation or 'trace' but a faith, a spirituality, and this perhaps explains why Meddeb encountered such resistance from many French Muslims (demonstrated, for example, by online critique and comment by readers of French Muslim websites such as *Oumma.com* or *Saphir News*). It is also plausible that this is an important reason why Meddeb became visible and audible in France's high-brow media and cultural landscape: to talk about Islam as a civilisation and as a culture is reassuring in a strongly secular state and society, since it corresponds to the hegemonic discourse relating to Islam in contemporary France. To talk about Islam as a publicly visible faith is altogether a more challenging act.

Meddeb's work is extensive, and although this chapter has focused on only a selection of his non-fictional works, it is nevertheless possible to identify some recurring preoccupations. Meddeb's emphasis on an Islam which is ailing, a Quranic text which he argues is above all a literary, created text, his performative stances as a secular and atheist Muslim intervening into the French public sphere and his dismissal of the practices of many ordinary Muslims both within and beyond Europe (e.g. veiling, prayers, belief in the Quran as foundational divine text) could be seen to have a disenfranchising effect on those Muslims who do not adopt secular language. Those Muslims cannot benefit from the resultant cultural or symbolic capital or power (Bourdieu 1991) that this sort of language can confer on its users. Furthermore, and returning to Said's analysis of Orientalism in intellectual discourse (Said 1978), Meddeb's sustained attempts to strategically locate himself with regard to the Muslim world is not without its consequences. One of these is arguably that he engages in a process of what I have called self-orientalisation, whereby the symbolic violence of Orientalism is self-imposed on the postcolonial scholar. We see this in Meddeb when he tends to describe Muslims and the Muslim world in fairly monolithic terms and when he consistently argues that one of the main problems for Islam is its weak degree of 'occidentalisation'. Vincent Geisser also argues that Meddeb's work is illustrative of the 'complexe du colonisé' (colonised complex) as discussed by Albert Memmi in his *Portrait du décolonisé, portrait du colonisateur* (Geisser 2008 cites Memmi 1985). In addition, Meddeb's explicit claims to a certain cultural, intellectual and moral authority which, according to him, stems from his dual affiliations to France and Tunisia is also potentially problematic since it assumes that those scholars or Muslims who situate themselves at the interstice, in between cultures, are those who should be listened to, as opposed to those who may not have claims to 'la poétique de l'entre-deux, de l'interstitiel, de la traversée' (Meddeb 2002: p. 205) (the poetics of the in-between, of the interstitial, of the crossing). As a result, if one adopts Meddeb's lens to address the question of Islam and Muslims in France and Europe, it is possible to argue that those Muslims who do not engage in secular discourse, i.e. those who do not *perform* a secular Muslim identity in the public sphere characterised by a strong political and social secularism, are at best ignored or at worst subject to suspicion and rejection.

Notes

1 This chapter covers some material published in Kiwan (2017).
2 For example, after Abdelwahab Meddeb's death in 2014, Abdennour Bidar took over as presenter of Meddeb's weekly radio programme on Radio France Culture, *Cultures d'islam*.
3 Some of Meddeb's titles include *Talismano* (1979); *Phantasia* (1986); *Tombeau d'Ibn Arabi* (1987); *Aya dans les villes* (1999); *Matière des oiseaux* (2001); *L'Exil occidental* (2005); *La Conférence de Ratisbonne: enjeux et controverses*, with Christian Jambet and Jean Bollack (2007); and *L'Histoire des relations entre juifs et musulmans des origines à nos jours*, with Benjamin Stora (2013).
4 See www.abdelwahab-meddeb.com/biographie-abdelwahab-meddeb/; accessed 8 September 2014.
5 *Ce soir ou jamais* (2008) 'L'islam a-t-il besoin d'etre guéri?', France 3 Télévision, 30 January.
6 *Contre-prêches* brings together Meddeb's weekly *chroniques* broadcast from Tangiers by Radio Méditerranée Internationale – Médi 1.
7 See, for example, Anidjar (2006), Asad (2003), Berger (1999), Derrida (2002), Dupuy (2013), Gauchet (1997), Habermas (2010), Milbank (1990), Taylor (2007) and de Vries and Sullivan (2006). For a succinct discussion of post-secular critique from a phenomenological perspective, see Staudigl and Alvis (2016).

8 Meddeb is not alone in his admiration of Sufism, as we shall see in subsequent chapters on Leïla Babès and Abdennour Bidar (Chapters 3 and 5). This is significant in terms of considering whether there is a certain form of Islam that is more digestible for the French intellectual sphere.
9 In his 2006 *Contre-prêches*, Meddeb identifies a contemporary form of a 'désir d'Europe' in Turkey's ambitions to become a member of the European Union (Meddeb 2006: p. 285).
10 For a suggested English translation of *mondialité*, see Coombes (2014).
11 Meddeb's 2006 *Contre-prêches* illustrates well the spirit of critique that he sought to espouse. As the introduction to the anthology of the *chroniques* states, these *contre-prêches* are 'des expressions sur l'islam qui constituent non pas la norme mais l'écart, sur des œuvres qui comptent pour nous aujourd'hui en raison de leur audace' (Meddeb 2006: p. 9) (discussions about Islam which are marginal rather than the norm, about works which today are important for us because of their audacity).
12 The praise of a past Islamic 'golden age' is also discussed at some length by Meddeb in his reference to Islamic poetry and the classical Arabic poetic tradition. Yet in his discussion of this 'poetic revolution' (Meddeb 2002: p. 26), he seems to suggest that poets such as the ninth-century Abu Nuwas should be read first and foremost in the context of their comparability to poetic figures of the French canon such as Baudelaire, Verlaine, Rimbaud and Mallarmé.
13 See Bourget (2008) on her critique of Meddeb's invocation of Flaubert's *Correspondance* in relation to Orientalism.
14 See Ben Rhouma (2014) and 'Abdelwahab Meddeb intellectuel…' (2011) for articles that give a sense of how French Muslims responded to Meddeb's work. The CFCM (French Council of the Muslim Religion) is a national elected body and was set up by the French government in 2003 in order to serve as an official interlocutor to the French state in matters regarding Muslims and Islam in France.

2

Malek Chebel: Enlightenment Islam

Malek Chebel is a French-Algerian anthropologist, psychoanalyst and historian who has been based in France since the late 1970s. Chebel can be described as a public intellectual, who, in addition to his presence in the French media, has published widely (about forty-one books) on Islam in general and, more specifically, on the subject he refers to as *l'islam des Lumières* (Enlightenment Islam). Chebel was born in Skikda, Algeria in 1953 and came to France in 1977 to pursue a PhD in clinical psychopathology and psychoanalysis, which he obtained from Paris VII-Jussieu in 1980. He then went on to further doctoral study, obtaining a PhD in ethnology from Université René-Descartes in 1982 and finally a doctorate in political science from the Institut d'Études Politiques de Paris. He died in Paris in November 2016. Chebel's was a prolific career, not only because of the sheer number of his publications but also because of the interdisciplinary dimension of his work. His approach could be described as a project of cultural translation, where Chebel can be regarded as a cultural mediator who seeks to productively confront non-Western and Western concepts of religion, spirituality, modernity and humanism. Indeed, many of Chebel's works could be regarded as 'livres de vulgarisation' (Catinchi 2016) (popular texts) whereby he aims to explain various aspects of the Quran or Islam to a non-specialist French audience. Of specific significance is Chebel's foregrounding of a *language* of Islamic secularism, which I argue can be interpreted as an attempt to transform perceptions of Islam and thus to intervene in the *symbolic* relationship between the Republican ideology of *laïcité* and France's Muslim citizens.

The chapter will critically assess his work via engagement with a range of monographs, essays and articles published in France between 2002 and 2016. Despite the wide range of topics under discussion in Chebel's work, it is nevertheless possible to identify a number of recurring themes such as reason, subjectivity, secularism, the body, love and sexuality in Islam. Chebel's publications range from essays, monographs and scholarly debates (e.g. Chebel and Godin 2011) to the more didactic or popular education texts such as *L'Islam pour les nuls* (*Islam for Dummies*) (Chebel and Clark 2015) or *L'islam en 100 questions* (*Islam in 100 questions*) (Chebel 2015b). He also had a high-profile media presence and was a frequent guest on television and radio programmes such as *Hors Champs* and *Les Nouveaux chemins de la connaissance* on Radio France Culture, in addition to launching his own periodical *Noor* (light) in 2013, which was subtitled *Revue pour un islam des Lumières*. Chebel was also an active voice in the French political landscape, and publicly defended the 2004 law banning religious symbols from public schools (Mas 2004). In 2008 Chebel was decorated as a *Chevalier de la Légion d'Honneur* by President Nicolas Sarkozy who, at the time of the ceremony, declared: 'Grâce à vous, la France découvre, ou redécouvre, un islam qui connaît et aime la vie, le désir, l'amour, la sexualité' (Vécrin 2016) (Thanks to you, France is discovering or rediscovering an Islam which engages with and appreciates life, desire, love and sexuality). More recently, Chebel was a vocal critic of the 'voile intégral' which he described as 'une provocation' in an interview in *L'Express* (Faure 2010).

Chebel's approach diverges to some extent from that adopted by Abdelwahab Meddeb (see Chapter 1) in that he is primarily concerned with an anthropological, historical and psycho-social approach to Islam. Nevertheless, Chebel's consistent focus on *l'islam des Lumières*, the place of the subject and subjectivity in Islam, the relationship between reason and Islamic belief and practice, and love and sexuality in Islam – in works which were all published in France and in French by well-known and mainstream French publishing houses – suggests that, like Meddeb, he was playing to a non-Muslim French audience or 'superaddressee' in order to change negative perceptions of Islam or rather of Muslims in France. Indeed, in an interview with *L'Express* magazine during the burqa affair (Faure 2010), Chebel argues that he believes that it is not Islam itself that is challenged by certain commentators who claim it is incompatible with Republican values. Rather, he sees the main challenge for Islam as resulting from the attitudes and behaviours of certain French Muslims, in particular young Muslims, who are not, what he calls, 'des Français modèles' (model French citizens). The use of the term 'Français modèles' is striking and Chebel seems to understand it in fairly narrow terms: 'Quand ils vivent leur citoyenneté au plan collectif, dans les entreprises ou les associations, ce sont des Français modèles car ils évoluent dans un cadre structuré' (Faure 2010) (When they live out their citizenship in the collective sense, in the world of work or civil society associations, they are model French citizens because they are developing in a structured framework). Chebel points out that those who are not part of such a structured environment are at most risk of becoming Muslims who are most at odds with Republican values because they are socially isolated and unable to 'se contenir' (contain themselves). He argues that certain Muslims are unable to take advantage of the modernity that is offered to them by the Republic because they do not have any leaders or are unable to make the transition towards such modernity. Whether he is implicitly positing himself as such a leader is certainly up for debate, since he claims that intellectuals in France should take on such a role with regard to this issue: 'Pour que la situation s'améliore, c'est à nous, les intellectuels musulmans, de renflouer le stock de valeurs fondatrices qui existe en chacun d'entre eux' (Faure 2010) (In order for the situation to improve, it's up to us, Muslim intellectuals, to replenish the stock of fundamental values which exists in each one of us). Two initial remarks can be made about Chebel's claims in relation to the broader discussion of the place of Muslim public intellectuals in contemporary France. The first is that, as discussed in the Introduction, Chebel subscribes to the language of 'exemplarity' and thus appears to operate within a discursive or ideological framework which posits French Muslims' alterity as problematic (Mas 2006, Fernando 2009, Bracke 2011). Secondly, it seems that, like Meddeb (Chapter 1), Chebel regards the role of public intellectuals as potentially restorative in so far as they are able to speak on behalf of others. This position potentially situates Chebel within a Bourdieusian conception of the spokesperson as an 'oracle' with the associated symbolic capital and symbolic violence that can ensue when the oracle risks substituting themselves for those communities on whose behalf s/he attempts to speak (Bourdieu 1991).

It is arguable that Chebel's prolific body of work indeed seeks to replenish the 'stock' of fundamental values amongst ordinary French Muslims, in particular young people. On the one hand, Chebel does this in his attempts to demonstrate how *within* Islam, one finds ample evidence of the notions of tolerance and justice. However, Chebel's work goes beyond such a defensive stance and towards calls for far-reaching reform of Islam. The originality of Chebel's work lies in his anthropological and historical sensibilities that allow him to show how the 'problem' is not with Islam itself but stems rather from an imbrication of Bedouin Arab pre-Islamic and Islamic beliefs and practices, which have led to the perpetuation of a number of values that stifle individual subjectivity and freedoms – values that are central to a Western understanding of modernity. This historical and anthropological approach to Islam in order to understand where some of these areas of tension may lie for contemporary Muslims, particularly those living as minorities in Western contexts, is the starting point for his work on the subject in Islam.

The subject in Islam

Published by the prestigious Seuil editions in 2002, Chebel's *Le Sujet en islam* explores the relationship between Islam and what he calls 'la tradition occidentale' (the Western tradition). In Chebel's analysis, the term 'Islam' does not stand for a monolithic entity which is regarded as representative of the worldwide community of Muslims (*Ummah*) or as a byword for the Quran. Rather, the use of the term Islam refers to what he calls 'le fait religieux en tant que praxis historique particulière, sociale, collective, générale et par conséquent, dominante' (Chebel 2002: p. 21) (religion as a particular historical, social, collective, general and consequently dominant praxis). For Chebel, the major point of divergence between Islam and 'la tradition occidentale' lies in the different conceptions of the individual and individual autonomy. As for the notion of subjectivity, Chebel understands the subject in the following terms: 'Le sujet est entendu ici comme acteur social agissant, conscient et autonome' (Chebel 2002: p. 13) (The subject is understood here as an active, conscious and autonomous social actor). However, Chebel also underlines the importance of the collective in his understanding of the subject: 'Le sujet ne peut donc exister sans une collectivité de référence' (Chebel 2002: p. 13) (The subject cannot, therefore, exist without reference to a collective). On the concept of the subject *within* Islam, Chebel's starting premise is that it remains an elusive and risky phenomenon: 'Le sujet musulman, c'est l'Arlésienne non identifiée et non réclamée tout à la fois ... [qu'] il ne peut se nommer sans danger' (Chebel 2002: p. 14) (The Muslim subject is that elusive, unidentified and unclaimed entity ... [which] cannot name him or herself without risk). The risk arises from the fact that Chebel's understanding of the social subject is one that is likely to disrupt and transcend the established social order. He also refers to the notion of an absent subject in Islam because of the taboo or 'interdit' surrounding the Cartesian *cogito, ergo sum* ('je pense, donc je suis', or 'I think therefore I am') (Chebel 2002: p. 15). It is the very act of thinking which seems to present the risk and, of course, as an intellectual and a thinker, Chebel's own work is consequently marked by transgression. Chebel's own reflexivity about his project to theorise the place of the subject within Islam leads him to regard himself (in similar terms to Meddeb 2004; see Chapter 1) as 'un "mauvais" musulman, qui dissèque et qui scrute le comportement des semblables sur d'autres bases que strictement religieuses' (Chebel 2002: p. 21) (a bad Muslim who dissects and studies the behaviour of his fellow Muslims in other terms beyond strictly religious ones). For him, the '"bon" musulman' is the one who accepts and conscientiously applies all religious teachings. It is striking that Chebel inscribes his work within this binary framework of the 'good' and the 'bad' Muslim, since this is a phenomenon which makes up the discursive framework about French Muslims and Muslims living in France. However, the classification of Muslims in this latter context tends to posit the 'good' Muslim as one who *does* question religious teaching, whilst the 'bad' or dangerous Muslim is the one who is seen to be too accepting of religious dogma and reluctant to embrace the critical autonomy in relation to religion required of the 'good' French citizen (Laborde 2012).

For Chebel, the fact that the Quran was revealed to the Prophet Mohammed in Arabic has a particular significance, since the fact that the message of Islam was spread through the ancient language of the Bedouins and city dwellers of the Arabian Peninsula means that it bears the imprint of their collective conscience, collective representations and 'temperament' (Chebel 2002: p. 16). Here, Chebel is principally concerned with affect and the ways in which language has embedded, within its formal and morphological structures, a particular way of relating to and being in the world which goes beyond the mere materiality of what is being expressed. This in turn has had an effect on the ways in which the notion of individual autonomy or subjectivity have been circumscribed within the nexus of Bedouin pre- and post-Islamic cultures, practices and beliefs. According to Chebel, one example of this reticence to give space to the individual as the subject is the reluctant use of the pronoun 'I' (*ana* in Arabic) amongst many Muslims: 'Affirmer ce je pour soi-meme, c'est se précipiter dans le chaudron satanique, patauger dans la puanteur et se couvrir de pustulences. Le Je humain n'existe par lui-même que lorsqu'il est fondu dans la totalité du divin.' (Chebel 2002: p. 33) (To assert this 'I' for oneself is to throw oneself into the satanic cauldron and to contaminate oneself. The human 'I' only exists when it is submerged within the totality of the divine.) Chebel simultaneously links this distaste and suspicion of the pronoun 'I' with cultural, linguistic and familial structures that are common in Arab-Muslim societies as well as with Islam as a religion as well. First let us take the cultural-linguistic aspect. Chebel argues that if one conducts a study of common family names in Arab-Muslim societies, one notes the prevalence of the prefix – 'father of' (*Abu*), 'mother of' (*Umm*), 'son/daughter of' (*ibn/bint*) – which suggests the effacement of the individual in relation to the collective, i.e. the family. Chebel's thesis demands further consideration, not least because the prefixes he mentions in relation to family names are in no way unique to Arab-Muslim societies; the *-son* suffix in many British names (e.g. Robertson, Anderson) and their Nordic counterparts (e.g. Andersson, Eriksson) are just two examples of the ways in which family lineage is inscribed into names. Chebel is perhaps more convincing in his claim that the absence or elusiveness of the pronoun 'je' may stem from what he identifies as part of the Quranic tradition whereby nothing is separate from the notion of divine creation, the sole and supreme source of human existence. Chebel argues that unlike the Holy Trinity of God, Jesus and Man in the Christian tradition, which according to Roger Arnaldez encouraged the emergence of a doctrine of the person, the very concept of the Trinity is alien to Islam (Chebel 2002: p. 34 cites Arnaldez 1987: p. 49). Chebel asks whether the concept of the Holy Trinity in fact facilitates the development of the individual since, if Man is created in the image of God, then this enables a process of self-knowledge which remains out of bounds for the Islamic subject: 'Faut-il ressembler à Dieu pour mieux l'entendre ou le connaître, et par conséquent se connaître soi-même?' (Chebel 2002: p. 34) (Must we resemble God in order to better understand or know him, and consequently, ourselves?).

Chebel seeks to further contrast Western and Islamic understandings of individuation by alluding to two major moments in the historical development of individual consciousness: the Socratic maxim 'Connais-toi toi-même'

(Know thyself) and the Cartesian *cogito, ergo sum*. He contrasts these powerful ideas with the observation made by the Prophet Mohammed himself that he who knows himself is in a position to know God: 'Celui qui se connaît soi-même connaît son Seigneur' (Chebel 2002: p. 42 cites Balyâni (1982): p. 49) (He who knows himself knows his Lord). Chebel regards this claim as evidence that self-knowledge in Islam is not an end in itself, but rather is subordinate to the ultimate object of knowledge: God. Chebel thus argues that in order to know oneself, Islamic doctrine places the emphasis on God as the sole source of the individual's existence. It therefore follows that the notion of individual subjectivity has not been accorded much space within the Islamic tradition. Indeed, like Bidar (see Chapter 5), Chebel laments the representation of human beings in the Quran as being totally insignificant in the face of a God described as 'une entité divine surdimensionnée' (Chebel 2002: p. 47) (oversized divine entity). He cites numerous verses from the Quran which reinforce the notion of what Chebel calls 'la petitesse humaine' (Chebel 2002: p. 47) (human pettiness), whereby Man is defined by his wretchedness and feebleness. As we shall see in Chapter 5, this clearly resonates with Bidar's frustration regarding the notion of Man as a 'creature' within Islam (Bidar 2008/2012a).

However, unlike Bidar, who appears to explain the absence of individual subjectivity or autonomy from a perspective which focuses disproportionately on the textual premises of Islam, Chebel seeks to move beyond a purely scriptural approach to the question by undertaking a historiography of Islamic scholarship. Even here, Chebel laments the absence of the subject: 'Ni la notion de moi (*al-ana/aniyya*) ni celle d'individu (*fard, fardiyya*), et moins encore celle d'un sujet acteur de son destin, ne semblent constituer aujourd'hui des thèmes pouvant intéresser le chercheur musulman' (Chebel 2002: p. 45) (Neither the notion of me (*al-ana/aniyya*) nor that of the individual (*fard, fardiyya*) and even less so that of the subject as agent of their destiny, do not seem, today, to be of interest to Muslim researchers). Chebel identifies two major intellectual movements which made a lasting imprint on Islamic theology. The first, associated with thinkers such as Ibn Hazm (993–1064) and Al-Ghazzali (1058–1111) and medieval authors such as Ibn Taymiyya (d.1329), was concerned with establishing the word of God in what Chebel refers to as 'le terreau mental des Arabes, puis des musulmans' (Chebel 2002: p. 49) (the Arab then Muslim mental landscape). The second intellectual tradition, associated with thinkers such as Râzi (860–923), al-Farabi (872–950), Ibn Sina (980–1037), Ibn Tofail (d.1185) and Ibn Rushd (1126–1198), is described as being engaged in the study of how human beings are affected by speculations about the meaning of God. Chebel argues that Islamic philosophers rarely stepped beyond the conventional limits which were established for all Muslims. Indeed, many of these philosophers, who are referred to by Chebel as the 'philosophes du sérail' (Chebel 2002: p. 50) (philosophers of the seraglio) were themselves part of the power structures and political institutions in place; for example, Ibn Rushd was the *cadi* (judge) of Seville and Cordoba.

Nevertherless (and in a similar fashion to Meddeb; see Chapter 1), Chebel discusses the Mutazilites – the term Mutazilite coming from the Arabic expression *i'tazala anna* ('Il s'est séparé de nous' (It broke away from us)) – a philosophical movement founded by Wasil ibn Ata that developed in Basra and Baghdad between the eighth and tenth centuries. The Mutazilites argued that Reason had an important role to play in religious affairs and, most controversially, claimed that the Quran was created, thus going against the dominant view that the Quran was a divine entity. As Chebel shows elsewhere (Chebel 2006), for the Mutazilites the Quran was the *translation* of the divine will of God which took the form of a sacred book. In other words, for the Mutazilites the Quran is the creation of God but it is not God himself. The reasoning underpinning the claim that the Quran was created rather than embodying God himself stemmed from the belief that to make such a claim would amount to suggesting that there are multiple gods. Despite the rationale for arguing that the Quran was created, reflecting the desire to uphold the oneness and supreme authority of God, the Mutazilites' claim that the Quran was created was treated as blasphemy and their movement was a short-lived one.

Other aspects of the Mutazilite movement were suggestive of the beginnings of the elaboration of a philosophy of human free will existing as separate from God. The Mutazilites adopted a liberal understanding of the longest sura in the Quran, *Al-Baqara* (The Cow), which they interpreted as evidence that humans create and are responsible for their own acts. The sura in question that Chebel cites in French states: 'Dieu n'impose à chaque homme que ce qu'il peut porter. Le bien qu'il aura accompli lui reviendra, ainsi que le mal qu'il aura fait.' (Chebel 2006: p. 44 cites *The Qur'an,* sura 2, v. 286; English translation from the OUP 2004 edition) (God does not burden any soul with more than it can bear: each gains whatever good it has done, and suffers its bad).[1] The Mutazilites' emphasis on free will and responsibility meant that they were regarded by many of their contemporaries as heretics and, indeed, from the second half of the ninth century, they were persecuted and repressed. However, the interest and significance of the Mutazilite movement for Chebel lies in the fact that even as early as the eighth century there existed a profound interest in the notion of human free will, freedom and individual responsibility which emerged from *within* the Islamic tradition; these three notions which are readily associated with modernity were thus already present in eighth century Islamic thought.

Chebel's approach to the notion of subjectivity in Islam, then, is not one which starts from the point of view that Islam must somehow move towards modernity in order to compensate for a 'deficit' in humanist values which is inherent to it as a religion (which would appear to be the perspective of Meddeb 2002, who writes about *la maladie de l'islam*; see Chapter 1). Nor does he argue for a reinterpretation of key elements of the Quranic scripture in order to facilitate the emergence of an eclipsed humanism within Islam, unlike Bidar whose central claim is that the notion of *khalifat* has been wilfully misunderstood by theologians and religious authorities in order to limit the implications of *khalifat* to the lesser notion of Man as God's lieutenant on earth, rather than Man as God's heir (Bidar 2008/2012a; see Chapter 5). Rather, his stance is based on an anthropological and historicised attempt to understand why certain approaches to Islam – such as that of the Mutazilites, which foregrounded individual human responsibility and freedom as separate from God/the divine – were quashed and suppressed by a socio-political and cultural order which itself did not encourage individual freedoms and liberties. Furthermore, Chebel argues that the notion of the separation of political and theological power was clearly theorised by the Mutazilites, who claimed that imams were not infallible, unlike the Prophet. So Chebel's approach to the question of subjectivity in Islam can be regarded as holistic in so far as he is constantly shifting between varying levels of analysis, at once scriptural, textual, practical, anthropological, historical, socio-political and symbolic.

Chebel consistently attempts to write against a 'clash of civilisations' narrative, demonstrating how Islamic thought embraced Greek, Indo-Persian, Turkish, Mongolian, Chinese and other intellectual traditions. However, Chebel ends up contrasting Islamic and 'Western' culture by arguing that the individual has little status within Islamic thought and civilisation, comparing this state of affairs with the importance of 'l'individu occidental', whose ability to emerge was founded on the centrality of the notion of the private individual (Chebel 2002: p. 184), which contrasts sharply with the notion of the *Ummah* – the collective social unit within Islam, whereby the individual is regarded with suspicion. Chebel's insistence that equality is foregrounded at the expense of 'movement', or the emergence of the individual within Islamic thought (Chebel 2002: p. 183), resonates with Bidar's critique of Islam as engendering 'une égalité, mais d'esclaves' (Bidar 2008/2012a: p. 44) (a slave-like equality) (see Chapter 5). Indeed, a major point of convergence between these two intellectuals lies in their interest in the question of *la soumission* (submission). Against the critique they make of the lack of individual subjectivity within Islam, both Bidar and Chebel attempt to sketch out the contours of what they see as an Islam that is no longer fundamentally defined by the notion of total human submission to God.

However, whereas Bidar tends to suggest that 'un islam sans soumission' (Bidar 2008/2012a) is possible via a re-reading of the Quran (and the *Al-Baqara* sura in particular), Chebel's investigation, whilst ultimately concerned with a new era of scriptural interpretation (*nouvel ijtihad*) suggests that the lack of space for individual subjectivity within Islam as we know it today stems in large part from pre-Islamic, Bedouin cultural values and practices which became embedded in Islamic traditions. Chebel writes that the only possible subject in Islam is

God: 'Le Sujet-Un est d'abord Dieu … Ce Sujet-Dieu en islam ne délègue aucun pouvoir à ses représentants sur terre' (Chebel 2002: pp. 60, 67) (The Subject is first and foremost God … This God-Subject in Islam does not delegate any power to his representatives on earth). Chebel even goes so far as to argue that the 'croyant' (believer) cannot in effect become a subject, and that it is *Ibliss* (the devil) who in fact incarnates the figure of the subject who disobeys and questions the motivations of God:

> Si l'homme a besoin de l'autonomie que lui octroie éventuellement son insoumission – tel est le cas d'Ibliss, seul sujet véritable dans le Coran – le Sujet-Dieu n'a pas besoin de cette autonomie, dans la mesure où il est celui qui la décrète pour toute sa créature. (Chebel 2002: pp. 68–69)
>
> (If Man needs the autonomy that his own non-submission potentially affords him – this is the case of Ibliss, the only real subject in the Quran – the God-Subject has no need for this autonomy in so far as he decrees it for all his creation.)

The problematic relationship between the *croyant* and the *sujet* for Chebel lies in the fact that a believer (the 'être-de-croyance') is entirely consumed with rituals such as prayer and fasting: 'Or il ne peut y avoir de sujet si ce sujet est acté plutôt que qu'acteur de sa condition de croyant, tout comme l'individu-sujet, tout au moins idéalement, est d'abord acteur de sa propre condition' (Chebel 2002: p. 70) (Yet there is no subject if that subject is enacting their condition rather than being the actor of it, just as the individual-subject, in ideal terms, at least, is actor of their own condition). In a similar manner then to Meddeb and, as we shall see, Bidar, Chebel's discussion of religious ritual or what he sees as excessive ritualisation also adopts pathologising elements. He employs a psychological approach to the discussion of the relationship between individual and community within Islam, and although he does make some attempt to say that one cannot generalise, 'car evidemment, l'islam n'est pas monolithique' (Chebel 2002: p. 94) (because, evidently, Islam is not monolithic), he does nevertheless argue that the 'système éducatif musulman' (p. 93) (Muslim educational system) is somehow responsible for the lack of individual subjectivity in Islam: 'Dès son plus jeune âge, l'enfant musulman est immergé dans une réalité sociale et humaine qui n'accorde aucune place au doute, au questionnement ou à l'échec. Toutes les questions que l'enfant se pose obtiennent des réponses toutes immédiates ou définitives.' (Chebel 2002: p. 93) (From the youngest age, Muslim children are immersed in a social and human reality which accords no room for doubt, questioning or failure. All the questions that a child asks themselves receive immediate or definitive responses.) For Chebel, this explains, at least in part, 'l'agressivité du musulman' (p. 93) (Muslim aggressiveness) when faced with someone or something that challenges the stability of his/her belief system – summed up as the impossibility of self-criticism or *autocritique*. Chebel's focus on the supposed absence of self-criticism amongst Muslims/Islam aligns his work with that of Bidar, who has made this theme a fairly dominant one in his writings about the wave of terror attacks perpetrated in the name of Islam in France and the reactions of the French Muslim community (see Bidar 2015b and Chapter 5).

It is perhaps in Chebel's macro-psychological or psycho-social analysis of Islam that his work most resembles that of Bidar and Meddeb, in that he focuses on the absence of individual agency and responsibility in the face of an overpowering *Ummah*. Here, Chebel argues that the advent of Islam replaced the Bedouin individualism of the pre-Islamic era with a more passive collectivism, which is inimical to subjectivity: 'la *Ummah* a également atténué le lien conscient et actif que l'individu se doit d'avoir avec lui-même, comme une responsabilité vis-à-vis de soi, minant ainsi toute aptitude à discerner l'acte singulier de l'acte collectif, ou encore la volonté personnelle de l'observance muette d'un rituel' (Chebel 2002: p. 108) (the *Ummah* also attenuated the conscious, active link and responsibility that the individual owes to themselves, thereby eroding any aptitude to distinguish individual acts from collective acts, and furthermore, individual will from the mute observance of ritual). For Chebel, such confusion between individual and collective acts leads in turn to confusion between the political and spiritual realms of existence, hence the absence of a secular tradition in many Muslim-majority societies. More fundamentally, Chebel argues that the lack of clear distinction between the individual and the collective is the basis of the notion of submission: 'Tel est le dilemme du sujet en islam: exister de manière aporétique dans un contexte qui ne magnifie que les vertus de passivité du "moi", suspectes depuis l'insoumission de Satan, elles demeurent le lot des bannis et des mécréants' (Chebel 2002: p. 110) (Such is the subject's dilemma in Islam: a truncated existence in a context which magnifies only the virtues associated with individual passivity, which have, since the non-submission of Satan, been regarded as suspect; they remain the fate of the banished and the unbelievers). The fact that many of the religious practices (or rituals as he refers to them), such as fasting, almsgiving, pilgrimage, Friday prayers, circumcision and marriage, are practised collectively is further evidence that the individual private sphere is unable to emerge as distinct from community life. Chebel contrasts this state of affairs with what he calls 'l'individu occidental', for whom an autonomous private sphere of life was the condition *sine qua non* for the emergence of the 'Western' individual. Chebel's argument is problematic on two counts. Firstly, most religions are indeed based on collective experience and practice: the Latin origin of the word religion, *religare* – to bring together – is itself clear testament to the social function and meaning of religion and religiosity. This is discussed in more detail in Chapter 3 where Babès looks at Durkheim's work on the social meanings of religion. In Christianity, prayer and pilgrimage can be collective, marriage is collective. The same can be said for Judaism (including marking the coming of age of boys through *Bar Mitzvah* celebrations). In this sense then, Islam is not an exceptional religion, as argued by Babès in Chapter 3. Secondly, the notion of the 'individu occidental' as somehow essentially existing in complete opposition to the 'individu musulman' suggests that Chebel is here subscribing to an orientalist 'clash of civilisations' narrative, which he otherwise and elsewhere claims to circumvent via his historical-anthropological analysis.

This apparent lack of nuance is further in evidence in Chebel's discussion of the cohesive power of the *Ummah*, which he attributes to the fact that Islam has never regarded itself as a minority religion. This claim is of course accurate for Muslim-majority societies but it in no way accounts for the status of European Islam and the experiences of European Muslims. In this work, Chebel is arguably more interested in the notion of myth in the anthropological sense, whereby the *Ummah* in Islam constitutes the ultimate myth which prevents the emergence of the *sujet musulman*: 'la *Ummah*, omniprésente dès l'époque médinoise, fonctionne aussi bien dans le mythe que dans la réalité comme un corps opaque et contraignant: l'individu est déclassé par rapport à la collectivité' (Chebel 2002: p. 148) (the *Ummah*, which was omniprésent during the Medina period, simultaneously functions in myth and reality as an opaque and constraining body: the individual is downgraded by the collective). Salvation can only come to the faithful via the collective and through obedience to religious teachings. Chebel further argues that it is significant that there is no discrete word in classical Arabic for 'subject', just as there is some difficulty surrounding the equivalent Arabic term for *laïcité*. On the question of *laïcité* and that of those Muslims who do stand out from the collective – ranging from secular to agnostic or atheist Muslims – Chebel highlights their fragile social position: 'Ils constituent toujours la part indicible de l'islam, son point aveugle' (Chebel 2002: p. 168) (They always constitute the unspeakable aspect of Islam, its blind spot).

Chebel's focus on the *Ummah* is similar to Bidar's focus on the notion of submission (Bidar 2008/2012a), in that both thinkers see that the foregrounding of collective identity or equality within Islam affects or circumscribes the notion of individual freedoms. Whilst Islam is often hailed as an egalitarian religion because of its absence of clergy, Chebel argues that it is the lack of clergy which leads to the importance of Islamic law (sharia), which in effect compensates for this absence. The preponderance of law further reduces the opportunities for the emergence of an autonomous subject. Like Bidar, who writes of 'un Dieu qui écrase l'homme' (Bidar 2008/2012a: p. 46) (a God who crushes Man), Chebel also refers to 'un Dieu trop puissant' (Chebel 2002: p. 173) (an over-powerful God), arguing that a clergy would have enabled a challenging or questioning of what he refers to as 'quatorze siècles de culture monolithique' (Chebel 2002: p. 173) (fourteen centuries of monolithic culture).[2] This supposedly monolithic culture is responsible for what Chebel sees as the lack of a culture of disobedience within Islam: 'On peut affirmer que l'obéissance du musulman constitue l'essence même de sa religion et la part la plus intangible de sa foi … L'obéissance est la clé de voûte du dispositif de contrainte morale, douce, pacifique, presque anodine, qui s'exerce sur l'ensemble de la communauté musulmane.' (Chebel 2002: pp. 185, 187) (We can maintain that obedience constitutes the very essence of his/her religion and the most intangible aspect of his/her faith … Obedience is the cornerstone of the moral, muted, pacific and almost anodyne framework of constraint, which affects the Muslim community as a whole.) Once again, Chebel seems to be adopting an essentialising and Orientalist approach to Islam and 'le musulman', and although he concedes that all religious traditions involve some form of obedience to dogma, he does not go beyond Islam in his discussion of social compliance within religious communities. Furthermore, he conflates Islam and Arab culture in this move, claiming that 'les vertus cathartiques de la déobéissance ne sont pas suffisamment connues dans la société arabe' (Chebel 2002: p. 190) (the cathartic virtues of disobedience are not sufficiently recognised in Arab society). Chebel sees this lack of a culture of disobedience vis-à-vis Islam as one of the principle reasons for the absence of 'autocritique' (self-criticism). He also ties it to education in Muslim societies (which he refers to as 'la société islamique') whereby he laments the lack of emphasis on education for the sake of education. For Chebel, this is explained by the tripartite structure of Muslim societies ('les gens du sabre' – warriors, those involved in jihad; 'les gens du *calame* (letters)/plume' – intellectuals, theologians and lawyers; and 'les gens de la balance' – merchants; Chebel 2002: p. 192) which has foregrounded the *gens du sabre* at the expense of the other two groups, in particular via an instrumentalisation of the *gens du calame/plume*. He seems to attribute this state of affairs to the fact that power in Islamic societies was won in great part by force and hence was consequently maintained by force. Chebel's critical evaluation of the tripartite social structure and what he calls his cultural psychoanalysis of power in Islam is yet another aspect of his broader argument that the emergence of the *sujet* is thwarted. This leads him on to a broader discussion of the notion of *jihad* within Islam – which he argues is no longer relevant or pertinent for the contemporary period – an idea he pursues in much greater depth via his *Islam des Lumières* project (Chebel 2004) which advocates a new phase of interpretation of the Quran, a *nouvel ijtihad* (reform).

Once Chebel has identified a range of historical, anthropological and psycho-social reasons for the elusive Islamic subject, he articulates his vision for an Islam that would, on the contrary, foster the emergence of the *sujet*. Chebel evokes Sartre's ideas about Man's ability to be a demiurge, imagining a scenario whereby a transition from the status of 'sujet clivé' (divided subject) of the *Ummah* to a 'sujet actif' (active subject) could materialise (Chebel 2002: p. 270). The 'sujet actif' can be regarded as a synonym for the subject citizen, and for Chebel citizenship can only develop via a process whereby individuals 'tourne[r] le dos à la mosquée sans supprimer Dieu de son horizon vital' (Chebel 2002: p. 270) (turn their backs on the mosque without removing God from their horizon). It is in this final culmination of Chebel's reflections about the conditions under which the *sujet musulman* may emerge that the theme of *laïcité* is discussed. The *nouvel ijtihad*, referred to by Chebel as 'une véritable refonte de l'islam' (Chebel 2002: p. 279) (a veritable re-working of Islam), rests upon the assumption that the spiritual and political spheres are separate. So, in a similar manner to Meddeb, Chebel makes a strong case for *laïcité* as the *sine qua non* of freedom of conscience and action for all those who are part of the *Dar al-islam* (Territory of Islam).

It is curious that Chebel waits until the closing pages of *Le Sujet en islam* to address the position and experiences of those Muslims who live *outside* of the *Dar al-islam*. After all, this is a book published in French, in France for a French-speaking audience. In a similar fashion to Meddeb, Chebel seems to be writing for a French 'superaddressee' about Muslims and an Islam which is rendered even more 'Other' since most of his analysis is not grounded in the familiar French context. Nevertheless, he makes the point that it is perhaps via Muslims in the West that a 'recomposition mentale et idéologique' (mental and ideological recomposition) could take place and in turn have an impact on 'les pays d'origine' (Chebel 2002: p. 283). This ideological and mental recomposition would rest upon the principles of *laïcité*. Whilst Chebel sees that European Islam may provide the 'éléments de réponse' (Chebel 2002: p. 282) (some partial answers) for the emergence of an Islamic subjectivity, he is nevertheless mindful to argue that there have been many examples of a sort of *implicit laïcité* within the history of Islam, such as the Abbasid, dynasty of Baghdad, the Ummayyad dynasty of Cordoba and Granada and the Zirid dynasty of Tunisia. However, he returns to a fairly limited reading of these phenomena, arguing that these Muslim experiments of *laïcité* could not develop, due to a lack of economic and social 'maturity' (i.e. stability). Is Chebel subscribing to a self-orientalising logic in the manner of Meddeb (see Chapter 1) in claiming this? Or is he trying to find a middle ground between Orientalism and self-defensiveness by hailing the 'jeunesse musulmane d'Occident' as the likely purveyors of reform? His attempts to move beyond a binary approach lead him to pose the dilemma facing Muslims in the following terms: 'Comment peuvent-ils accéder à la modernité – et laquelle? – sans tourner le dos à leur foi?' (Chebel 2002: p. 285) (How can they gain access to modernity – however that is defined – without turning their back on their faith?). This is the task that he sets himself in his 2004 text, *Manifeste pour un islam des Lumières*.

Islamic reform

Chebel coined the term 'un islam des Lumières' in his text *Manifeste pour un islam des Lumières*. Here, he argues that the expression *islam des Lumières* might correspond in Arabic to *Al-Islam al-munawwar, Al-Islam al-munir*, in German to the term *Aufklärung* or in English to the Enlightenment. In *Manifeste pour un islam des Lumières*, Chebel proposes how Islam should be reformed from within and he thus presents himself as the inheritor of other historic and contemporary Islamic reformist movements such as the nineteenth-century *nahda* (awakening or renaissance) and other thinkers ranging from the twelfth to the twenty-first century, such as Ibn Rushd, Mohammed Iqbal (Afghanistan), Mohamed Talbi (Tunisia), Mohammed Arkoun (France), Bichara Khader (Belgium), Muhammad Said al-Ashmawy and Nassar Abu Zayd (Egypt) and Mohammed Abed Al-Jabri (Morocco). His twenty-seven proposals cannot all be discussed in detail here, but the key point he makes is that it is incumbent upon Muslim scholars to engage in a process of scriptural reinterpretation of the Quran, known as *ijtihad*, so that it is made more compatible with the current historical period: 'il s'agit d'adapter l'islam à la modernité' (Chebel 2004: p. 26) (it is a question of adapting Islam to modernity). This adaptation seems to be a one-way process: Chebel claims that calls for modernity to adapt itself to Islam are akin to Islamist, i.e. extremist positions.

Chebel's rationale for launching his manifesto is ambiguous for two reasons. Firstly, many of the proposals in the *Manifeste* cannot be described as theological, as they are not strictly speaking about a reinterpretation (*ijtihad*) of the Quran, despite his assertion that such a process is fundamental. Instead, many of the proposals (approximately a third of them) are more social or political in nature and seem to be broad generalisations about Muslim-majority societies and what they 'need' to 'change' in Chebel's view; examples include combatting corruption, embracing new technologies and raising environmental awareness. The second ambiguity in Chebel's manifesto is the lack of clarity regarding his audience: is he addressing a French audience in a move which, in a similar manner to *Le Sujet en islam* (2002) somehow contributes to a certain 'othering' or Orientalisation of Islam, or is his audience a Muslim-French one or simply a Muslim/Islamic world readership? The latter scenario is of course of limited possibility since this is a work published in French by a Parisian publishing house. Indeed, it would seem that Chebel is addressing a French or Francophone readership in order to *inform* them about Islam, which is primarily constructed as being a non-European entity.

Chebel starts his *Manifeste* with a preamble which he entitles 'Le constat' (Observation) whereby he suggests that his motivation for writing this text stems from his claim that in the absence of the rule of law in 'Muslim countries' and the major upheavals that have shaken the Arab world in particular, Muslims have reacted in predominantly two ways: 'Certains choisissent le repli et l'immobilisme ... Ce repli est adopté par la plupart des musulmans qui manquent d'un minimum de connaissances et qui ne peuvent juger la religion qu'à travers les discours redondants que les imams tiennent habituellement à la mosquée' (Chebel 2004: p. 12) (Some choose withdrawal and opposition to change ... This withdrawal is adopted by most Muslims who have minimum knowledge and who can only understand religion via the redundant sermons that imams habitually deliver at the mosque). The second category of Muslims which Chebel identifies concerns a minority, albeit a more active one, and this is the category of the 'islamistes' (Chebel 2004: p. 12): 'D'un côté, un islam modéré, non revendicatif et surtout peu politisé qui caractérise le plus grand nombre. De l'autre, un islam militant et très politisé.' (Chebel 2004: p. 13) (On the one hand, a moderate Islam, which is non-dissenting and above all, depoliticised, reflecting the majority. On the other hand, an activist and highly politicised Islam.) Chebel's choice to reduce the heterogeneity and variety of Muslim beliefs and practices to a binary opposition between what he calls 'les musulmans identitaires' (identity-focused Muslims) and 'les musulmans modérés' (moderate Muslims) (Chebel 2004: p. 14) does seem to suggest that his intended readership or imagined superaddressee is one with little knowledge or experience of Islam or Muslims. This makes it all the more problematic when one takes into account that Chebel saw himself as a spokesperson for Muslims in France (he talks about listening to Muslims themselves; p. 10) as well as an intellectual with the capacity to shift French Muslims' values, as he claimed in his 2010 interview with *L'Express* magazine (Faure 2010). Nevertheless, a potentially more generous assessment of Chebel's position would acknowledge his claim in the same *Express* interview that he sees that the 'problem' is not caused by Islam but rather by its 'pratiquants'. Indeed, this may be why he makes a clear proposal calling for the revocation of *jihad* when it is understood as 'holy war' rather than a personal inner quest for self-discovery: 'Cette proposition vise à substituer à la guerre sainte (*djihad*) une veritable ascèse intérieure, un sacerdoce orienté vers le bien, un véritable approfondissement de la foi, et non pas une diversion obtenue à la pointe de l'épée' (Chebel 2004: p. 39) (This proposal aims to substitute holy war (*jihad*) with a real form of interior self-discipline, a calling which is oriented towards the good life, a profound development of faith, rather than a mere diversion enacted by the sword). Chebel's proposal also has a more socio-political aspect beyond the individual/interior dimension, in that he calls for the creation of a Muslim non-governmental organisation which would promote peace and what Chebel calls 'une véritable culture de paix au sein de l'espace musulman et partout si nécessaire' (Chebel 2004: p. 41) (a genuine culture of peace at the heart of the Muslim world and everywhere if necessary). Whilst Chebel's proposal can be argued to be a laudable one, it is striking that he seems to see peace or a 'culture of peace' as something which is primarily missing from the Muslim world. Given such a partial approach, one cannot help thinking of Meddeb's work which in its own way contributes, perhaps unwittingly, to the undermining of millions of the faithful worldwide.

Chebel's focus on the role of reason, secularism, freedom of conscience, *jihad*, women, individualism and humanism seem to be most representative of what Chebel is trying to achieve via his call to reinterpret the Quran. Chebel's intellectual project to sketch out the dimensions of an Enlightenment Islam can thus be understood in relation to the notion of translating secularism into Islam. However, the process of translation is multi-directional, since Chebel points out at the start of *Manifeste* that the expression *islam des Lumières* refers simultaneously to the European Enlightenment of the eighteenth and nineteenth centuries and to the symbolism of light which is present within the Quran and in Islamic thought, particularly amongst Islamic mystics such as Ibn Arabi whereby *lumière* can be understood as an invitation towards knowledge, as in sura 24 entitled *An-Nur* (Light), cited by Chebel:

> Dieu est la lumière des cieux et de la terre! Sa lumière est comparable à une niche où se trouve une lampe. La lampe est dans un verre; le verre est semblable à une étoile brillante. Cette lampe est allumée à un arbre béni: l'olivier qui ne provient ni de l'Orient, ni de l'Occident et dont l'huile est près d'éclairer sans que le feu la touche. Lumière sur lumière! Dieu guide, vers la lumière, qui il veut. Dieu propose aux hommes des paraboles. Dieu connaît toute chose. (Chebel 2004: p. 11 cites *The Qur'an*, sura 24, v. 35; OUP 2004 translation, p. 223).

> (God is the Light of the heavens and the earth. His Light is like this: there is a niche, and in it a lamp, the lamp inside a glass, a glass like a glittering star, fuelled from a blessed olive tree from neither east nor west, whose oil almost gives light even when no fire touches it – light upon light – God guides whoever He will to his Light; God draws such comparisons for people; God has full knowledge of everything.)

Despite the importance of the notion of light and knowledge in the Quran itself as highlighted above, Chebel argues that one of the main explanations for the difficulties that Islam encounters today is the disdain with which rationality is regarded by many Muslim societies: 'Ce phénomène tient au fait que les sciences rationnelles ne sont pas encore considérées comme faisant partie du savoir-faire oriental … un enseignant universitaire est si dénigré aujourd'hui qu'il éprouve de la honte à donner son titre' (Chebel 2004: p. 32) (This phenomenon is due to the fact that the rational sciences are still not regarded as part of Eastern savoir-faire … a university teacher is today so denigrated that they are ashamed to divulge their title). Chebel argues that this suspicion is particularly the case for disciplines such as philosophy, although he does not specify which countries he is referring to, thus creating a rather sweeping impression. However, although he argues clearly that in order to develop an *islam des Lumières*, it is necessary to 'affirmer la supériorité de la raison sur toute autre forme de pensée ou croyance' (Chebel 2004: p. 30) (affirm the superiority of reason above all other forms of thought or belief). He makes the point quite clearly at the end of the book that rationality is to be 'reinvented' in order to enhance faith: 'C'est bien cette direction que toute réforme de l'islam doit prendre: réinventer la rationalité et le sens de l'histoire pour mieux vivre sa foi' (Chebel 2004: p. 198) (It is certainly this direction that any reform of Islam must take: via a reinvention of rationality and the sense of history in order to foster positive relationships with one's faith). So he is attempting to go beyond a simplistic opposition between faith and reason: 'la foi n'est pas antinomique au changement, elle est seulement sa première condition' (p. 198) (faith is not contradictory to change; it is simply its primary condition). Nevertheless, he does not give much indication in the chapter of how this reinvention might take place.

It is left to readers to assume that Chebel places the notion of rationality at the heart of his understanding of the individual and individual subjectivity. Indeed, proposal 13 in his *Manifeste* returns to the central theme addressed in *Le Sujet en islam* whereby Chebel calls for a dismantling of what he calls 'l'attitude islamoïde', defined in the following terms: 'Le comportement "islamoïde" consiste donc à rejeter en bloc toute innovation inconvenante, tout en donnant le change à quiconque s'avise de critique tel ou tel précepte islamique' (Chebel 2004: p. 101) (The 'Islamoid' attitude involves the wholesale rejection of any improper innovation, whilst simultaneously pulling the wool over the eyes of anyone who dares to criticise Islamic precepts). Instead, Chebel calls for a clear divide between public and private spheres in order to foster collective responsibility and personal engagement, and to combat what he calls 'la pensée fixiste des musulmans' (Chebel 2004: p. 100) (the fixity of Muslim thought). So what he calls 'le primat de la politique en matière de gestion de la cité' (Chebel 2004; p. 104) (the primacy of politics in terms of the organisation of the civic community) is central to his discussion of the secularisation of Islam, which is translated into Arabic as *ilmaniyya*. Here Chebel makes quite concrete proposals regarding what he sees as a necessary separation between politics and religion and, like Meddeb, he cites the West ('L'Occident') as the example *par excellence* of successful secularisation – a process which he associates with its power. Furthermore, Chebel laments the dearth of modern reformist thinkers in Islam equivalent to the European tradition of Montaigne, Hobbes, Nietzsche, Montesquieu, Marx, Einstein and Freud.

One of Chebel's proposals which reflects his constant reference to the European Enlightenment concerns the question of freedom of conscience (proposal 16): 'Faire de la liberté de conscience et la liberté de pensée des vertus musulmanes' (Chebel 2004: p. 117) (To make freedom of conscience and freedom of thought Muslim virtues). Although the proposal makes it seem that these concepts are somehow external to Islamic tradition, Chebel is actually more nuanced than his proposal suggests, since he shows that previous Islamic reform movements such as the Mutazilites or the Ikhwan as-Safa (tenth to twelfth century) had already explored, albeit without success, the notion of freedom of individual conscience. Nevertheless, the process of translating secularism into Islam is, for Chebel, primarily concerned with the development of what he calls 'un nouvel humanisme' (Chebel 2004: p. 120). Here, Chebel's argument resonates with that of the philosopher Bidar (see Chapter 5) in so far as he argues that the notion of *les droits de l'homme* are not in themselves alien to the Quran and that, indeed, human rights principles which we associate with non-religious and Western values could actually be enriched or revived via contact with Islam:

> Y a-t-il contradiction entre le respect des individus et plus largement des droits de l'homme et les prescriptions coraniques? Rien dans le Coran ne s'y oppose, pas plus d'ailleurs que dans le *hadith* du Prophète, ni même dans la tradition observée par certains souverains musulmans au temps où l'islam avait une perception apaisée de lui-même. L'Homme n'est devenu secondaire que lorsque les logiques d'enfermement idéologique ou d'exploitation industrielle (grand capital) l'ont assujetti à des normes de production, de consommation ou de fonctionnement qui dépassent sa vocation première. C'est en cela que l'islam pourra innover, en revenant à une meilleure appréciation de l'homme dans sa multiplicité et en faisant sienne cette même multiplicité, aujourd'hui combattue, minorée ou suspectée. (Chebel 2004: p. 185)

> (Is there a contradiction between the respect for individuals and more broadly, human rights and Quranic teachings? Nothing in the Quran would appear to go against such ideals, no more than in the *hadith* about the Prophet in any case, nor in the traditions observed by certain Muslim sovereigns when Islam was at one with itself. Man [sic] only became secondary when the logic of ideological limitation or industrial exploitation (mass capital) subjected him to the norms of production, consumption or function which were irrelevant to his initial vocation. This is how Islam could innovate, by coming to a more fine-tuned appreciation of Man [sic] in his multiplicity and by embracing that very multiplicity, which is currently fought, minimised or regarded as suspect.)

So Chebel's emphasis on humanism means that he sees no necessary contradiction between humanism, the divine or 'le sacré'. On the contrary, Chebel compares 'l'homme' to a 'source infinie', claiming that it is possible to measure the 'génie' of a civilisation or a religion by its ability to 'promouvoir le divin' (Chebel 2004: p. 185) (promote the divine).

Despite Chebel's certainty regarding some aspects of his reformist proposals, he is surprisingly cautious in other areas, notably with regard to his discussion of the status of women in Islam. Unlike some of his other very concrete proposals, Chebel holds back from proposing specific change where women are concerned, preferring instead to present his stance as an invitation for further reflection: 'Est-il temps d'appeler à une égalité absolue de droits et de devoirs entre l'homme et la femme, ainsi qu'à la reconnaissance de la dignité de celle-ci en tant que croyante et actrice à part entière de la vie sociale, religieuse, économique et intellectuelle?' (Chebel 2004: p. 74) (Is it time to call for absolute equality of rights and responsibilities amongst men and women, as well as the recognition of the dignity of women as believers and actors in social, religious, economic and intellectual life in their own right?) He is critical of the headscarf, using the limited number of references to it in the Quran as his evidence, and he praises the reform of the Moroccan civil code in women's favour, but aside from this there is not much focus or detail from him on this significant issue. Indeed, Chebel has worked consistently on the question of sex and love in Islam, so this omission in analytical depth is all the more curious. More broadly speaking, it is possible to argue that the whole of the *Manifeste* is just what it claims to be, in that it is a broad programme about the change its author wants to see and what he wants his readership to see. It is fair to say that this text, which is perhaps one of the least 'scholarly' in his repertoire, is the one that Chebel is perhaps best known for. The *islam des Lumières* formula was an effective one in the French context and in a sense it became Chebel's 'calling card'. His launch of the *Noor* (the magazine/cultural review of the *islam des Lumières* project) is further testimony to the fact that it was via *islam des Lumières* that he was able to communicate most effectively as a public Muslim intellectual.

Islam and Reason

In a prolongation of his reflections in his *Manifeste pour un islam des Lumières*, Chebel again picks up the theme of reason and rational, critical enquiry in his 2006 essay, *L'Islam et la raison: le combat des idées*. However, unlike other recent secular Muslim thinkers such as Meddeb, Chebel did not argue that Reason or rationality are somehow external to Islamic thought and, indeed, in the introduction to his text *L'islam et la raison*, he states that the object of the book is to 'exhume' the ideas of free-thinkers that have been part of the history of Islam:

> L'idée de ce livre est simple: l'histoire musulmane conserve le souvenir d'expériences innovantes, rebelles et intelligentes qui ont ouvert des voies, posé des jalons. Mais qui se souvient encore de ce passé? Exhumer les réflexions des libres-penseurs, de théologiens curieux et de savants profanes qui ont cherché à doter la troisième religion monothéiste d'une approche rationnelle exigeante, en phase avec la réalité de leur temps, tel et le projet de cet ouvrage. (Chebel 2006: p. 7)

> (The idea behind this book is simple: Muslim history preserves the memory of innovative, bold and erudite experiences, which opened up pathways and marked major achievements. But who still remembers this past? The exhumation of free-thinkers' reflections and curious theologians' or non-religious scholars' ideas who sought to provide the third monotheistic religion with a rigorous rational approach, in step with the realities of their epoch, such is the aim of this project.)

So Chebel's understanding of Reason is not a phenomenon that is alien to religious faith; indeed he makes the case quite clearly for Reason being a 'force alternative' (Chebel 2006: p. 9) which facilitates religious faith: 'la pluralité des opinions et des croyances prépare l'avènement d'une force alternative, celle de la Raison, une force qui croit d'abord en la disponibilité individuelle pour s'emparer intuitivement de l'entité Dieu' (Chebel 2006: p. 9) (the plurality of opinions and beliefs lays the ground for the emergence of an alternative force, namely Reason, a force which believes primarily in individual availability in order to intuitively take over from the God entity).

Chebel's overall approach in his 2006 text can be described as both a historical and a speculative interrogation which poses the following question: what might have been if Islam had embraced the numerous missed opportunities to reform itself and engage in a humanist and secular religiosity? He identifies three major phases in the history of ideas in Islam: the introduction of Islam in the seventh century, the development of Islamic law between the eighth and ninth centuries, and intellectual autonomy from the ninth to the tenth century. He provides an overview of the different 'acteurs de la controverse' (Chebel 2006: p. 7) (actors of controversy), starting from the period immediately following the death of the Prophet Mohammed, through to the Mutazilites, the Mutakallimun and Ikhwan as-Safa movements, as well as the experiences of Al-Andalus and Sufi Islam.

Chebel shows how, in the immediate aftermath of the death of the Prophet Mohammed, the political power struggles amongst his followers led to a limitation of possibilities for an Islam initially at ease with the notions of Reason, individual free will and the separation between political and religious spheres. He resorts to pathologising terms as he describes this period in terms of the 'maladies d'enfance' (childhood illnesses) of Islam (Chebel 2006: p. 24) and argues that in their desire to maintain a fragile and new faith in a political and cultural context beset by rivalries and the risk of a return to the polytheism of the past, the Prophet's successors quashed dissent: 'D'une certaine façon, la philosophie avait perdu sa première manche face à la politique, de sorte que la foi de quelques-uns a neutralisé les postures audacieuses de ceux qui voulaient sortir l'islam de ce premier enfermement doctrinal' (Chebel 2006: p. 19) (In a certain manner, philosophy lost the first round to politics in so far as the faith of a minority neutralised the audacious positions of those who sought to extract Islam from this first phase of doctrinal closure).

Following his initial discussion of the period following the death of the Prophet, the remainder of *L'islam et la raison* focuses on ninth- and tenth-century developments in Islam's intellectual culture. Chebel's 'tour d'horizon' of the rationalist thinkers in Islam starts then with a consideration of the Mutazilites, citing one of the key figures of the movement, Al-Jahiz, as follows: 'Cinquante doutes valent mieux qu'une certitude' (Al Jahiz, *Le Livre des animaux*, Chebel 2006: p. 36) (Fifty doubts are worth more than one certitude). He argues that central to the ideas developed by the Mutazilites were notions of human freedom, free will and responsibility. He also discusses the Mutakallimun movement (theologians specialised in the art of logic, discourse and dialectics) and the Baghdad-based thinker Al-Ghazzali (1058–1111) in particular, who is described as embodying the renewal of Islamic thought via his ability to reconcile mysticism and faith with Reason (his writings were influential in fields as varied as philosophy, speculative theology, mysticism, rhetoric, law and politics). Chebel argues that Al-Ghazzali's concern for all forms of Muslim expression afforded him a particular stance with regard to power, and thus he participated in what Chebel sees as the the 'ré-illumination de l'islam' (Chebel 2006: p. 64) (re-illumination of Islam).

A further key movement associated with such renewal via rationalist enquiry discussed by Chebel is the ninth-century movement known as the *Ikhwan as-Safa* (the Brothers of Purity) who are compared to the *philosophes* of the *Encyclopédie* project in eighteenth-century France due to their emphasis on pluralism and critical thinking. They simultaneously drew on the Prophet's and *hadith*'s calls to Muslims to educate themselves, the Prophet having claimed that 'S'instruire est l'un des devoirs du musulman' (Chebel 2006: p. 72) (Educating oneself is one of the duties of Muslims). The group remained anonymous for fear of reprisals in ninth-century Basra (Iraq) and this may explain in part their short-lived existence and influence. However, they did produce an *encyclopédie* which tackled the fundamental issue of the relationship between the power of an all-mighty God and that of his creation, Man, where a philosophical and gnostic approach was foregrounded. The *Ikhwan as-Safa Encyclopédie* influenced Muslim Spain's intellectuals, such as Maslama Al-Majriti in the tenth century and subsequent generations of Muslim scholars who went on to publish their own encyclopaedias in areas beyond mysticism, alchemy and gnosis in order to include the 'profane' sciences such as history, geography and language. For Chebel, the *Ikhwan as-Safa Encyclopédie* and the movement in general constitute a good example of how *raison* and faith can be articulated within Islam. Indeed, he points out that 'la plupart de ces penseurs, philosophes, théologiens ou linguistes, ont été de parfaits musulmans, respectueux du dogme et de la tradition. Mais tous refusaient le diktat d'une lecture formatée, artificielle et privée des vertus éclairantes du cœur.' (Chebel 2006: p. 82) (most of these thinkers, philosophers, theologians or linguists were perfect Muslims, who respected religious teachings and tradition. But they all refused the diktat of a formatted, artificial reading, deprived of the enlightening virtues of human emotion.) Chebel concludes that the *Ikhwan as-Safa* demonstrated that it is possible to return to the fundamental texts and teachings (via *ijtihad* – reinterpretation and reform), interrogate them and go beyond them without dismantling faith in the process.

Such a spirit of tolerance is something that Chebel identifies as being part of Islamic intellectual culture, citing the experience of Muslim Spain or what he refers to as 'l'esprit de Cordoue' (spirit of Cordoba) whereby tolerance constituted a model that inspired a range of elites including emirs, viziers, scholars and poets. For Chebel, Al-Andalus represents one of the rare and unparalleled examples of Islamic humanism due to the successful co-existence between different religious groups there. He laments the generalised ignorance of the contribution of Arab civilisation to the West and the way in which it served as a bridge between Ancient Greece and the European Renaissance. Of course, Chebel contemplates that today the 'spirit of Cordoba' is non-existent and locates it as possibly emergent in Paris, Brussels, New York or Berlin. On the question of what he sees as the necessary reform of Islam, Chebel argues that this cannot be done without the West since the spirit of Cordoba, Granada or Seville (synonymous for tolerance) is now situated in the non-Muslim world. And yet, it is problematic to claim that tolerance only exists in the West. This is a significant generalisation which does not take account of the individual agency and subjectivity that Chebel is apparently so keen on. Instead, it favours an essentialist approach to cultural norms which does not acknowledge the complexities of Muslim lives and experiences of tolerance in multiple locations. Certainly, for a French Muslim readership who may experience discrimination due to their faith or presumed faith, to claim that the West is the cradle of tolerance is highly contentious, in addition to being a-historical given the West's myriad colonial histories.

This tendency to seek 'salvation' in the West is not always apparent, however, and fundamentally Chebel is keen to demonstrate that Islam has, within its own cultural and intellectual history, successfully articulated religion and tolerance, as well as religion and rational, critical enquiry, to the extent that in many ways the European Enlightenment was facilitated by the work of Arab and Persian intellectuals who translated Greek scholars (Chebel 2006: p. 122). Similarly, Chebel's approach to Sufi Islam as 'une forme d'humanisme musulman' (Chebel 2006: p. 103) (a form of Muslim humanism) that moves beyond ritualistic forms of religiosity and submission whilst simultaneously favouring rational and philosophical enquiry means that he sees in Sufi Islam a possible vehicle for renewal, which whilst facilitating the Enlightenment of Others (the Renaissance), has not enjoyed its own Enlightenment. Chebel here is very careful to argue that this 'missed opportunity' is not due to the Quran or Islam itself but rather to the socio-political and historical conditions under which it developed. Despite his tendency for pathologising language (similarly to Meddeb, Bidar and, to a lesser extent, Babès), such as referring to the *autisme* of Islam, Chebel is confident in the future. For him, the crux of Islam's renewal along humanist and rationalist lines lies in its acceptance of *laïcité*, the essential separation of the political and religious spheres. This is the condition *sine qua non* of any future *islam des Lumières* and a process of *ijtihad*; in this Chebel assigns an important role to the West, once again, but this time to Muslims *in* the West for it is *they* who, according to Chebel, have the ability to bring about change and, in turn, influence *le monde islam*.

Performing cultural encounter

Perhaps Chebel sees himself as one of those Western Muslims who can bring about such change. This is certainly suggested in the title of his 2011 dialogue with philosopher Christian Godin, *Vivre ensemble: éloge de la différence*. Yet this encounter is characterised by much ambiguity. For example, in his dialogue with Godin he pointedly remarks that he is frustrated by the frequent debates about the 'in/compatibility' of Islam and *laïcité* in contemporary France: 'La laïcité est en quelque sort le ticket d'entrée dans le trio gagnant du sommet ... C'est comme sur un champ de bataille: l'islam doit se démettre ... et venir endosser le manteau de la laïcité' (Chebel and Godin: 2011: p. 247) (Secularism is somehow the entry ticket to the winning trio at the summit ... It is like a battlefield: Islam must submit ... and embrace secularism). He thus appears to suggest that *laïcité* becomes problematic shorthand for anti-religious rhetoric and suspicion of Islam and Muslims as opposed to tolerance and recognition of religious liberties and pluralism. Ultimately, Chebel makes a strong statement in favour of *laïcité* because of the protection it can provide to religious minorities such as Muslims: 'Je suis un défenseur déclaré à titre personnel de la laïcité. Je n'ai pas rédigé un seul article sur l'islam sans rappeler cette référence.' (Chebel and Godin 2011: p. 245) (I am a self-declared defender of secularism. All of my writings on Islam recall this principle.) Chebel seems to judge it necessary to state this – to present himself as an exemplary Muslim (see Mas 2006, Fernando 2009 and Kiwan 2013). Only once this has been done is he then able to go on to critique what he regards as some of the lacunae within current understandings and applications of *laïcité,* namely regarding religious clothing: 'Ces gens-là se disent: Je suis francais, et je n'ai pas le droit de porter le vêtement que je veux?' (Chebel and Godin 2011: p. 250) (These people say: I am French and I can't wear what I want?).

Chebel's stance when faced with Godin is thus markedly different to many of his other public interventions on the issue of the headscarf. Indeed, Chebel was a vocal supporter of the 2004 law banning religious symbols, arguing in *L'Express* in 2010 that the *burqa* was a 'provocation': 'Ce que les gens doivent comprendre, c'est que la première religion du pays, c'est la laïcité. Toutes les autres sont personnelles, et doivent se vivre dans la sphère privée. Hors de la mosquée, le Musulman devient un citoyen.' (Faure 2010) (What people must understand is that the majority religion of the country is secularism. All other religions are personal and must be lived out in the private sphere.) The stark contrast between Chebel's positions in 2010 and 2011 must be linked to the different performative contexts of his statements. It is notable that, when making a solo public intervention in *L'Express*, he is keen to unequivocally align himself with a strong interpretation of *laïcité* – one which is itself endowed with its own religious traits. In *Vivre ensemble: éloge de la différence*, Chebel is in dialogue with a non-Muslim philosopher who is fairly critical of Islam and who adopts a universalist, difference-blind approach to identity politics. As a result, the dialogue between Chebel and Godin becomes a sort of performance of cultural encounter. Indeed, the *avant-propos* of the text suggests that the notion of cultural encounter is central to their debate: 'car notre formation dans et par une culture particulière – musulmane pour l'un, occidentale laïque pour l'autre – ne signifie pas l'enfermement dans cette culture' (Chebel and Godin 2011: p. 9) (because our grounding in a particular culture – Muslim for one, Western for the other – does not mean being enclosed in that culture).

Cultural encounter is not necessarily a smooth process, and in some ways the dialogue between Chebel and Godin resembles a confrontation. When faced with Godin's difference-blind universalism, for instance, Chebel takes up the challenge of advocating diversity: 'Ce qui fait notre identité, c'est la diversité des differences' (Chebel and Godin 2011: p. 20) (The range of differences is what makes up our identity). Unlike his sometimes essentialist statements about 'le musulman' or 'le monde musulman' in *Le Sujet en islam*, *Manifeste pour un islam des Lumières* or *L'Islam et la raison*, Chebel repeatedly takes an anti-essentialist stance in *Vivre ensemble*, arguing that 'il n'y a pas d'identité absolue' (Chebel and Godin 2011: p. 25) (there is no absolute identity). Chebel also develops a much more critical stance in relation to the question of individual autonomy in this text than he does in *Le Sujet en islam* (2002), even going so far as to allude to the 'illusion d'autonomie' (illusion of autonomy) as a principle (Chebel and Godin 2011: p. 62), whereas in his 2002 text he suggests that autonomy is a tangible goal to be strived for within Islam in order to facilitate the emergence of individual subjectivity.

Furthermore, Chebel is more critical of the West when faced with Christian Godin's claims that human rights discourse is universalist, and he instead argues that human rights must take into account cultural particularisms: 'Les droits de l'homme ne seront pas applicables ni appliqués du tout tant qu'on arrivera pas à comprendre les schémas chinois, africains, arabes et musulmans de la pensée' (Chebel and Godin 2011: p. 101) (Human rights will neither be applicable nor applied at all as long as we cannot comprehend Chinese, African, Arab and Muslim systems of thought). Chebel presents himself as far more sensitive to ethnocentric claims in this dialogue with Godin than he does in his own single-authored works. Godin, on the other hand, is convinced that the overcoming of ethnocentrism has de facto been achieved in the West (Chebel and Godin 2011: p. 109), whilst Chebel remains convinced about what he calls the 'violence symbolique' (p. 115) of Western domination in the world and the problematic absence of a human rights agenda that takes into account the rights of the stranger.

Chebel ultimately seems to occupy a more nuanced and complex position in the conversation with Godin than he does in some of his earlier works, and the dialogue format perhaps encourages Chebel to be more self-reflexive about his own motivations and perspective. In the company of Godin, Chebel thus describes himself as 'occidentalisé' (westernised) and explains how this has created a backlash against his work, particularly *Le Sujet en islam*. However, whereas Chebel seeks to illuminate what he regards as some of the shortcomings of Islam in *Le Sujet en islam*, in his encounter with Godin Chebel is keen to demonstrate that human will (subjectivity) and ethics are clearly articulated in the Quran via the notion of *khalifat*, whereby human beings are expected to be the lieutenants of God on earth. Here, Chebel's vision for an Islamic humanism are, like Bidar's, anchored to the concept of the *khalifat*, but Chebel does not go as far as Bidar in his interpretation of this concept (see Chapter 5). In his insistence that Islam already articulates a humanist vision from *within*, Chebel simultaneously rejects the notion of some sort of irreconcilable opposition between East and West, saying that the notion of a 'clash of ideologies' would be more accurate than the notion of a 'clash of civilisations' (Chebel and Godin 2011: p. 223), since civilisations mutually fertilise and influence each other more than they come into conflict with one another. This statement yet again marks a departure from Chebel's stance in *Le Sujet en islam* whereby he seemed to subscribe to such a clash. In a similar move regarding the status of women in Islam, in *Manifeste pour un islam des Lumières* Chebel regards this as something that requires reform. Yet in Godin's presence, Chebel makes a point of defending the status of women in the Quran, whom he says are addressed as '[Ô] croyantes' (Oh believers!) rather than according to their biological status as women. He interprets this as a potentially progressive aspect of the Quranic text: 'il y a un droit possible pour l'affranchissement des femmes dans la mesure où le Coran n'a pas figé leur statut au fait qu'elles soient femmes' (Chebel and Godin 2011: p. 309) (there is a potential right to female enfranchisement in so far as the Quran does not define their status in terms of them being women).

A further apparent development in Chebel's thought which emerges through the performed cultural encounter with Godin is his claim that there is not one Islam but rather many Islams and many diverse ways of being Muslim; in short, there is no such thing as a 'civilisation arabo-musulmane'. This is certainly not the approach that Chebel constructs in *Le Sujet en islam*, *Manifeste pour un islam des Lumières* or *l'Islam et la raison* where he consistently makes reference to the idea of a 'civilisation arabo-musulmane' which has developed through an imbrication of anthropological and theological influences.

Despite his apparent inconsistencies, depending on the context, Chebel fundamentally seems to be arguing in favour of the recognition of France's Muslims. On the issue of integration and assimilation, Chebel claims that many of the Muslims in the *banlieues*[3] have turned towards a ritualistic practice of Islam in the face of social exclusion and discrimination as a mode of resistance and opposition, rather than one of disintegration (Chebel and Godin 2011: p. 273). Chebel thus seems to be trying to understand why young people born and brought up in France would adopt orthodox or even extremist beliefs, so he applies a sociopolitical lens to his analysis when faced with Godin.

Pathologising tropes?

However, when Chebel publishes as an individual, he reverts back to a much more critical stance with regard to Islam. Indeed, the very title of his 2015 book-length essay *L'Inconscient de l'islam* is indicative of what we might call an internal approach to what Chebel regards as the problems that face Islam and Muslims in the contemporary period. Chebel's main premise in *L'Inconscient de l'islam* is that in order to understand 'la folie actuelle d'une partie de la communauté' (Chebel 2015a: back cover blurb) (the current madness of a part of the community), it is necessary to drill down into the twin notions of 'la faute' (sin) and 'la transgression' (transgression) which are omnipresent in the contemporary Muslim world. Chebel proposes doing this via a historical-anthropological investigation of the link between religion, politics and freedom within Muslim doctrine in order to further understand a number of contemporary 'ills'.

In *L'Inconscient de l'islam* then, Chebel's approach is in some ways similar to Meddeb's (and Bidar's) pathologising stance, since his starting point for trying to understand the 'folie actuelle' (current madness) afflicting a part of the community today is to consider what he refers to as 'la structure mentale' (cognitive structure) of Islam as it developed in the Arabian Peninsula from the eighth to the thirteenth century (Chebel 2015a: p. 7). To evoke the notion of *folie* is very similar to Meddeb's *maladie de l'islam* and Bidar's own discussion of the 'cancer' of Islam (Meddeb 2002; Bidar 2015b), suggesting a certain level of essentialisation on the part of the author.

Chebel's central focus then in *L'Inconscient de l'islam* is how the twin concepts of 'la faute' and 'la transgression' structure the ideology of holy war (*jihad*) and the suicide bomber, the status of women and mothers and the place of ideas and the written word in Muslim communities. On the issue of *jihad* and the spread of Islam, Chebel claims that, with the exception of Omar, for Uthman's and Ali's caliphates, 'il s'agissait avant tout de peupler le harem du souverain de jeunes femmes venues d'ailleurs afin de régénérer le sang de la race. Exit l'idée de l'expansion de l'islam, l'heure était l'assouvissement d'un désir de puissance et d'un désir sexuel.' (Chebel 2015a: pp. 8–9) (it was a question above all of populating the sovereign's hareem with young women from elsewhere so as to inject new blood into the tribe. This marked the end of the expansion of Islam and the start of a period characterised by meeting the needs of a desire for power and sex.) Chebel dedicates an entire chapter to this claim, entitled 'La guerre pour les femmes', and unlike in his encounter with Christian Godin in 2011, when Chebel suggested that the Quran referred to women as 'croyantes', thus potentially liberating them from their biological status, Chebel argues here that women in the Quran are portrayed as trapped between the twin poles of error and transgression: 'Certes, le Coran évoque régulièrement la femme, mais uniquement pour l'enfermer entre la *faute* et la *transgression*' (Chebel 2015a: p. 20) (The Quran certainly regularly evokes women, but solely to enclose them in the notions of sin and transgression). He then goes on to discuss how the sexuality of women in Islam has been controlled within the context of *jihad* and imposed regardless of whether they are 'femmes libres', 'concubines', 'captives de guerre', 'femmes de mauvaise vie', 'femmes-utérus' or 'succubes' (free women, concubines, war captives, women of ill repute, surrogate women or succubi). Chebel's claims conflict somewhat with his later argument that the harem (as mainly described by European travellers such as Eschyle, Sismondi, Baudier, Florian, Tavernier, Chardin, l'Abbé Bergier, Montesquieu, Nerval and Loti, whose work Chebel draws on in his essay) could be conceived of as a 'lieu de résistance' because of the rivalries that may have existed between women from different cultures: 'Combien de régicides et d'assassinats non résolus ont été fomentés par ces co-épouses ou des concubines jalouses?' (Chebel 2015a: p. 30) (How many unsolved regicides and murders were plotted by jealous co-wives and concubines?).

Beyond the discussion of *jihad*, Chebel does address the ideology of the *kamikaze*, but he does so in a surprisingly superficial manner, including a very short chapter on 'Idéologies du kamikaze ordinaire' where he simply claims that within Islam it is clear that the suicide bomber cannot and should not benefit from any funerary rituals, since his/her act casts them out from the community of believers. On the question of war more broadly, Chebel restates that within Islam the only justifiable wars are wars of self-defence and that the suicide bomber represents a figure of inhumanity (Chebel 2015a: p. 58).

In his discussion of the perversion of *jihad* and the ideology of the *kamikaze*, Chebel is clearly concerned with broader themes of masculinity within Islam. It is thus not surprising that he engages in a fairly substantial discussion about the relationship between mothers and their sons in Arab and Muslim societies. Chebel claims that Muslim culture more generally bears the imprint of Arab Bedouin culture since Islam developed in the Arabian Peninsula. His central argument hinges on the concept of 'le ma(n)ternel' which he defines as

> un processus d'introjection symbolique, ou de 'dévoration', de l'enfant mâle par sa propre mère pour que celle-ci puisse se construire par son truchement et trouver sa place dans le rhizome familial. Le 'n' de manternel symbolise le sentiment éprouvé par la mère qui fonctionne comme une 'mante religieuse', au lieu d'adopter un sentiment maternel ordinaire. (Chebel 2015a: p. 59)

(a process of symbolic introjection, or 'devoration', of the male child by his own mother so that she is able to develop herself through his intervention and find her place in the familial rhizome. The 'n' in *manternal* symbolises the sentiment experienced by the mother, who functions as 'a praying mantis', rather than through a more ordinary maternal sentiment.)

There are a number of problems with Chebel's discussion, not least its potential misogyny about cannibalistic or predatory mothers, but also the vast generalisations Chebel is making about 'Arab culture', 'Islamic culture' and the mysterious notion of 'un sentiment maternel *ordinaire*' (emphasis added). His central claim is that mothers in Arab societies use their sons to gain the social status they would otherwise be denied within a patriarchal family structure. These mothers' permissiveness with regard to their sons and their idolisation of them produces little boys who are 'tout-puissant' (all-powerful) and emotionally immature, which Chebel regards as a societal problem: 'la relation archaïque "mère–enfant" est fondatrice d'un ordre complexe qui fonctionne comme une préfiguration de l'individualité arabe, de ses avatars d'égoïsme disproportionné, et de l'agressivité dont l'homme fait preuve à l'égard de ses filles, de ses sœurs et des amantes' (Chebel 2015a: p. 67) (the archaic 'mother–child' relationship is the foundation of a complex social order which operates as a prefiguration of Arab individuality, its disproportionately egotistical misfortunes and the aggressiveness that men display towards their daughters, sisters and lovers). Chebel makes no attempt to nuance his generalisations; indeed he argues on the contrary that this relationship occurs in all families due to 'le mimétisme ethnique et social' (Chebel 2015: p. 70) (ethnic and social mimicry). Chebel thus appears to be taking part in a process of self-orientalisation, in a similar manner to that adopted by Meddeb (see Chapter 1) since he claims that the problematic mother–son relationship in Arab-Muslim societies explains 'la fragilité affective et émotionnelle du monde arabe face au progrès' (Chebel 2015a: p. 64) (the affective and emotional fragility of the Arab world in the face of progress).

So it would seem that for Chebel the Arab-Muslim world is not marching in tune to progress, and he confirms this in his claim that orality continues to dominate within Islam, in both religious and cultural terms. He argues that the Quran is generally seen as the only legitimate book in a culture where 'l'écrit est absent' (Chebel 2015a: p. 86) (the written word is absent). He traces a lineage of suspicion towards writers running from the era of revelation, right up to the contemporary period. The era of revelation refers to the period when the *suras* and *ayas* that make up the Quran were revealed to the Prophet Mohammed by the Angel of Revelation, Gabriel:

> En dehors de la 'Révélation', point de salut pour l'écrit profane, les écrivains étant suspectés de déviationnisme, puisqu'à travers leur création, ils réfutent la pensée

mimétique et ses conventions étroites. Aujourd'hui encore, tout écrivain qui ose écrire un livre risque d'être pris pour un anti-prophète. (Chebel 2015a: p. 86)

(Beyond the 'Revelation', there is no salvation for profane writing, given that writers are suspected of being deviant, since, through their creation, they refute mimetic thought and its narrow conventions. Today still, any writer who dares to write a book risks being labelled an anti-prophet.)

Beyond Chebel's problematic statements about the written word versus orality, given that in his other works such as *L'Islam et la raison* (2006) he has shown that there *is* a significant Muslim intellectual tradition based on the written word, it is tempting to argue that he sees himself as an intellectual who risks being accused of being 'un anti-prophète'. He seems to locate the 'salvation' of Islam as something that may take place in and through writing, and points to the example of *Les Mille et une nuits* as a text that, through its sensuality and complexity, could serve an effective counter to hatred and xenophobia. In his exaltation of the power and status of literature (and the written word in general), Chebel joins Meddeb in the attempts to transform perceptions of Islam, but also makes a plea for protection of the individual freedoms of the writer. He poses the question: 'Le créateur humain sera-t-il éternellement maudit en islam?' (Chebel 2015a: p. 110) (Will human creativity be eternally damned within Islam?). Chebel was perhaps reflecting on his own trajectory and status as writer and public intellectual, but in the framing of this question Chebel seems to place himself at a crossroads between a defence of Islam and a relentless critique of its practitioners. It remains to be seen whether this is a tenable position for an intellectual who claimed to speak on behalf of others of Muslim heritage.

The 'reassuring' scholar

Chebel's attempts to alter the image of Islam for a non-Muslim majority continued right up until the end of his career and his untimely death in 2016 via the publication of a monograph entitled *Mohammed, prophète de l'islam* (2016). Chebel claims that the rationale of the book is that it is imperative for more to be known about the Prophet Mohammed's life, even if this is a risky pursuit for an intellectual in the broader context of Islamic fundamentalism. The risk involved in his project could be attributed to the fact that Chebel's approach presents what he calls 'le double prophète' – one who is the major figure of Islam for 'les croyants' and another who will be subjected to 'une deconstruction critique' (Chebel 2016: p. 18) (a critical deconstruction). Chebel states in the introduction to the book that he is aware that 'his' religion is a source of anxiety for people: ' "ma" religion angoissait le monde entier' (Chebel 2016: p. 10) (' "my" religion was a source of anxiety to the whole world). He thus sets out to produce a biography of the Prophet Mohammed that places emphasis on how the Prophet valued human experience including 'l'amour des biens matériels, la sexualité et l'exercice du pouvoir' (Chebel 2016: p. 11) (a love of material goods, sexuality and the exercise of power). This allows Chebel to insist on the dual nature of Islam, as a religion which is simultaneously mystical and quasi-secular in the sense that it accepts that its sacred dimension may be enriched by profane elements. It is significant that in this 2016 text, Chebel is for the first time explicit about who he thinks his audience is, claiming that any biography of the Prophet should be addressed to Muslims and non-Muslims in a universalist manner. Keen to reference crossover points and commonalities, Chebel's biography emphasises the links that Mohammed's life had with both Judaism and Christianity; indeed, the overarching approach that Chebel adopts in *Mohammed, prophète de l'islam* is one which draws out the complex nature of Islam and its multiple and shifting influences.

One key example of Chebel's attempt to draw attention to the internal diversity of Islam is in his discussion of the Constitution of Medina, which was established *c.* AD 642 once the Prophet Mohammed had established the city as his base and negotiated a political treaty between opposing tribes based there. The Constitution text is the only known source that codified relations between Jews and Muslims in Medina, and Chebel argues that the popularity of the Constitution stemmed from the fact that it was regarded as a 'projet de nation' which was founded simultaneously on belief and a sense of justice. Chebel draws on W. Montgomery Watt's two-volume biography of the Prophet which similarly paints a positive portrait of the Medina Constitution:

> Ceci est un traité de Mohammed le Prophète. Il concerne les liens de bon voisinage que les Qûraychites qui ont migré de La Mecque à Médine, entretiennent avec les gens de Yathrib, ceux qui les suivent et les belligérants qui leur font la guerre. Ils forment [tous] une communauté unique qui est distincte des autres peuples. (Chebel 2016: p. 116 cites Watt 1957, 1958).
>
> (This is the treaty of Mohammed the Prophet. It concerns the neighbourly relations that the Quraysh, who migrated from Mecca to Medina, maintain with the Yathrib people, those who follow them and the belligerent who make war with them. They all form a unique community which is distinct from other peoples.)

Chebel's emphasis here is on a prophet whose religion can and should be associated with tolerance of diversity and the promotion of peaceful co-existence amongst different communities of belief. Indeed, Chebel dedicates a chapter to the Biblical references which can be found in the Quran and discusses the Prophet's awareness of Biblical heritage and his own place within monotheistic history. Chebel (2016: pp. 206–207) cites the Prophet as having claimed: 'Je ne suis pas venu pour effacer ce qui a été envoyé avant moi, je suis venu pour le confirmer et le compléter' (I did not come to erase what was sent before me, I came to confirm and complete it). It is significant that Chebel does not provide the source for this statement, and indeed there is a problematic use of sources throughout this text as whole. Regardless of the ambiguity surrounding the sources for some of the claims and statements of the Prophet, it appears that Chebel's insistence on some of the continuities between the Quran and the Bible, and the Torah for that matter (in terms of the figures common to all, such as Abraham), is possibly intended to reassure his non-Muslim readership (the superaddressee). In any case, Chebel's consensual approach here stands in sharp contrast to some of his earlier writings which made strong claims about the homogeneity and insularity of Islamic and pre-Islamic Bedouin culture (see, in particular, Chebel 2002, 2015a).

Chebel's discussion of the place of war in Islam's history in this biographical work also appears to be at odds with his discussion of the role of war in *L'Inconscient de l'islam* where he argues that war was a central feature of Islam's development and that, by and large, it was motivated by a desire to ensure the survival of tribes via exogamous marriage (Chebel 2015a). In his biography of the Prophet Mohammed, Chebel argues that war arises from divine commandments that the faithful should fight those who attack them. In other words, war is recast as being fundamentally about self-defence. So in relation to the question of co-existence between Jews, Christians and Muslims in Medina, Chebel argues that reconciliation was actively sought by the Prophet Mohammed, that historical records show that he did not seek the conversion of Jews and that he did to a certain extent engage in inter-faith dialogue with Jews and Christians (Chebel 2016: p. 134). Whilst war was ultimately declared by the Prophet Mohammed on the Jewish Banû Qaynûqa, Banû Nadhir and Banû Qûrayza tribes of Medina, Chebel seeks to remind the reader that this event should be regarded as arising from divine intervention:

> Un 'ordre de Dieu' l'y amena: 'Combattez dans la voie de Dieu ceux qui vous combattent, mais ne soyez pas des provocateurs, car Allah n'aime pas les transgresseurs.' (Chebel 2016: p. 135)
>
> (An 'order from God' steered him there: 'Fight in the way of God, those who fight you, but do not be instigators, for God does not like transgressors.')

Furthermore, Chebel argues that war between Muslims and Jews in Medina was in some ways a 'fatality' which could not be avoided (Chebel 2016: p. 137). This once again seems inconsistent with the approach adopted by Chebel in 2002 and 2015 whereby he resists any notions of passivity, arguing instead for greater individual autonomy within Islam (Chebl 2002). Indeed, in *Mohammed, prophète de l'islam*, Chebel seems to defend war or armed proselytising as long as certain restrictions are followed, such as the prohibition on killing women, children, the elderly, the disabled, slaves or animals (Chebel 2016: p. 147). Chebel reminds the reader that the Quran views war as 'just' if it brings polytheists into the realm of monotheism and that 'le conflit le plus glorieux' (Chebel 2016: p. 153) (the most glorious conflict) was that which would conquer the enemy without shedding a drop of blood. Chebel therefore does not interrogate the very logic underpinning war. Instead he portrays the Prophet Mohammed as a spiritual leader who did not advocate excessive use of force. He also claims that the first Muslims who surrounded the Prophet regarded war as the necessary means to achieve peace. Chebel does not critically examine the problematic logic that war seeks peace as its ultimate aim and this his position here is divergent to that expressed in *L'Inconscient de l'islam* where he appears extremely sceptical of the very notion of war.

Such apparent contradictions in Chebel's analysis also arise with regard to his discussion of the Prophet's harem, which he describes in *Mohammed, prophète de l'islam* as: 'un esprit où règne la loi du père' (Chebel 2016: p. 196) (a spirit whereby reigns the law of the father), whereas he had argued, problematically, in *L'Inconscient de l'islam* that the harem could, in some respects, be regarded as a space for feminine resistance. So Chebel seems to oscillate between critique and reassurance; this also applies to his discussion of 'la société et morale en islam' (society and morals in Islam) whereby he refers to the 'personnalité musulmane' (Chebel 2016: p. 228) (the Muslim personality) as being one where doubt is not encouraged. Yet he simultaneously exalts the tendency within Islamic communities to promote the notion of 'l'amour d'autrui' (love of the other) or 'l'amour du prochain' (love of the neighbour) (Chebel 2016: p. 225). Similarly, Chebel seems to want to reassure his readership about sharia law, claiming that it is only practised in a minority of states (Chebel 2016: p. 253). Given Chebel's shifting stance between critique of and reassurance about of Islam, it is fitting that he ends his biography of the Prophet Mohammed with a chapter entitled 'Le Grand Malentendu' (The Great Misunderstanding) wherein he cites numerous Western canonical writings, such as Voltaire's *Mahomet ou le Fanatisme*, Dante's *Inferno* and Victor Hugo's *La Légende des siècles*, that have portrayed the Prophet in unfavourable terms. He argues that the tragedies which afflict our current era stem from the 'great misunderstanding' which exists between Islam and the West, a misunderstanding which also has something to do with the very late translation of the Quran into European languages (more than five centuries after the revelation – 1143 for the Robert of Ketton edition; 1647 for the De Ruyer French edition; 1698 for the 'édition aggressive' by Ludovico Marracci; Chebel 2016: p. 259). He laments the fact that much of the critical European literature surrounding the life of the Prophet Mohammed focused in Orientalist fashion on the Prophet's sensuality and his harem. One wonders whether in focusing so much of his own research and writings from the 'inside' on love and sexuality in Islam, Malek Chebel sought somehow to answer back to the many layers of historical *malentendu* surrounding not only the life of the Prophet Mohammed but also Islam more broadly. The question remains of course whether Chebel was successful in his endeavour to 'answer back', or whether his legacy is shot through with its own ambiguities and impasses, arising from his status as a 'good' Muslim intellectual within a French public sphere characterised by an increasingly antagonistic relationship with Islam and French Muslims.

Notes

1 Chebel does not indicate which French edition of the Quran he is citing. The English translation featured above is from the Oxford University Press edition, translated by M.A.S. Abdel Haleem, 2004.
2 See Chapter 3, in which Leïla Babès argues on the contrary that Catholicism's tradition of a powerful and structuring clergy in fact constitutes an exception rather than the reference. Here, then, Chebel seems to be writing for a French audience or superaddressee in an almost apologetic sense about differences between Islam and Catholicism.
3 The term *banlieues* or suburbs has a particular socio-cultural significance in the French public imagination, since these outskirts of France's large cities are mainly associated with North African and Sub-Saharan African migrant populations and their descendants. From the 1980s onwards, the *banlieues* have been increasingly portrayed in the media and by the political class as being the locus of a range of social problems, such as unemployment, crime, religious extremism and, sporadically, civil unrest, such as during the 2005 riots.

3

Leïla Babès: spirituality, affect and women

Leïla Babès, who was born in Guelma, Algeria is Professor of Sociology of Religions at the Université Catholique de Lille and is well known for her consistent foregrounding of a spiritual rather than legalistic approach to Islamic belief and practice. Her ideas about *lived* Islam – which she observes through ethnographic research – in addition to her concern for women's equality within Islam are key features of her work (Babès 2000; Babès and Oubrou 2002). Babès is interested in what she calls 'une intériorisation de la foi' (Babès ed. 1996: p. 129) (internalisation of faith) and has been a fierce critic of the so-called *voile islamique* and *voile intégral*. Yet unlike other critics of the headscarf, such as the 'ex-Muslim' Chahdortt Djavann (author of *Bas les voiles!*; Djavann 2006), Babès nevertheless maintains a position as a secular Muslim public intellectual who argues that Islam can be a progressive and positive phenomenon if its reactionary and conservative spokesmen are sidelined. Her weekly radio editorials on Medi1 Radio (*Points de vue*) provide a critical commentary on current affairs, with the expressed aim of deconstructing discourses and mechanisms of domination at work in the field of politics, religion and culture. This chapter will demonstrate how Babès' contributions are significant in that they go well beyond the almost obsessive nature of French public debates regarding so-called 'Islamic dress' – the 'external' face of Islam, with the associated anxieties about women's bodies and their outward appearance – to contemplate the 'interiority' and lived experience of Islam, a narrative which runs counter to political constructions or dominant discursive frameworks of Islam as a monolithic entity in contemporary France.[1]

Whilst Babès' work shares many concerns with that of Bidar, Chebel, Meddeb (and, to a lesser extent, Bouzar) the main distinguishing feature of her research is its sociological approach, which is focused on the practice and lived experience of Islam in all its diversity. This is not to say that Babès is not interested in theological or historical issues. On the contrary, her work seeks to articulate a nuanced knowledge of the Quran, *hadith* and the history of Islam with an approach that examines the spiritual lives of Muslims, particularly in contemporary France. One finds throughout her work (in the form of monographs, essays, media interviews and blogs) a consistent interest in three aspects of Islam: what Babès refers to as *la foi, le rite* and *la loi*: faith, rituals (practices) and religious law.

Spirituality, affect, passion

In Babès' earlier works one finds a consistent examination of the notions of faith and spirituality and how this is experienced in 'lived Islam' as opposed to 'a constructed Islam' (based on official or orthodox norms and doctrines). Throughout her early work in particular, she is keen to demonstrate that Islam should not be seen as the exception within the broader field of the sociology of religions, arguing that many of the internal developments and shifts affecting contemporary Islam are also to be found in other monotheisms. Indeed, in her 1996 edited volume entitled *Les Nouvelles Manières de croire: judaïsme, christianisme, islam, nouvelles religiosités* (Babès 1996), her aim is to explicitly point to these areas of convergence across a number of religious traditions in contemporary France. For Babès, one of the major indicators of a shared tendency, particularly between Islam and Christianity, is the process of secularisation. Babès refutes the widely held assumption that Islam is somehow not concerned with or affected by secularisation and instead argues that what we are seeing in contemporary French Islam in particular is a clear shift towards secularisation, which plays out in frequently contradictory terms. For Babès, secularisation does not entail the disappearance, privatisation or decline of religion, but rather the transformations and re-compositions that take place within religious beliefs and practices. The principle characteristics of secularisation are differentiation and individualisation, where what is important is personal experience, yet this does not exclude some rather paradoxical tendencies, such as the increased internalisation of religious practice for some but much greater social visibility for others. By highlighting the inconsistencies of secularisation in general and within Islam in particular, Babès consistently points to the diversity of lived Islam.

In order to demonstrate this diversity, Babès presents in *Les Nouvelles Manières de croire* the findings of an empirical study that she carried out with young French Muslims aged between 20 and 40 years in the Nord-Pas-de-Calais region in 1992. The starting point for the qualitative interviews that she conducted with a small sample of about twenty individuals was to pose the question: 'Qu'est-ce qu'être musulman?' (What does it mean to be a Muslim?). Babès found that there were generally two types of Islam being practised amongst her cohort: 'un islam coutumier' (customary Islam), which focused above all on the social and inherited aspects of Islam, foregrounding notions of *le rite* (rituals) and *la loi* (religious doctrine) and concerning only a minority of subjects in her sample, and 'un islam sécularisé' (secularised Islam), characterised by an individual and spiritual approach (Babès 1996: p. 123).

Beyond the apparent dichotomy between *la loi/le rite* (*islam coutumier*) and *la spiritualité* (*islam sécularisé*), Babès also introduces a third aspect which has characterised recent developments in the modern and contemporary era, namely the 'intellectualisation' of Islam. However, unlike for Meddeb, Chebel or Bidar, intellectualisation is not necessarily synonymous with progress. Indeed, for Babès, the process of the 'intellectualisation' of Islam goes hand-in-hand with its deculturation and the decline of what she refers to as 'la religion populaire', characterised by religious brotherhoods (orders) common in Sufi Islam or the veneration of saints (Babès 1996: p. 126). Indeed, Babès proposes that one of the effects of the so-called intellectualisation of Islam in the Maghreb and above all in Algeria from the 1930s onwards was the emergence of a reformist movement (*islâh*, meaning reform) which promoted reason and science – hence the suspicion towards 'la religion populaire', which was considered to be 'backwards'. However, Babès is not convinced that the process of rationalisation associated with the Algerian reformist movement could ever be seen as being complete, given that for her it is deeply problematic to associate reason with faith, as the reformists have tried to do. In this sense then, Babès is at odds with someone like Chebel who consistently makes the case for the promotion of the reform of Islam (*l'islam des Lumières*) and *l'islam de la Raison* (Chebel 2004, 2006). Babès goes even further in her critique of the intellectualisation and reformist movements in the Maghreb and Algeria in particular, by arguing that the reformist movement sowed the seeds of Islamic fundamentalism which emerged in Algeria during the 1980s and 1990s and subsequently developed in France amongst French-Algerian populations.

However, Babès argues that those within her sample of interviewees in Nord-Pas-de-Calais who practice a more spiritual Islam which foregrounds faith (*la foi*) rather than doctrine (*la loi*) are able to articulate a more universalist religiosity:

> La focalisation de ce discours spiritualiste sur la catégorie de Dieu, le Dieu monothéiste, permet de redonner à l'islam l'universalité qu'un réflexe définissant celui-ci comme la religion des arabes, et auquel les acteurs eux-mêmes avouent avoir participé, tendait à masquer. (Babès 1996: p. 131)

> (The focus of this spiritualist discourse on the category of the monotheistic God gives back to Islam a universality that tended to be masked by a reflex defining it as the religion of the Arabs, a tendency which those concerned admit to having partaken in.)

The individualised and spiritual approach to Islam is testament to the modernity of the ways in which young French Muslims practice their faith, according to Babès. She argues that it is 'la volonté de distanciation par rapport au consensus communautaire' (Babès 1996: p. 131) (the desire for distance from the community consensus) that lies at the heart of the modernity of their practice.

Similarly, Babès argues that spiritualist approaches to Islam that have developed amongst young French Muslims such as those who took part in her study are alternatives to what she calls 'le caractère ritualiste' (the ritualistic character) or 'des automatismes' (automatic gestures) (Babès 1996: p. 133). Whilst it may appear that Babès is subscribing to a potentially reductive image of modernity here, she does make the point that modernity should not simply be understood as 'le contemporain, ni la dernière trouvaille' (Babès 1996: p. 135) (contemporary or the latest finding). Rather, she attempts to develop a more nuanced understanding of modernity, premised on Mohammed Arkoun's idea of a critical separation between faith and science and the reconciliation of a critical stance regarding religious heritage ('intellectualisation') and faith (Babès 1996: p. 135 cites Arkoun 1993). Taking this reflection further in *L'islam positif* (1997), Babès argues that in its time, the Quran could be seen as being modern in relation to the *Jâhiliya* (the 'age of ignorance' in pre-Islamic Arabia). However, she argues that religious traditions should move in sync with human and societal development so that religious *doxa* does not become fixed in an intransigent manner. She thus rejects any simplistic opposition between modernity and tradition, arguing instead that

> il n'y a pas de rupture entre modernité religieuse et tradition religieuse, puisque la première ne se constitue pas *ex-nihilo*, en faisant table rase de la seconde, mais tente de repenser ses contenus. S'il y a rupture, celle-ci se fait, non avec la tradition, mais avec une certaine tradition, celle du sens unique. (Babès 1997: pp. 193–194)

> (there is no rupture between religious modernity and religious tradition, because the former is not constituted out of nothing, by wiping out the latter, but it attempts to rethink its contents. If there is a break, this is made, not with tradition, but with a certain tradition, that of a uniform meaning.)

Babès returns to the theme of spirituality, individualisation and 'distanciation' within Islam in her monograph entitled *L'Islam positif* (1997) which looks at the religious practices and beliefs of young French Muslims in much more detail than *Les Nouvelles Manières de croire*. The title of the monograph is itself significant, since it quite clearly demonstrates Babès' desire to communicate something about Islam that goes against the negative discursive frameworks which abound in France. Indeed, in her introduction, she states that it is her aim to move away from the study of Islam which is premised on the notion that it is a religion that somehow necessarily exists in an antagonistic relationship with the State, *laïcité* and French society. Babès warns of the unwanted or perverse effects which can arise when researchers focus on the negative social representations of Islam, namely that those images become even more entrenched and widespread even if the intention is to deconstruct those images. So she is arguing that researchers should acknowledge that they have a certain responsibility to push back against a broader pathologisation of Islam and its discontents, setting her apart from Meddeb, Chebel and Bidar's focus on *la maladie de l'islam* (Meddeb 2002; Chebel 2015a; Bidar 2015b). Instead, Babès seeks to focus on 'les modes du croire' (Babès 1997: pp. 7–8) (the modes of belief) in all their everyday banality, as well as the transformations affecting French Islam from within.

Babès' choice to examine 'la religiosité populaire' (popular religiosity) can also be seen as a means by which to counter Orientalist approaches, which tend to essentialise the Quran in an a-historical manner, paying scant attention to internal developments within lived Islam and its regional variations. In this sense, Babès appears to stand apart from Meddeb and Bidar in her clear interest in Islam beyond scripture (although Meddeb is also interested in 'l'islam vernaculaire' with regard to the veil; see Meddeb 2004: p. 197). In addition, her work is distinct from that of Chebel who consistently focuses on the Arab and Bedouin cultural features of Islam, which arguably runs the risk of essentialism. Rather than focusing on any supposed essential qualities or 'specificities' that define Islam, either via the Quran or via some of its cultural-historical aspects, Babès seeks to highlight the universality of Islam as she did in *Les Nouvelles Manières de croire*, drawing attention again and in much more detail to the process of secularisation and pluralisation within Islam. Furthermore, dismissing the notion that Islam should somehow constitute a separate branch within the sociology of religions, Babès also examines the links between Muslims and non-Muslims.

Indeed, Babès is keen to show that there is a desire amongst young Muslims for dialogue with Christians which has emerged in recent years via inter-faith association meetings, festivals and networks. Much of her fieldwork for *L'Islam positif* was taken up with an ethnography of the annual Christian-Muslim meetings held at the *Centre spirituel du Hautmont* near Tourcoing in northern France during the early 1990s. Although she frames Muslim-Christian dialogue in positive terms, she nevertheless argues that it is the Christian groups who tend to hold the upper hand in these encounters, in so far as it is they who choose the themes for the events, all the while making sure to avoid any topics deemed too 'sensitive', such as the status of women. Furthermore, Babès is lucid about the possible motivations for Muslims seeking out Christian-Muslim dialogue, arguing that some Muslims desire to be seen in a certain light by their fellow Christians as ideal modern Muslims or the 'beur irréprochable' (Babès 1997: p. 65) (irreproachable French-North African), recalling the problematic assumptions regarding the 'interpellation' (Althusser 1971) of 'le bon musulman' (the good Muslim) or 'le musulman modéré' (the moderate Muslim) which are discussed by Mas (2006) and Fernando (2009; 2014), among others. Despite her reservations about these encounters, Babès is tempted to see that there is a possibility of *rapprochement* between Christians and Muslims via the potential emergence of '*une spiritualité islamo-chrétienne*, voire monothéiste, voire encore universelle' (Babès 1997: p. 63; emphasis in the original) (*an Islamic-Christian,* even monotheistic or universal *spirituality*), which is fostered via communal prayer during inter-faith events, for example.

Whilst Babès appears to be seeking to reassure her French readership that French Muslims can peacefully co-exist and build links with their fellow Christians, by stating that often the initiative for encounters and meetings comes from Muslims themselves, she nevertheless recognises that such inter-faith dialogue is in some ways an inevitable consequence of religious pluralism. Babès is also keen to show that, within Islam itself, there is an obligation for Muslims to take into account previous Abrahamic religions, so whilst the inter-faith encounters between Muslims and Christians may stem from a desire on the part of Muslims to reach out to Christians, there is also a sense that this is a religious obligation. She quotes one of her interviewees who clearly expresses such a view: 'Si on veut être musulman, il faut être respectueux et tolérant vis-à-vis des autres religions' (Babès 1997: p. 108) (If one wants to be Muslim, one has to be respectful and tolerant of other religions). Like Chebel in his debate with philosopher Christian Godin (see Chebel and Godin 2011), Babès makes a point of highlighting the shared heritage between Islam and Christianity, such as the important status given to Jesus and Mary in the Quran (Babès 1997: p. 108).

So Babès' emphasis on shared heritage, inter-faith encounters and pluralism fits into her broader integration-framed approach whereby she argues that Islam should not be seen as an exceptional religion existing on the margins of French society. Rather she interprets the growing visibility of Islam and demands for recognition by Muslims in France as illustrative of integration. She also does not see a contradiction between embracing what she refers to as 'l'éthique islamique' and civic engagement: 'l'adhésion à l'islam se fait conjointement avec la revendication de la citoyenneté' (Babès 1997: p. 151) (the allegiance to Islam is made conjointly with the claim to citizenship). She foregrounds the notion of individual choice in religious matters amongst young French Muslims, alluding to de Beauvoir's famous claim regarding gender by arguing that '*On ne naît pas (ou plus) musulman, on le devient*' (Babès 1997: p. 157; emphasis in the original) (*We are not (or no longer) born Muslim, we become Muslim*). In highlighting the importance of choice, Babès' presents her analysis of the secularisation of French Islam as being antithetical to sociologist Émile Durkheim's canonical understanding of the relationship between faith (*la foi*) and ritual (*le rite*) as discussed in *Les Formes élémentaires de la vie religieuse*. Indeed, Babès suggests that *le rite* comes after *la foi*, unlike Durkheim, for whom *le rite* comes before *la foi* (i.e. the collective act of worship/religiosity is what inculcates faith rather than the other way round). Babès thus claims to refute Durkheim's approach to religious faith as something that is socially instilled and maintained in order to argue that it is *individually* pursued as a first step towards collective practice (Babès 1997: p. 190 cites Durkheim 1985: p. 596). It is interesting to note Babès' fairly liberal stance on Muslim visibility and demands for recognition in this 1997 work as compared to her stance some years later in *Le Voile démystifié* (2004) wherein she clearly makes the case against the growing visibility of Islam via a virulent critique of *communautarisme* and any sort of link between Islamic ethics and citizenship in the French context. Indeed, in her debate with Tareq Oubrou (Babès and Oubrou 2002), her essay on the veil (Babès 2004), and in her media appearances and interviews, Babès clearly seems to have shifted and become much more critical of notions of faith-based understandings of citizenship and demands for faith-based political recognition in the public sphere. Such a shift would suggest a 'hardening' on certain questions in response to the political climate, the 2004 law on religious symbols and the 2010 law on full-face coverings, as well as a desire to publicly distance herself from those she refers to as 'les prédicateurs' (preachers), amongst whom she includes Tariq Ramadan.

Babès' increasingly vocal rejection of the vision of European Islam as promoted by Tariq Ramadan fits into the broader agenda that she wants to address: the question of the reform of Islam. Unlike Malek Chebel, who makes the issue of reform one of the central features of his work through his *islam des Lumières* project, Babès argues that the reformist movement in Islam has in large part been responsible for sowing the seeds of Islamic fundamentalism in Muslim-majority countries because of its denigration of 'la religion populaire', non-canonical forms of religiosity and the religiosity of women. Babès is at pains to point out that the reformist movements of Islam have ultimately led to Islamic fundamentalism because of their over-rationalist, over-intellectualised approach to the Quranic text – their 'scripturalisme' which leads to a 'processus d'idéologisation de la religion musulmane' (process of ideologisation of the Muslim religion) conceived above all as collective norms and *doxa*, rather than individualised spiritual practices (Babès 1997: p. 183). However, she claims that this is not because of some essentialist message of the Quran itself, since in her view, the Quranic text features much evidence which would run counter to many fundamentalist claims, such as the non-separation between politics and religion. Rather, her argument is that the obstacle to the secularisation of Islam lies in the lack of democracy in many Muslim-majority countries as well as a process of deculturation which has taken place in the Maghreb and then been transplanted to France. Babès defines deculturation as follows:

> La déculturation, cela veut dire que l'on passe d'un monde où la religion est vécue suivant les modalités à la fois particulière et de l'imaginaire musulman, à un monde régi par la force du concept, le but étant, sinon un changement radical de la société, tout au moins un changement des mentalités. (Babès 1997: p. 160)
>
> (Deculturation implies a shift from a world where religion is experienced according to both specific modalities and modalities of the Muslim imaginary, to a world ruled by the force of the concept, the goal being, if not a radical change in society, then at least a change in mentalities.)

Babès counters the widely accepted argument that deculturation processes amongst French-born second-generation descendants of Maghrebi immigrants in France have led to the growth of Islamic fundamentalism in France. She turns that argument on its head by showing that the deculturation of Islam as a legacy of the reformist movements in the Maghreb (Algeria in particular) was itself transplanted to France via immigration and then taken up by the younger generations. In other words, it is not immigration which has led to deculturation but deculturation *itself* which has migrated.

Against this Islam characterised by deculturation and its external facets – *la loi* (religious doctrine) – Babès continues to focus instead on the internal dimensions of Islam – *la foi* – in her monograph entitled *L'islam intérieur: passion et désenchantement* (Babès 2000). By adopting an ethnographic approach to 'l'islam vécu' (lived Islam), Babès examines 'l'intériorité de l'islam' (the interiority of Islam) in all its everyday aspects, whether via henna ceremonies and the sharing of couscous or the more spectacular albeit non-orthodox practices associated with 'la religion populaire', such as the saint tradition, trance or *marabout* miracles. It is significant that Babès is critical of both 'les intellectuels laïques' and 'les orthodoxes'(secular intellectuals and the Orthodox) whom she accuses of not taking these practices seriously and approaching them as falling into the category of 'l'irrationnel' (Babès 2000: p. 8) (the irrational). It is particularly notable that Babès distinguishes herself from secular intellectuals, described by her later in the work as 'incapables de penser l'islam' (Babès 2000: p. 30) (incapable of thinking about Islam) given that in her later publications, media interventions and interviews, Babès presents herself as being a secular intellectual – perhaps due to the polemics over the 2004 law on religious symbols and the 2010 law on full-face coverings. This is not to say that earlier in her career Babès was more sceptical about *laïcité*. She has been a consistent defender of *laïcité* as a principle that allows freedom of conscience, whilst simultaneously proposing that Islam can and should be regarded as 'une religion du croire qui postule le primat du coeur' (Babès 2000: p. 32) (a religion of belief which postulates the primacy of the heart). Babès' attachment to *laïcité* is thus premised on her conviction that Islam should be understood and experienced in terms of *la foi* – the internal spiritual world of Muslims as opposed to social visibility and the demand for religiously determined rights based on Muslims' understanding of *la loi* of Islam. Her understanding of *laïcité* is not an anti-religious stance at all; rather her references to *laïcité* have much in common with Jean Baubérot's (2012) understanding of it, i.e. as a framework within which the separation of the State and religion is the condition upon which religious freedoms can flourish. Babès' promotion of an 'islam intérieur', where notions such as 'le croire', 'le coeur', 'le for intérieur' and 'le vécu' (belief, heart, conscience and lived experience) (Babès 2000: p. 187) as well as 'la passion' (Babès 2000: p. 12) are central, certainly sit well within a secular context such as France, and the fact that her stated intended readership encompasses both Muslims and non-Muslims is telling in that sense. Her project seems then to be defined by a desire to educate Muslims about alternative forms of Islam, unknown to the generations born in France who are heavily influenced by post-reformist and scripturalist Islam associated with 'les prédicateurs' (preachers), whilst simultaneously demonstrating to a non-Muslim readership that the image of Islam as an a-cultural and austere religion, predominantly defined by religious law and doctrine, is inaccurate.

So whilst Babès could be regarded as 'toeing the party line' as far as *laïcité* in France is concerned, arguing that Islam should be an interior, spiritual experience, from another perspective she is arguably engaged in a more subversive project. Indeed, she argues that 'lived Islam', which is simultaneously described and promoted as some kind of ideal religiosity, can also be understood as 'déviant' (deviant) and 'égaré' (wayward) (Babès 2000: p. 11). Her central focus on the category of 'la passion' as a 'style de vie, langage, culture' (Babès 2000: p. 18) (style of life, language, culture) is also significant since she argues that in many more conventional understandings of Islam, 'la passion est subversive' (Babès 2000: p. 12) (passion is subversive). Religiosity expressed as passion – *le coeur, le for intérieur* – also largely concerns women's practice of Islam; for example, the saint Jilâni is an important figure of 'la religiosité féminine' and therefore stands in sharp contrast to a more doctrinal Islam that is dominated by men. Nevertheless, even though 'passion' may be part of a 'culture dominée' (dominated culture), she also describes it as 'résistante' (Babès 2000: p. 18) and indeed argues that Muslim women could be seen as possible agents of renewal within Islam via their tendency to embrace non-canonical forms of religiosity. Babès thus suggests that this form of Islam could be a useful alternative to the 'islam des notables', 'des gestionnaires' and the 'logiques clientélistes' (Islam of the notables, managers and clientelist dynamics) which are the most visible forms of Islam in contemporary France (Babès 2000: p. 183).

So, via her clear promotion of 'un islam intérieur' and the concept of religious passion, Babès articulates a vision of Islam that is both subversive (associated with women, pre-Islamic culture, magic, trance and popular religiosity) and moderate. It is subversive within the context of a post-reformist and intellectualised Islam that is deeply suspicious of 'la religion populaire', yet within the broader French context it is arguable that Babès' vision of Muslim religiosity as being internalised (invisible) and spiritual as opposed to doctrinal and externalised (visible) defines her project as universalist and hence supportive of the political status quo in France. So, despite arguing that researchers should preferably adopt a sociological approach to the study of Islam and Muslims in France due to the complexity and plurality of lived Islam which it uncovers, Babès argues against any notion that Muslims might be regarded as a 'social group', stating that 'La communauté musulmane de France n'est pas un objet réel en tant que tel, c'est-à-dire une totalité concrète clairement circonscrite et identifiable' (Babès 2000: p. 178) (The

Muslim community of France is not a real thing as such, that is, a concrete, clearly delineated and identifiable entity). She instead argues that the notion of 'une communauté de foi' (a community of faith) is far more useful than the concept of 'un véritable groupement social' (a true social grouping) (Babès 2000: p. 179). Babès seems, then, to conform both to the image of the unconventional or heterodox Muslim within an Islamic context and to the moderate or conventional Muslim in the French context. Despite her numerous divergences with fellow Muslim intellectuals in contemporary France, such as Abdennour Bidar and Abdelwahab Meddeb in particular (who tends to gloss over any notion of plurality or lived experiences amongst Muslims in favour of a monolithic conception of Islam and 'le monde musulman'),[2] Babès ultimately speaks the same language as her contemporaries – a resolutely secular and universalist one. As such, Babès corresponds to the profile of the 'reassuring' Muslim scholar in a similar manner to Bidar, Meddeb and Chebel.

Secular and divine law

Babès' stance as a secular, universalist scholar of Islam and as a Muslim intellectual is particularly evident in her published debate with the Bordeaux imam, Tareq Oubrou, in *Loi d'Allah, loi des hommes: liberté, égalité et femmes en islam* (2002). At the start of *Loi d'Allah*, Babès returns to her argument made in *L'Islam intérieur* regarding the lack of discussion *within* Islam in order to present the encounter with Oubrou as a 'débat polémique et fraternel' (Babès and Oubrou 2002: p. 8) (a polemical and fraternal debate) between 'une intellectuelle attachée à la critique scientifique des textes et à une conception moderne de la liberté' (an intellectual attached to the scholarly critique of texts and modern conception of freedom) and 'un chef spirituel ouvert aux adaptations nécessaires ... dans le cadre de la loi islamique' (a spiritual leader open to necessary adaptations ... within the Islamic legal framework) (Babès and Oubrou 2002: back cover blurb). In this extensive debate of some 350 pages, the themes of individual freedoms, the status of women and gender equality become contexts in which Babès is able to interrogate or even 'police' Oubrou with regard to his stance on a number of issues, ranging from reformist movements in Islam to the veil and apostasy. So, in contrast to the published dialogue between Chebel and Godin (Chebel and Godin 2011; see Chapter 2), where it was Chebel who was trying to prove his secular and universalist credentials in the *face-à-face* with Godin, here it is Babès who is putting Oubrou to the test, and although the encounter is, on the whole, a constructive one, it is significant that some years after the publication of *Loi d'Allah*, Babès' position regarding Oubrou's stance on issues such as the status of women in Islam and the veil in particular is markedly less generous.

The first part of the debate in *Loi d'Allah* is structured around the question 'L'islam est-elle une religion de la contrainte'? (Is Islam a religion of constraint?)

and Babès pursues her earlier position expressed in *Les Nouvelles Manières de croire*, *L'Islam positif* and *L'Islam intérieur* in arguing that the ethical foundations of Islam have been overtaken by its legal dimensions: 'Pour moi, l'islam est un message éthique qui s'est dégradé en religion de la loi, c'est-à-dire de la contrainte' (Babès and Oubrou 2002: p. 18) (For me Islam is an ethical message which has deteriorated into a religion of laws, that is, of constraint). The use of the image of degradation is clearly not anodyne and is chosen by Babès to illustrate her explicit rejection of punishments applied for deviation from religiously established societal norms: 'Pouvons-nous, aujourd'hui, accepter la peine de mort réservée aux apostats, les mains coupées, le statut discriminatoire de la femme, et prétendre que nous respectons la liberté, le pluralisme et les droits de l'homme?' (Babès and Oubrou 2002: p. 19) (Can we, today, accept the death penalty for apostates, hand amputation, the unequal status of women, and claim that we respect freedom, pluralism and human rights?). Furthermore, although she states for the first time in her academic publications that she is 'croyante' (a believer), she also positions herself as a French intellectual expressing solidarity with her fellow Muslim intellectuals in Egypt, Sudan, Yemen, Jordan, Pakistan, Saudi Arabia and Afghanistan who are or have been persecuted by the courts as well as by civil society for blasphemy and apostasy. The main problem, as Babès sees it, is that the Quran's message should be regarded as ethical rather than juridical and that the blurring of the categories of the human and the divine has led to 'une sacralisation de l'oeuvre humaine dans l'interprétation du Texte coranique' (Babès and Oubrou 2002: p. 23) (a sacralisation of human endeavour in the interpretation of the Quranic Text). Whilst clearly at odds with Abdennour Bidar's stance on the textual interpretation of the Quran (see his discussion of *khalifat* in the *Al-Baqara* sura in Chapter 5), Babès makes this point to reinforce her stance that where human beings have become too involved in a process of juridical or legislative interpretation of the Quran, this had led to a 'closing down or folding inwards' of Islam – its transformation into a 'religion de la contrainte' (a religion of constraint), although she does point out that sura 2 of the Quran includes the following statement: 'Pas de contrainte en religion' (*The Qur'an*, sura 2, v. 256; OUP 2004 translation, p. 29) (There is no compulsion in religion).

Babès argues that the resistance against such a legalistic model of constraint could be located within European Islam, and she presumably includes herself within such a movement, along with intellectuals such as Bidar and Chebel who also refer to European Islam as being a force for renewal and change of 'le droit musulman' (Muslim law) in Muslim-majority countries (Babès and Oubrou 2000: p. 29). Babès is a sharp critic of the absence of freedom of expression in Muslim-majority countries and she sees this as the result of the 'tyrannie de la communauté sur la liberté individuelle, conjuguée à l'instrumentalisation politique' (Babès and Oubrou 2002: p. 57) (tyranny of community over individual liberty, together with political instrumentalisation). So, for her, the reason why apostasy continues to be a difficult issue in Islam is not *because* of Islam but due to a lack of democracy and the persistence of 'un reflexe de despotisme' (Babès and Oubrou 2002: p. 57) (a despotic reflex). In her attempt to resist a legalistic degradation of Islam, Babès could be described as somehow 'testing' Oubrou, who as an imam represents the views of religious leaders. For example, Babès quizzes Oubrou about whether he is a member of the *Frères Musulmans* (Muslim Brotherhood) movement (Babès and Oubrou 2002: p. 37) and whether he admires Hassan-al-Banna, its founder (Babès and Oubrou 2002: p. 179). On several occasions, Babès seems to want to pin Oubrou down, particularly on his stance in relation to the question of the death penalty for apostasy in Islam. The following extract exemplifies Babès' stance: 'Si je vous ai demandé si vous condamniez cette loi de l'apostasie, ce n'est pas pour vous contraindre à me suivre dans cette voie, mais pour avoir une réponse claire (par oui ou par non) à ce propos' (Babès and Oubrou 2002: p. 50) (If I asked you if you condemned this law on apostasy, it was not to force you into following my approach, but in order to receive a clear response (via a yes or a no) on this issue). On the question of the veil, Babès pressurises Oubrou in order to extract as unequivocal a response from him as possible. For example, after some fairly extensive discussion about the signification of veiling in the Quran and its relationship to the general requirement of modesty for both men and women, Babès appears to become somewhat exasperated, directly asking her interlocutor the following question: 'Oui ou non, le voile est-il pour vous obligatoire?' (Babès and Oubrou 2002: p. 211) (Yes or no, in your opinion, is the veil compulsory?). When Oubrou declines to provide direct answers to his interlocutor's questions, Babès defends her incisive approach as being in the interests of intellectual transparency and integrity (Babès and Oubrou 2002: p. 38). It is striking that Babès is so intent on achieving clarity regarding Oubrou's stance on issues such as the veil, blasphemy and apostasy, especially given that she so consistently makes the case elsewhere for complexity in matters regarding Islam and Muslims.

Despite these numerous and repeated attempts on Babès' part to unearth Oubrou's 'true' position, the two interlocutors do engage in an extensive discussion of the status of women, covering issues such as 'la mixité' (social mixing of men and women), the veil in the Quran and the legal status of women in relation to men. In each case, the approach of Babès is to try to establish that the Quran does not contain explicit or specific commandments. For example, Babès claims that the social prohibition surrounding the mixing of men and women does not arise from scripture and that no religious text in Islam requires the physical separation of men and women. Instead, she sees the source of the prohibition, exclusions and discriminations that many women face as arising from the reformist movement associated with the absence of political freedoms across 'le monde musulman' (Babès and Oubrou 2002: p. 160). In addition, she points out that as far as the veil is concerned, there is no clear requirement in the Quran for it to be worn and that the Prophet Mohammed did not seek to veil his wives, but came under pressure from his inner circle of followers such as Omar, stating that: 'rien dans le texte coranique n'indique une quelconque obligation pour les femmes de se voiler, la prescription ne concernant que les épouses du Prophète et les femmes des croyants, c'est-à-dire les femmes mariées avec les compagnons du Prophète' (Babès and Oubrou 2002: p. 191) (nothing in the Quran indicates any obligation for women to veil, the prescription only concerning the wives of the prophets and the wives of the believers, that is to say, women married to the companions of the Prophet).

Like Chebel, Babès argues that the Quran is liberating for women since in the Quran women are not conceived in solely biological terms but as Muslims: 'Avec l'islam, la femme émerge comme sujet croyant' (Babès and Oubrou 2002: p. 220) (With the advent of Islam, women emerge as believing subjects). Whether Chebel would agree with her that women become subjects under Islam is questionable, but there is clearly convergence between the two thinkers with regard to the transformation of women's status which occurs after the revelation. Furthermore, as in the discussion of the veil, Babès is keen to highlight the fact that the Prophet held women in high regard.

The veil

Babès returns to the discussion about the veil that she had with Tareq Oubrou in a 2004 essay entitled *Le Voile démystifié*. The timing of this essay was of course significant as it coincided with the passing of the law prohibiting religious symbols in public schools. Whilst the law stipulates that *all* religious symbols are prohibited, it is widely accepted that the legislation was passed in order to tackle the headscarf worn by female Muslim school pupils in particular. Indeed, the events that triggered the establishment of the government-appointed Stasi Commission to examine the proposals on religious symbols concerned the exclusion of two sisters from their high school in Aubervilliers for refusing to remove their headscarves inside school premises. The choice of title for Babès' essay reflects her desire to deconstruct the ways in which the headscarf is generally seen by those who both defend and reject it as a religious requirement. Babès argues that this is a gross misunderstanding akin to a process of 'mystification'. In her prologue to the essay, Babès is clear in her condemnation of French Islamic organisations such as the *Conseil francais du culte musulman* (CFCM) and the *Union des organisations islamiques de France* (UOIF) who claim that the veil is a religious prescription: 'Il s'agit là d'une des plus grandes mystifications que des musulmans aient jamais produites sur leur propre religion' (Babès 2004: p. 5) (This is one of the greatest mystifications that Muslims have produced about their own religion). She is particularly sceptical of the CFCM, which she argues should be restricted in its role of organising the Islamic faith for Muslims in France, as opposed to representing or seeking to represent Muslims in France: 'Ces "représentants" n'ont aucune légitimité à engager leurs positions doctrinales – qui ne reflètent que leurs opinions et leurs affiliations idéologiques – au nom de l'islam et des musulmans de France qui ne partagent pas, loin s'en faut, leurs idées' (Babès 2004: p. 6) (These 'representatives' have no legitimacy to commit their doctrinal positions – which simply reflect their opinions and their ideological affiliations – in the name of Islam and French Muslims who don't share their ideas at all). In her criticism of the CFCM's confusion over its mission (faith-based organisation or sociopolitically representative group), Babès upholds a position which converges with that of Bouzar (see Chapter 4) and re-asserts her universalist opposition to any form of 'communautarisme'.

Le Voile démysitifé is clearly aimed at a French readership (the text's superaddressee) who it is assumed know little of the Quran, so Babès takes it upon herself to educate her assumed non-Muslim readership about what the text says or does not say. She underlines the fact that in the 6000 verses of the Quran, only 200 have a 'legislative' character, and even those verses do not necessarily have a religious character: 'Une chose est claire: le voile n'entre pas dans cette catégorie de la foi, du dogme et du culte, comme l'affirment mensongèrement certains "religieux"' (Babès 2004: p. 10) (One thing is clear: the veil does not enter into this category of faith, dogma and religion, as certain "religious" figures dishonestly claim). Instead, Babès returns to the categories that structured her discussion of Islam in *Les Nouvelles Manières de croire* (1996), *L'Islam positif* (1997) and *L'Islam intérieur* (2000), namely the foundational importance, in her view, of 'le rapport vertical, individuel qui s'établit entre le croyant et Dieu' (Babès 2004: pp. 9–10) (the vertical, individual relationship which is established between the believer and God) where the only element that can and should be judged by God is innermost conscience. Babès refutes entirely the claim by some veiled women that the practice of veiling might be regarded as a spiritual undertaking (Babès 2004: p. 11). Two remarks can be made about this claim. First, it is arguable that in her unambiguous rejection of the veil as spiritual (she argues that such a claim is simply 'faux' (false); p. 11), Babès runs the risk of excluding alternative understandings of spirituality which do not correspond to her own. Secondly, Babès appears to use the fact that many of the women who do claim that the veil is a spiritual practice belong to the UOIF – a conservative movement close to Tariq Ramadan and the Frères Musulmans' approach to Islam – as a means of dismissing their perspectives. The UOIF has become a sort of shorthand in French public discourse to denote Islamists. The most recent evidence of this was made clear when presidential candidate Emmanuel Macron sought to distance himself from the declared support of the UOIF in the run-up to the 2017 election for fear that he would appear 'soft' on *communautarisme* or, worse still, on Islamic fundamentalism in the face of Marine Le Pen's *Front National*.

It is striking that in a book-length essay on the veil Babès does not include any reference to the lived experiences and perspectives of the women concerned – which conflicts with her otherwise consistent promotion of 'un islam vécu' in all her published works. Surely a sociological approach to the study of Islam, which Babès defends vigorously in *Les Nouvelles Manières de croire*, *L'Islam positif* and *L'Islam intérieur*, should also include the empirical study of those practices of Islam with which the social scientist disagrees. However, the voices of those veiled women are silenced here, just as they so often are in the broader discussion of the veil in France. That Babès, a specialist in Islam and a self-declared 'believer' also partakes in this silencing of certain women – the women who do not correspond to her vision of what Islam should look like – suggests that Babès seeks to speak in the name of Islam as a public intellectual with strong normative claims that promote a universalist, individual, secularised Islam. This is not problematic in itself, but if she is to take the plea for a sociological approach to Islam to its logical conclusion, her work in *Le Voile démystifié* would also have included the perspectives and views of those who *do* wear the veil. As such, one can regard this text as a clear position statement on the issue and, given that her stance firmly promotes the curtailing of religious freedom as far as religious dress is concerned, it would seem that as a public intellectual Babès reinforces rather than interrogates the political status quo.

For Babès, the practice of veiling is neither a religious requirement nor a spiritual engagement, but rather a reflection of the objectification of women's bodies as 'troublesome' objects of sexual desire from which men feel the need to be 'protected': 'Le mot d'ordre est le suivant: le corps de la femme est objet de désir sexuel, elle doit donc le voiler pour assurer la tranquillité des hommes' (Babès 2004: p. 11) (The watchword is as follows: women's bodies are the object of sexual desire, and so they must therefore conceal them in order to ensure men's peace of mind). On this basis, Babès argues that any attempt to legitimise the veil amounts to an absurd form of communitarian discourse (Babès 2004: p. 12) which should have no place within the secular space of the State. Her endorsement of *laïcité* could not be clearer: 'La laïcité s'impose à tous, et c'est ce qui rassemble les citoyens autour des mêmes valeurs, quelles que soient leurs croyances religieuses' (Babès 2004: p. 13) (Secularism applies to everyone, and it is what binds citizens together around the same values, regardless of their religious beliefs). She argues that the Republic should not have to adapt its secular principles for any 'community' for fear of offending Muslim sensibilities or stigmatising Muslims. It is clear that Babès is sceptical about the process of stigmatisation since she places the term in inverted commas and ends the essay by arguing that those Muslims who complain of discrimination regarding their right to wear a headscarf should recognise that the 'real' discrimination at play is the perpetuation of inequality between men and women: '[qu']en matière de droits de l'Homme, ce n'est pas la liberté religieuse qui est menacée mais bien l'égalité des sexes, et que la France n'a pas à rougir de continuer à défendre cette valeur fondamentale face aux pressions, quelles qu'elles soient, et d'où qu'elles viennent' (Babès 2004: p. 122) (in terms of Human Rights, it is not religious liberty which is threatened but rather the equality of the sexes, and France must not be embarrassed about continuing to defend this fundamental value in the face of pressure, whatever form it might take and from wherever it may emerge). Such a stance could be the argument of someone from the right of the political spectrum who is unsympathetic to Islam or claims of anti-Muslim discrimination (see Bruckner 2017), although Babès does present herself here as a Muslim ('moi, une musulmane'; Babès 2004: p. 83). Indeed, Babès' dismissal of the stigmatisation of Muslims fits into her broader rejection of the concept of Islamophobia, which she claims arises out of 'la vieille rengaine de la victimisation' (Babès 2004: p. 79) (the familiar refrain of victimisation).

Playing 'victim' would seem for Babès to go hand in hand with the 'ethnicisation' and 'communautarisation' of Islam whereby certain Muslims in France come to think of themselves as part of a specific community – the *Ummah*. For Babès, those who adopt such a stance are 'islamistes', i.e. fundamentalists, and she laments the marginalisation of the Sufi tradition via 'l'éradication pure et simple de l'héritage spirituel, patrimoine non pas d'une religion, mais de toute l'humanité' (Babès 2004: p. 91) (the pure and simple eradication of spiritual heritage, not from religion, but from humanity as a whole). Babès is always striving for a universalist vision of Islam, and her reference to humanist heritage links her thinking to that articulated by Bidar in his work on Islamic humanism as a basis for the renewal of universalism (see Chapter 5). However, her focus on the universal leads her to disqualify the specific claims of many Muslims and hence, just as she is sceptical about the notions of Islamophobia, she is equally dismissive about the notion of Islamic feminism, which she reduces to Muslim women's desire to wear the veil:

> Mais en quoi toute cette énergie dépensée et le fait de porter le voile sont-ils porteurs de féminisme? Que demandent ces femmes à part le droit d'être voilées? … Entreprennent-elles de faire une nouvelle lecture des textes religieux? Se servent-elles des ouvertures qui existent dans ces mêmes sources pour revendiquer le droit à diriger la prière – pour les hommes comme pour les femmes, cela va sans dire – à être des mufties autorisées à délivrer des fatwas (avis juridiques)? Elles ne demandent rien de tout cela. Et pourtant, ces fonctions ne leur sont pas explicitement interdites, du moins pas par tous les exégètes, et encore moins par les textes fondateurs (Coran et tradition prophétique). (Babès 2004: pp. 108–109)
>
> (But how is all this spent energy and the wearing of the veil feminist? What are these women demanding, apart from the right to be veiled? … Do they intend to undertake a re-reading of the religious texts? Do they use openings which exist in these sources in order to make claims for the right to lead prayer – for men and

women, that goes without saying – to become muftis who are authorised to declare *fatwas* (legal judgements)? They don't make any demands of the sort. And yet, these functions are not explicitly prohibited for women, at least not by all exegetes, and even less so by the foundational texts (Quran and prophetic tradition).)

Babès does not acknowledge that there are Muslim feminists who do lead prayers, such as Amina Wadud in the United States (see Bouzar's discussion of Wadud in Chapter 4) but beyond that, one does not get the impression that her claims are based on sociological research. *Le Voile démystifié* thereby marginalises the voices of those who are being scrutinised by Babès. Furthermore, what does it signify for a Muslim woman who makes feminist claims to dismiss the feminist claims of other Muslim women? It would seem that by questioning the credibility of 'Islamic feminism', Babès runs the risk of establishing a hierarchy of feminisms, or at least a binary opposition between authentic and inauthentic feminisms. In this sense, Babès seems to be reproducing the schism and exclusionary politics which arises between some secular feminists who dismiss the notion that feminist struggles can be articulated with religious belief since, in their view, religion is the embodiment of patriarchy. Yet, Babès herself symbolises this reconciliation of religion and feminism in her claims that the traditional ethics outlined in the Quran actually improved women's condition in the seventh century and continue to have the potential to do so in the contemporary period: 'En vérité, si la femme est placée au centre du dispositif islamique, c'est bien parce que c'est par elle que passe la liberté, source de perversion de la mythique "*Umma*"' (Babès 2004: p. 99) (In truth, if women are placed at the centre of the Islamic system, it is surely because it is via women that liberty transits, and liberty is a source of perversion of the mythical '*Ummah*'). However, in her non-recognition of the declared feminism of veiled Muslim women, Babès is also potentially denying the subjectivity of these women. In the same way as the labels of 'good' and 'bad' Muslim symbolically structure public discourse about Islam in France (and the West), here we see the how the labels of 'real' and 'bogus' feminist can take hold of discussions about women and Islam, thus obscuring the complexities of the 'lived Islam' of which Babès is such a keen advocate.

So, for Babès, the main reason for the prevalence of the veil in France today is to be found within Islamist groups, which she associates with the historical reformist movements that undertook a process of *ijtihad* (from the 1930s onwards in the Algerian case) leading to a 'scripturalist', prescriptive and austere form of Islam, devoid of spirituality. Babès thus diverges quite sharply from the position of Chebel, who was a firm advocate of a *nouvel ijtihad*, as well as from Bidar, who undertakes his own reinterpretation of the Quran via his re-reading of the *Al-Baqara* sura and the principle of *khalifat* in particular. Babès regards the veil as a phenomenon that is the result of social pressure, which not only concerns France but Belgium and Germany as well: 'Dans les quartiers … une femme non voilée est amenée un jour ou l'autre à se voiler pour être acceptée comme une "bonne musulmane".' (Babès 2004: p. 114) (In socially deprived neighbourhoods … a non-veiled woman eventually veils herself in order to be accepted as a 'good Muslim'). As for the counter-argument, which states that women voluntarily choose to wear the veil, Babès regards this as 'servitude volontaire en somme, qui peut aller jusqu'au syndrome de Stockholm' (Babès 2004: p. 115) (basically voluntary servitude, which may go as far as Stockholm syndrome) in a move reminiscent of Meddeb's discussion of the veil (see Chapter 1). Babès' rejection of the veil and any potential rationale underpinning it is unequivocal and arguably lacking in nuance. *Le Voile démystifié* is, in this sense, a political pamphlet and it begs the question of to what extent an intellectual with no Muslim 'background' could write the same type of essay without being accused of anti-Muslim sentiment. Does such a stance enable discussion across the different constituencies which make up contemporary French Islam or does it rather serve to further polarise and isolate competing versions of religiosity amongst French Muslims? Is such an approach similar to the symbolic violence done by public intellectuals via their 'oracle effect' (Bourdieu 1991)? In her defence, Babès did attempt to foster dialogue about different understandings of Islam and Muslim experience via her debate with Tareq Oubrou in *Loi d'Allah, loi des hommes* (2002), but her pointed criticisms of Oubrou in *Le Voile démystifié* published just two years later seem to suggest that a meaningful exchange was an elusive endeavour. Perhaps one of the *effets pervers* of her unambiguous rejection of the veil in *Le Voile démystifié* is that she ends up doing what she had previously condemned in her earlier work, that is, sociological description that focuses excessively on the negative portrayals of Islam and unwittingly reproduces those negative stereotypes it seeks to dismiss. The Babès of 2004 thus seems to stand in sharp contrast with the Babès of 1996, 1997 or even 2000, where she consistently foregrounded a discussion of Islam focused on the positive and innovative aspects of the lives of young Muslims. It is undoubtedly the case that the geopolitical climate changed post-2001, but that is not to say that those positive and innovative practices have disappeared. Herein lies the dilemma of public intellectuals working on Islam in a politically fraught context such as contemporary France: should they be primarily reactive and respond in a normative manner to spectacular and high-profile political events and phenomena (from the veil to terrorism) or should they intervene on a much slower time-scale in an attempt to provide more complex and nuanced analyses which may have less 'impact' in the short term?

It seems that Babès has adopted both these strategies throughout her career, and if *Le Voile démystifié* represents one of those responsive or circumstantial interventions, her next book, *L'Utopie de l'islam: la religion contre l'État* (2011) attempts to understand contemporary Islamist extremism via an in-depth historical and theological examination of Islam from the time of the revelation to the present day.

Religion and the political

In *L'Utopie de l'islam,* published in 2011, Babès sets out to present a genealogy of Islamist terrorism that has afflicted the contemporary period. She argues that although the violence carried out in the name of Islam impacts Muslims above all in terms of numbers of victims, and despite the fact that such violence emerges from a perversion of Islamic sources, its roots lie within the troubled relationship between 'le religieux' and 'le politique' in Islamic history. Babès seeks to explain the contemporary crisis via a historical study of the foundations and development of political power in Islam, which in her view has been profoundly affected by the central tension which underpins a 'utopian' vision of Islam. The utopia of Islam is defined by Babès as the fundamental contradiction between the concepts of *dîn* (religion) and *dunya* (world or politics) as well as the concepts of justice and religious imperialism. If we take the first utopia – the confusion over *dîn* and *dunya* – Babès argues that these two entities are not easily reconcilable:

> Le politique est au cœur de l'islam depuis ses origines. L'islam est *dîn* et *dunya,* religion et monde, et cette seule équation, qui ouvre déjà sur le pouvoir, se double sur le versant théologique d'une contradiction qui n'a jamais été résolue: comment concilier la vie ici-bas, avec ses richesses et ses plaisirs offerts aux hommes, et le salut dans l'Au-delà? À cette question, une tendance cyclique, récurrente, lancinante, répondra en posant qu'il faut corriger ce monde pour le transformer à l'image de l'Autre. (Babès 2011: p. 15)

> (Politics has lain at the heart of Islam since its origins. Islam is *dîn* and *dunya,* religion and world, and this sole equation, which already impinges on power, is reinforced in theological terms by a contradiction which has never been resolved: how to reconcile worldly experience with the riches and pleasures offered to humans and salvation in the realm of the ever-after? This question is cyclically and pointedly answered over and over again via the claim that the present world must be enhanced in order to transform it into the image of the Other world.)

It is, according to Babès, the recurrent, cyclical struggle (*jihad*) to transform the world in the imagined image of the afterlife which explains the existence of 'une longue tradition insurrectionnelle' (Babès 2011: p. 14) (a long tradition of insurrection). Furthermore, the 'période fratricide' (era of fratricide) or the *fitna* (discord) which characterised the third and fourth caliphates with the assassination of both Uthman and Ali, whilst clearly accepted as a defining moment in the history of Islam by Babès, only obscures a much more profound discord which has affected Islam for fourteen centuries: the irreconcilable ideals of Islamic justice and the State. Babès writes: 'L'histoire de l'islam a été ponctuée par des guerres que des musulmans, au nom du premier, ont livrées aux représentants du second, pour accomplir, réaliser, restaurer, réformer, le "vrai" islam, reproduisant exactement ce que d'autres avaient fait avant eux' (Babès 2011: p. 15) (The history of Islam has been punctuated by wars, which Muslims, in the name of

Islamic justice, delivered to the representatives of the State in order to accomplish, undertake, restore and reform the 'true' Islam, reproducing exactly what others had done before them). She evokes the notion of a 'fronde permanente' (Babès 2011: p. 15) (permanent civil war), which has drawn on various theological and political reference points, such as the Day of Judgement, reform, and a wide-ranging collection of Quranic verses and *hadiths* in order to legitimise the principle of the 'duty of revolt'.

This tendency and long tradition of rebellion and violence in the name of the Islamic utopian ideal of justice and equality is described as a 'guerre auto-destructrice' (Babès 2011: p. 15) (self-destructive war) which has constituted the greatest obstacle to the establishment of a stable and secularised state. No clear consensus has ever been achieved regarding the *type* of justice that the Quranic message advocates. Babès opines: 'Le Coran n'est en rien un programme de redistribution, mais seulement un message éthique d'obligations de dons et d'entraide' (Babès 2011: p. 16) (The Quran is not a programme of redistribution, but solely an ethical message of obligations and mutual assistance). This utopian ideal of some sort of social justice which is to be fought for on earth has unleashed a cycle of revolt and suspicion towards the State within Islam throughout its history and, in Babès' view, explains the permanent failure of political Islam. Beyond this assessment of the internal development of Islam, Babès argues that the spread of Islam, via conquest, beyond the Arabian Peninsula also created a further irreconcilable utopia in that the imperialist spread of Islam inevitably involved the oppression of the lands and populations under its control, so the Quranic message of social justice was compromised in that sense as well: 'ou l'empire se déploie dans sa logique d'État séculier, par le renoncement à l'idéal islamique, ou c'est la propagation du message de la foi qui devient la priorité, dans un rapport d'*indifférence* au monde ... le *dîn* et le *dunya* ne peuvent se conjuguer que dans l'affrontement' (Babès 2011: p. 88; emphasis in the original) (either the empire deploys itself within a logic of the secular state, via the renunciation of the Islamic ideal, or the spread of the message of faith becomes the priority, in a relationship of *indifference* to worldly affairs ... the religious realm and the temporal world can only be articulated via confrontation).

After her discussion of the historical development of Islam and the utopian, unrealisable reconciliation of an Islamic ideal of social justice on earth via political Islam, Babès turns her attention to the contemporary manifestations of political Islam's utopian quest. She argues that, as a political discourse, political Islam or Islamism actually negates or cancels out the political because it is lacking in any sort of reflection regarding political institutions. For Babès, Islamism is characterised by a delusion that the civil political sphere and the 'intimate' religious sphere can be fused together. Such a fusion of the political and the religious registers explains the failure of the State to realise a project based on the notion of social justice because, in Babès' view, such an endeavour is inevitably hampered by the absence of secularisation, here understood as the autonomy of politics from the religious sphere. Such a project is also, in any case, rendered impossible by the fact that it is a divine model: 'Comment en effet réaliser un modèle divin, par définition parfait, lorsqu'on est de simples mortels?' (Babès 2011: p. 267) (How, in fact, can a divine model be established, which is by definition perfect, when we are but simple mortals?).

Whilst Babès conceded that political Islam or Islamism may not have succeeded in taking power on a grand scale across the Muslim world, they have nevertheless managed to impose a certain 'ordre moral' (moral climate) in many countries. This Islamist moral climate is most visibly identifiable through the veil, which Babès refers to as 'l'arme absolue' of 'cette sous-culture de la sharîa' (the ultimate weapon of this sharia sub-culture) (Babès 2011: p. 267). Babès thus returns to the critique of the veil which she developed in *Loi d'Allah* and *Le Voile démystifié*, and notably adopts pathologising language and terms used by Meddeb in particular (see Chapter 1) – referring, for instance, to 'la contagion' on more than one occasion – to discuss the spread of Islamist ideology via the socially constraining and mimetic processes of 'la foule' (the mob) and 'la meute' (the pack) across the Muslim world (Babès 2011: p.268). However, where Babès hailed the French state to halt the spread of what she considered to be Islamist ideology in *Le Voile démystifié*, here Babès seems to suggest that the 'solution' to the 'contagion' can be found amongst Muslims themselves, and women in particular:

> Ces poches de résistance se manifestent un peu partout. Les femmes elles-mêmes recourent à mille et une ruses pour détourner les significations du voile, n'en respectant que la Lettre. Il suffit d'observer les libertés que les femmes iraniennes prennent avec le tchador pour s'en convaincre ... Aucun État, aucun pouvoir islamique, ne peut résister, ni à l'usure du pouvoir, ni à l'instinct de vie de peuples. (Babès 2011: p. 269)
>
> (These pockets of resistance crop up almost everywhere. Women themselves resort to a thousand and one tricks in order to hijack the meanings of the veil, only respecting the letter, not its spirit. One only has to observe the liberties that Iranian women take with their chador to be convinced ... No state and no Islamic power is able to resist the erosion of power nor peoples' instinct for life.)

So, for Babès, it is clear that the political sphere should take precedence over the religious sphere in order to facilitate a process of secularisation of Islam whereby what is essential is *la foi* rather than *la loi*. In Babès, we have an intellectual who is in tune with her French secular context; she does not call into question Republican universalism, but rather consistently challenges contemporary forms of French Islam. Her refusal to seek to understand the socio-economic processes which can contribute to the emergence of deeply conservative and fundamentalist forms of Islam amongst the younger generations in France is curious for a sociologist who recognises the importance of empirical and ethnographic research. However, on the other hand, Babès' universalist, Republican and secular stance on Islam confirms the broader picture of the Muslim intellectual landscape in contemporary France as presented in this book: questioning universalist paradigms in such a political context is simply beyond the pale. What becomes, then, of the expectation that intellectuals speak truth to power (Ahearne 2006: p. 335)?

Notes

1 I would like to thank Leïla Babès, who agreed to be interviewed by me in October 2015 in Lille.
2 See, for example, Bidar (2015b, 2016) and Meddeb (2002, 2008), as well as Chapters 1 and 5.

4

Dounia Bouzar: public intellectuals as policy experts in times of crisis

The work of Dounia Bouzar and her engagement in the political debates about Muslims in France raises significant questions about the relationship between Islam, secularism and feminism. Bouzar is an anthropologist of religions: a public intellectual, an activist, a public 'expert' and a public policy advisor. Bouzar was born in 1964 in Grenoble into an academic family. Her father was of Algerian, Italian and Moroccan origin and her mother was French Corsican. She explains in *L'Une voilée, l'autre pas* (2003), co-written with Saïda Kada, feminist activist and member of the organisation *Femmes françaises et musulmanes engages* (FFME), that she has not always been a Muslim and that she was, prior to her conversion, extremely critical of Islam for what she saw as its mistreatment of women. Bouzar could be described as a Muslim feminist in that her work has consistently been concerned with what she calls 'la condition féminine', including questions such as the headscarf, women's equality in the private and public spheres and, more recently, the indoctrination of young Muslim women into groups such as Al Jabhat al-Nusra and so-called Islamic State (or ISIS) in Iraq and Syria. She has published widely on the topic of Islam, religious diversity and *laïcité* (ten books, numerous articles and many media appearances) and she is the founding director of *Bouzar Expertises: Cultes et Cultures* – a consultancy organisation set up in 2009, having previously worked as an *éducatrice spécialisée* (specialist youth worker) then as a *laïcité* researcher at the *Ministère de la Justice* from 1991 to 2009. From 2003 to 2005, she sat on the *Conseil Français du culte musulman* and in 2013 she was nominated by the government to be a member of the *Observatoire de la laïcité*. Following the publication of her 2014 book *Désamorcer l'islam radical: ces dérives sectaires qui défigurent l'islam*, Bouzar founded the *Centre de prévention contre les dérives sectaires liées à l'islam* (CPDSI). This chapter will focus on Bouzar's recent writings from a feminist perspective, taking into account the following themes in particular: disruptive discourses in the public arena, the notion of *la femme-alibi*, the experiences of women who intervene in the public arena and finally the relationships between feminism and anti-racism.

Disruptive discourses in the public arena

In one sense, it would be fairly straightforward to argue that, given the level of media visibility that Bouzar enjoys in addition to her growing recognition within numerous official and government-backed organisations, we cannot necessarily regard her as a women who is 'speaking truth to power' (Ahearne 2006: p. 335). However, such an assessment of her intervention in the public arena is reductive and overlooks the various dimensions of her work. Indeed, the book for which Bouzar became most well known, a co-authored publication with Saïda Kada, *L'Une voilée, l'autre pas* (2003) could be regarded as a disruptive mode of intervention in the public debates about the Islamic headscarf in schools – a debate which was fairly binary in nature in the 2003–2004 period. Indeed, the authors state clearly their concern for the need to articulate their views as two French Muslim women with divergent perspectives on the question: 'On le sait, la liberté passe par l'accès au savoir, et la libération par la prise de parole. C'est pourquoi il était indispensable, en tant que femmes françaises et musulmanes, de nous faire entendre sur ce sujet.' (Bouzar and Kada 2003: p. 15) (We know that liberty is obtained via access to knowledge, and liberation via speaking up. That is why it was indispensable for us, as French Muslim women, to make ourselves heard on the subject.) Kada is an activist who wears the headscarf and Bouzar is a self-identifying Muslim who chooses not to wear it. At the time of publication, Bouzar was a researcher and civil servant working for the *Protection judiciaire de la jeunesse* (Youth Justice Protection). The main premise underlying the book is that, despite a lengthy public debate about the headscarf in France, the voices of the girls and young women concerned were inaudible. Hence their book is structured around the voices of those women, through a series of *témoignages* (testimonies). These accounts of personal experience are then interpreted and debated by Bouzar and Kada who integrate them into a broader context. Bouzar and Kada adopt a personal stance on the issues they discuss, and their positions as French Muslim women, as activist and researcher/civil servant, respectively, are thus incorporated into their analyses. The personal, professional and political registers are therefore woven into their discussions in a self-reflexive manner. The format of the book is not unusual; well-known figures often engage in such published debates (see Meddeb and Petit 2004; Chebel and Godin 2011; Babès and Oubrou 2002) and it is arguable that given their relatively unknown status at the time of publication, Bouzar and Kada knowingly subvert this textual genre.[1] A further way in which we can consider Bouzar as attempting to disrupt dominant discourse in *L'Une voilée, l'autre pas* is through her challenge of the binary nature of debates concerning French Muslims in general and French Muslim women in particular. Bouzar critiques the two polarised 'options' which are used with regard to women of North African heritage: 'On ramène les "beurettes" aux deux seules alternatives de femme "arabe musulmane soumise" ou de "femme athée dite occidentalisée". On part du principe qu'elles doivent choisir un modèle ou un autre.' (Bouzar and Kada 2003: p. 59) (We reduce the '*beurettes*' to two sole alternatives: the 'submissive Arab Muslim' woman or the 'so-called Western atheist woman'. The basic premise is that they must choose one model or the other.) Indeed, Bouzar makes the point that amongst young women Islam can be a means by which they enter into a process of individuation within patriarchal family structures. So, for Bouzar, the notion of Muslim feminism is not a contradiction in terms (unlike for Leïla Babès; see Chapter 3): 'Ainsi l'islam devient, pour les filles subissant ce type de discriminations, le moyen de faire valoir des droits et une reconnaissance qui n'existent pas toujours dans les cultures d'origine … c'est au nom de l'islam qu'elles ne se soumettent plus' (Bouzar and Kada 2003: p. 95) (So for women subjected to this type of discrimination, Islam becomes a means by which to claim rights and recognition that do not always exist in the cultures of origin … it is in the name of Islam that they are no longer submissive). This is an important point, since feminist movements in France have been fundamentally defined by their rejection of religion as an ideology of patriarchy. Hence the regular clashes between secular white feminists and young women of North African or Muslim heritage, a scenario which has been explored by sociologists such as Nacira Guénif Souilamas and Eric Macé in *Le Féministe et le garçon arabe* (2004). Going beyond the 'feminism versus Islam' debate, Bouzar argues that a turn *towards* Islam for both young women and men can in fact be regarded as part of a process which facilitates a necessary intergenerational conflict:

> C'est justement un des points positifs que je vois dans ce processus de renouement avec l'islam: les jeunes – filles et garçons d'ailleurs – peuvent enfin vivre leur conflit de générations. Et dans la structuration d'un adolescent, l'importance de la confrontation positive avec la génération précédente permet de se mesurer et de grandir. Et c'est comme ça que le monde avance. (Bouzar and Kada 2003: pp. 96–97).
>
> (It's precisely one of the positive aspects that I see in this process of reconnection with Islam: young people – both girls and boys – can finally experience their clash of generations. And for adolescent development, the significance of positive confrontation with the preceding generation facilitates self-awareness and growing maturity. And that's how the world moves forward.)

So Bouzar firmly rejects and thus disrupts the dominant discourse prevalent amongst secular feminists and the institutions that represent the Republic such as the *Ministère de l'Education nationale*, which tends to regard Islam as bad for women and bad for integration. She is a vocal critic of the position adopted by the association *Ni Putes Ni Soumises*, in particular what she considers as their attempts to demonstrate that Islam cannot be 'French', illustrated by their organising of a public event about the need for Muslim and North African women from the *banlieues* to become autonomous. It was striking that the speakers who were invited to this event were women from Saudi Arabia, Morocco and Algeria, as though there were no Muslim women from *within* France who were up to the task:

> Aborder la question sous cet angle renvoie les jeunes à leur condition d'étranger, comme si les banlieues faisaient partie du Maghreb. Cela revient à lier les analyses concernant la situation des filles issues des quartiers à ce qui se passe dans les pays d'origine. Cette appropriation fait fi des dizaines d'années d'installation des familles en France, qui ont abouti à la revendication des jeunes d'être français. (Bouzar and Kada 2003: p. 115)

> (Approaching the question from this angle suggests that the young people are foreigners, as if the *banlieues* were part of the Maghreb. This amounts to linking the analyses of the situation for girls in working-class neighbourhoods to what is happening in their countries of origin. This association overlooks the many decades that families have been settled in France, which has led in turn to the claim by these young people to be regarded as French.)

This perception by the association *Ni Putes Ni Soumises* that Islam is somehow foreign to France is, according to Bouzar, replicated by the process that led to the establishment of the *Conseil français du culte musulman* (CFCM). She claims that there is a disjuncture between the stated aims of the French government to facilitate the establishment of 'un islam *de* France' and the nomination of an Algerian national to preside over it along with a significant number of executive committee members who came to France as adults and whose first language is Arabic rather than French. Finally, the decision to determine electoral colleges based on the sizes of the mosques concerned automatically gave more weight and clout to those larger mosques that are funded by foreign states. In sum, Bouzar argues that: 'Les liens avec les pays d'origine sont prédominants dans ce processus d'établissement d'un islam de France' (Bouzar and Kada 2003: p. 117) (Ties with the countries of origin are dominant in this process of establishing a French Islam).

Indeed, Bouzar's intellectual project sets out to disrupt the assumptions that Islam is somehow 'foreign' to France or to Republican citizenship, an assumption that continues to structure much of the public debate concerning Islam and Muslims in contemporary France. In her discussion of the political involvement of the descendants of North African migrants, following the political disillusionment of the generation involved in the 1983 *Marche pour l'égalité et contre le racisme*, Bouzar reflects on the growing relevance of Islam in the political involvement of those who could be described as the 'third generation', i.e. the younger brothers and sisters of those who went on the *Marche*. In her discussion with Saïda Kada surrounding her involvement in the association *DiverCité*, she questions and challenges the omnipresent opposition of Islam and secularism, arguing that Islam and French citizenship in the sense of civic engagement should not be seen as incompatible:

> À la différence des 'années beurs', vous ne reprenez pas le concept de citoyenneté tel qu'il est traditionnellement conçu dans l'histoire de France: c'est comme si vous l'aviez 'désethnicisé' lui aussi, vous en faites une notion politico-philosophique transversale qui se construit au-delà de l'histoire et de la civilisation française ... En clair, tu revendiques le fait que la notion de citoyenneté soit comprise dans ta référence musulmane et pas uniquement dans les valeurs dites françaises. (Bouzar addressing Kada in Bouzar and Kada 2003: p. 147)

> (Unlike during the 'beur years', you don't accept the concept of citizenship as it is traditionally conceived in French history: it's as though you had 'de-ethnicised' this as well, as though it was an intersecting politico-philosophical concept which develops beyond the history of French civilisation ... Clearly, you make the claim for the notion of citizenship to be inclusive of your Muslim identification and not solely in reference to so-called French values.)

Bouzar is aware of the political genealogies of the notion of a 'statut musulman', which emerged as a result of the French colonial experience in North Africa and in Algeria in particular, where Muslim Algerians were not granted French citizenship rights despite Algeria being a *département* of France from 1830 to 1962. As such, she is attentive to the legacy of the colonial period, which is illustrated by what she refers to as 'le paramètre "islam" [qui] apparaît comme révélateur d'un fonctionnement normatif dans la continuité "ancien colonisé/ancien colonisateur"' (Bouzar in Bouzar and Kada 2003: p. 152) (the 'Islam' parameter [which] is revelatory about the continuing normative function of the 'former colonised/former coloniser'). This colonial legacy blurs perceptions of the involvement of French Muslim in the political sphere, who are erroneously perceived as Muslims struggling for recognition of 'le droit à la différence' (the right to be different), that is, as religious minorities rather than as French citizens of Muslim heritage or faith. Bouzar claims that what defines and structures the involvement of French Muslims in political struggles is equality, a demand for equal treatment as citizens rather than as Muslims, although these citizens are not seeking to minimise their faith or Muslim origins as those of the *primo-arrivant* or *beur* generation generally did:

> La demande d'égalité dépasse la question religieuse: il ne s'agit plus d'égalité de traitement demandé *en tant que musulman*, mais d'une égalité pure *en tant que citoyen français*, de la même égalité pour tous, que l'on se réfère à l'islam ou à n'importe quoi d'autre. (Bouzar in Bouzar and Kada 2003: p. 154; emphasis in the original).

> (The demand for equality goes beyond the religious question: it is no longer a question of equal treatment *as a Muslim*, but rather of pure equality *as a French citizen*, the same equality for all, whether we make a claim to Islam or to anything else.)

Bouzar addresses Kada directly here once again and disrupts the dominant perception that those Muslims who become involved in politics do so necessarily as Muslims first and foremost and as part of a transnational '*ummah*', that is, at the expense of their allegiance to the national (here, French) community: 'Votre inscription dans la citoyenneté se distingue nettement d'une adhésion à un islam transnational politique ... La revendication de l'islam vous a permis de vous "franciser"' (Bouzar in Bouzar and Kada 2003: pp. 156–157) (Your investment in citizenship is distinctly separate from membership of a transnational political Islam ... The claim to Islam has allowed you to 'Gallicise' yourself). Bouzar's stance thus stands in sharp contrast to the position of Leïla Babès, who consistently argues that the only relevant framework for political engagement is a secular national community (see Chapter 3).

The link that Bouzar and Kada establish between 'Frenchness' and 'Muslim values' is central to the process of disrupting public discourse about Islam in France. Their main claim is that Islam should be seen as a banal element of 'French' national values, as part of the 'patrimoine commun' (Bouzar and Kada 2003: p. 201) (common heritage) and that to continue to regard Islam as somehow exterior or foreign to French national identity is to condemn French society to a polarised future, characterised by inequality. The authors make it clear in their conclusion that it is high time that Islam and Muslims are regarded as French, with an emphasis placed on the Republican principle of equality, which, it is argued, flows from a process of the recognition of Islam. Bouzar and Kada make a clear distinction between what they call 'le religieux' and 'la référence musulmane', indicating that whereas 'le religieux' is theological in nature, 'la référence musulmane' is more cultural in nature and is thus inflected by the dual concerns of individual subjectivities and beliefs that are explicitly articulated with Republican civic principles such as *laïcité*: 'Il ne s'agit pas de faire pénétrer le religieux à l'intérieur de la République, ni d'instaurer des particularismes quelconques, mais bien de laisser une place à la référence musulmane au même titre que les autres et de se l'approprier collectivement' (Bouzar and Kada 2003: p. 200) (It is not a question of introducing the religious into the Republic, nor of establishing any specific particularisms, but rather of leaving a space for Muslim identity in a similar fashion to all others and to collectively claim ownership of it). So the notion of 'la référence religieuse' as far as Islam or any other religion is concerned relates to issues that go well beyond the religious sphere of influence or 'competence' and extends out to questions such as 'le rapport à l'autre, à la famille, à l'éducation, à la raison, à la société, à la politique…' (Bouzar and Kada 2003: p. 200) (relations with the Other, family, education, reason, society and politics).

In the challenge posed to a bipolar vision of the world whereby 'the West' is erroneously regarded as the sole location of modernity and Islam as the location of archaism, Bouzar and Kada attempt here to outline the importance of the notion of individual will: 'Être moderne, c'est "dire je" – ne pas laisser le clan décider pour soi – et utiliser la raison pour remettre en question des traditions ancestrales' (Bouzar and Kada 2003: p. 199) (To be modern means to 'say I' – to refuse to let the clan decide for you – and to use reason to question ancestral traditions). Although the authors claim that Islam does not always facilitate their understanding of what it means to be modern ('l'islam ne mène toujours pas à la modernité'; Bouzar and Kada 2003: p. 199 (Islam does not always lead to modernity)), they are at pains to point out that Islamic scripture can and does defend the cause of women. Indeed, they spend most of the last part of the book on this question. As such, in Part III, entitled 'Ce que dit l'Islam sur les Femmes' (What Islam says about women), Bouzar and Kada explore a range of problematic areas concerning women in the Quran and Islam, such as gender equality, the headscarf (the multiple and divergent interpretations regarding its necessity or otherwise), relations between men and women in public and private spaces, women and work, maternity, the couple, the Quranic concept of *qiwamah*, which pertains to notion of the 'responsibility' of men to provide for the material needs of his wife and children, violence and women, inheritance, marriage and marital consent, bearing legal witness, polygamy, divorce, excision, personal hygiene, contraception, abortion and sexuality. They cite a number of verses in the Quran and *hadith* which indicate that, at the time of the revelation, Islam provided women with some degree of emancipation as compared to the pre-Islamic period. Furthermore, it is their view that it is still possible today for Muslim women of North African heritage to draw on the Quranic scripture in order to emancipate themselves from patriarchal family 'traditions' which are cultural or regional as opposed to religious in nature (e.g. regarding a woman's right to an education, to choose her husband, to divorce, to work, to be respected or to reject female genital mutilation).

However, despite or perhaps because of their close attention to what the Quran says on a number of issues relating to the status of women in Islam, the authors do not fully introduce the notion of the 'je moderne' which they argue so clearly in favour of in their conclusion. Another problem with the analysis is that it remains silent on certain issues which do not fit the broader aim of trying to demonstrate a positive status for women in Islam. For example, although the authors point out that marriage in Islam should involve the consent of the bride and that Muslim women are within their rights to demand divorce, nothing is said about the difficult question of child custody or the ways in which women can be treated unfavourably in this domain in the event of a marriage breakdown. The authors' own discussion remains circumscribed by the Quran, what it says and how it has been interpreted by a number of established religious scholars (including the well-known Muslim feminist scholar Fatima Mernissi). So the 'je moderne' seems to get lost here and as such shows a clear distinction between the work of Bouzar and Kada and that of Abdennour Bidar in *Self islam: histoire d'un islam personnel* (2006), which explains how, for him, being a Muslim is about defining one's relationship to God, rather than being defined by the scripture and its interpretations (see Chapter 5). Bidar goes further, then, in his articulation of an 'un islam pour notre temps' (Islam for our time) (to use his words) than Bouzar or Kada. But in a sense, we could in fact invert that reasoning by arguing that Bouzar and Kada's stance is more audacious in the secular Republican context since they do not set out to *laïciser* (secularise) Islam or to make it French/palatable for a French superaddressee.[2] Instead, they argue that French Muslims who follow Quranic scripture and the principles of Islam should not be regarded as exterior to the 'patrimoine commun' of French society. Bidar seems to want to make Islam French, whereas Bouzar and Kada here appear to be engaged in a different endeavour, namely to make Muslims French.

Indeed, one of the key aspects of Bouzar's intellectual project since 2003 has undoubtedly been the emphasis she has placed on demonstrating that Muslims are de facto part of French society. This approach is clearly developed in her monograph, *Monsieur Islam n'existe pas: pour une désislamisation des débats*, which was published one year after her co-authored book with Saïda Kada. In the monograph, Bouzar explores the challenges involved when talking about and on behalf of Islam and Muslims in the contemporary French context. This work seems to mark a departure from the stance adopted in *L'Une voilée, l'autre pas*, which was perhaps affected by the divergent views held by Bouzar and Kada. In *L'Une voilée, l'autre pas*, a significant amount of discussion focused on what the Quran says about women's status within the family and society, with close attention paid to individual suras and *hadiths* in order to demonstrate that women could be regarded as equal to men in Islam. However, in *Monsieur Islam*, Bouzar's starting point is to raise the question of how it is that young French citizens who were born and educated in France come to organise their lives around a notion of strict Islamic guidelines: 'La question n'est pas de savoir "ce que l'islam dit ou ne dit pas", mais de comprendre pourquoi ce jeune, né en France, socialisé à l'école de la République, a envie de penser que "l'islam dit plutôt ceci ou plutôt cela"' (Bouzar 2004, back cover blurb) (The issue is not about finding out 'what Islam does or doesn't say', but understanding why a young person born in France and socialised in the school of the Republic wants to think in terms of 'Islam says this or that').

Monsieur Islam n'existe pas discusses research carried out within twelve Muslim associations in the Lyon, Lille, Paris and Nord regions for a research project commissioned by the *Institut national des hautes études en sécurité* (INHES), thus demonstrating Bouzar's peculiar position as a public intellectual who, certainly at the outset of her research career, was working within rather than outside existing political institutional structures. The epigraph at the start of the book, drawn from Amin Maalouf's *Les Identités meurtrières* (1998), sets the tone and reveals it to be quite a different one to that developed in *L'Une voilée, l'autre pas*: 'On donne souvent trop de place à l'influence des religions sur les peuples et leur histoire, et pas assez à l'influence des peuples et de leur histoire sur les religions' (We often give too much space to the influence that religions have on people and their histories, and not enough space to the influence that people and their histories have on religions) (Bouzar 2004 cites Maalouf 1998: p. 7). Bouzar makes her position clearly distinct from that developed in the book co-authored with Kada and draws on Olivier Roy's approach to Islam in France: 'Ce qui m'importe ici, ce n'est pas le Coran mais ce que les musulmans "disent que le Coran dit". Comme le propose Olivier Roy, laissons le Coran aux théologiens et revenons aux musulmans et à leurs pratiques concrètes.' (Bouzar 2004: p. 9 cites Roy 2002: p. 12) (What concerns me here is not the Quran but rather what Muslims 'say that the Quran says'. As suggested by Olivier Roy, let us leave the Quran to theologians and return to Muslims and their actual practices.) Bouzar therefore states from the outset that her research is not about 'les musulmans de France' (p. 9) because that would be based on a flawed assumption that it is possible to refer to a group with certain collective characteristics, whereas the book (in a very similar manner to Babès 1996, 1997; see Chapter 3) is concerned with individuals and question of 'Qu'est-ce que c'est, être musulman, en 2004, dans une société laïque?' (Bouzar 2004: p. 11) (What is it to be Muslim, in 2004, in a secular society?) Given that her approach is based on individual practices, rather than a textual engagement with the Quran, it follows that she is not motivated by locating theological justifications of key current issues in France, such as gender equality: 'Soyons clairs: ce qui permet avant tout l'émancipation des femmes, ce n'est pas plus le Coran que la Bible ou la Torah en eux-mêmes, mais avant tout le développement économique et social des pays qui permet leur relecture' (Bouzar 2004: pp. 10–11) (Let us be clear: what facilitates the emancipation of women above all is not the Quran, any more than the Bible, or Torah in themselves, but most of all the economic and social development which enables their re-reading).

So whilst Bouzar, who is an anthropologist of religions rather than a theologian, does not seek to engage in a process of exegesis or a study of the Quranic scripture, she does make the case quite clearly for a need to revisit the Quran – alluded to in the notion of 'relecture'. One of Bouzar's main points is that insufficient space is accorded to the re-reading and reinterpreting of the Quran in a contemporary French context, and that this lack of space and time to revisit the texts arises from a dual constraint that is imposed on French Muslims. The first of these constraints emerges from the climate of institutional suspicion which weighs down on French Muslims, who are interpellated (in the Althusserian sense) by the French state to define themselves in ways that promote the notion of compatibility between Islam and the Republic: 'Mais lorsque les discours institutionnels et politiques cultivent une suspicion permanente et automatique sur la compatibilité de l'islam avec la République, ils participent à la surenchère de "l'extase islamique" et retardent la reflexion herméneutique nécessaire' (Bouzar 2004: p. 173) (But when institutional and political discourse cultivates permanent and automatic suspicion regarding the compatibility of Islam and the Republic, they partake in the political one-upmanship around 'the Islam spotlight' and delay necessary hermeneutic reflection). The second constraint is self-imposed by the French Muslim association leaders who are the subject of *Monsieur Islam n'existe pas*:

> 'L'approche islamisante que nous avons croisée tout au long de nos interviews – sorte d'extase islamique – correspondrait d'abord au résultat d'une ignorance théologique généralisée. Sommés à tout moment de prouver leur soumission à la République, ces leaders se justifient par un islam qui coïncide avec les exigences des situations rencontrées, sans avoir le temps d'en élaborer les assises théologiques ou doctrinaires.' (Bouzar 2004: pp. 171–172)

> (The Islamising approach that we encountered throughout our interviews – a kind of Islamic ecstasy – appears to primarily be the consequence of generalised theological ignorance. Constantly expected to prove their submission to the Republic, these leaders justify themselves through an Islam which coincides with circumstantial demands, without having the time to develop their theological or doctrinal foundations.)

Bouzar seeks to challenge dominant discourse about Muslims in France via her study of Muslim associations by insisting on the 'francité' (Frenchness) of her interlocutors against a discursive landscape which has since the 1990s tended to construct French Muslims as being somehow external to the French nation, either because they are misleadingly linked to international events involving political Islam by the media or are considered to be under the influence of foreign Muslim powers by the French state. This dynamic is exemplified by the repeated recourse to foreign-born Muslim 'leaders' or experts in the exercise leading to the establishment of the CFCM or during the Stasi Commission's hearings ahead of the 2004 law banning ostentatious religious symbols in France's public schools. Bouzar argues that the 'third generation' of North African-origin activists, that is, those who are the 'petits frères et petites soeurs' (younger brothers and sisters) of those who were involved in the *Marche pour l'égalité et contre le racisme* in 1983 have adopted what she calls a 'nouveau discours religieux' (new religious discourse), which she identifies as representing the approach taken by Tariq Ramadan, an intellectual who until recently enjoyed a widespread following amongst this generation of activists (Bouzar 2004: p. 46). This new religious discourse is characterised by the overlapping of the definitions of citizen and Muslim which allows these association leaders to be active citizens in French society, without renouncing their Muslim identification: 'Dans cette logique il devient possible de se définir exclusivement par l'islam et de participer pleinement à la société, puisque l'engagement social devient lui-même une preuve de foi' (Bouzar 2004: pp. 46–47) (According to this logic, it becomes possible to exclusively define oneself in relation to Islam and to partake fully in society, because civic engagement becomes in itself an indicator of faith).

Bouzar (like Babès in Chapter 3 and Meddeb in Chapter 1) is critical of Tariq Ramadan and the 'nouveau discours religieux', since she argues that it leads to a rather prescriptive approach which leaves little room for multiple, individual or dialectical interpretations, although it does of course insist on the essential modernity of Islam. However, Bouzar is keen to critique what she sees as a process whereby the 'new religious discourse' justifies an inherent Islamic modernity as illustrated in the Quran without necessarily seeking to modernise the actual religious issues concerned. Indeed, Bouzar challenges the tendency of certain association leaders to seek evidence for the modern and positive aspects of Islam (such as gender equality) exclusively in the Quran – a process that is described as involving 'des detours interprétatifs étonnants qui peuvent ressembler à de la "haute voltage herméneutique": pour prouver un principe général' (Bouzar 2004: p. 72) (astonishing interpretative detours which can resemble 'high-voltage hermeneutics' in order to prove a general point). Instead, Bouzar draws on Bordeaux mosque imam Tareq Oubrou and Islamic Studies scholar Mohammed Arkoun to argue in favour of revisiting canonical theological knowledge and involving the study of the historical, human and social processes which have created those canons in the first place (Bouzar 2004: pp. 69, 97 cites Babès and Oubrou 2002 and Arkoun 1975). She is critical of what she regards as an anachronistic approach to the Quran amongst the association leaders she interviewed: 'estimer que les textes sacrés ont *conçu* des valeurs modernes est en soi un contresens puisqu'une telle position projette vers le passé des productions actuelles, souvent résultats de luttes sociales' (Bouzar 2004: p. 140; emphasis in the original) (to claim that the holy texts *conceived* of modern values is in itself a misinterpretation because such a position projects current issues, which are often the result of social struggle, back into the past). Similarly, Bouzar seems to have doubts about the potential to articulate a universal vision of social struggle when the association leaders she encountered tend to foreground their 'islamité' and to limit their own religiously inspired social action through a static relationship with the Quran and Islam ('ce que l'islam dit' (what Islam says)): 'Mais peut-on passer par une religion pour s'inscrire dans une nation? (Bouzar 2004: p. 155) (But can we inscribe ourselves into a nation via a religion?).

However, Bouzar makes it clear that she does not place sole 'blame' for these disjunctures and limitations on the association leaders themselves. On the contrary, she argues that these pitfalls that seem to characterise the social action and discourse of French Muslim association leaders is compounded, if not indeed caused by, the ambient Republican discourse: 'En acculant "Monsieur Islam", devenu une entité, à décliner sa véritable identité-sur-le-champ, ils empêchent les musulmans de se constituer en véritables sujets' (Bouzar 2004: p. 173) (By pushing 'Mr Islam' – a label which has subsequently become a 'social phenomenon' – to immediately divulge his true identity, Muslims are prohibited from becoming real subjects). In this claim, Bouzar's approach seems to resonate with an Althusserian conception of negative subject formation, whereby the (Muslim) subject is hailed by the powers that be and as such has very limited space in which to articulate itself in a fully autonomous manner (Althusser 1971). In such a move, Bouzar is perhaps the only figure in this volume to explicitly recognise this issue, although she does not refer to Althusser herself.

Indeed, Bouzar argues that social relations in France have undergone a process of Islamisation, thus echoing a similar process of ethnicisation in the 1980s, and this is clearly demonstrated by the tendency of politicians to seek explanations for France's social problems amongst the post-migrant youth in the *banlieues* within the religious framework of Islam: 'Les députés de la République ont ouvert le Coran au sein de l'Assemblée nationale ... Des comportements de jeunes définis comme le produit de l'islam' (Bouzar 2004: pp. 180–181) (Elected deputies of the Republic opened up the Quran in the National Assembly ... Young peoples' behaviour defined as the product of Islam). This is part and parcel of what Bouzar sees as a two-stage process of reductionism, the first in the 1980s, when young people were expected to maintain their *islamité* within the private sphere, and the second today, where the situation has shifted to one where their *islamité* is accepted but becomes their defining feature, at the expense of all other aspects of their experience. In other words, Bouzar argues that these individuals are seen first and foremost by the political class as Muslims, rather than French citizens.

Despite these criticisms, what Bouzar shows through her study of association leaders is that they have internalised the fundamental Republican principle of *laïcité*:

> Tous les responsables associatifs interviewés, quelle que soit leur relation aux textes sacrés, estiment que si le Coran contient des éléments de doctrine en rapport avec la question sociale, il ne prévoit pas les modalités de leur mise en œuvre. Une différence est faite entre les principes moraux destinés à réguler le comportement des humains et les règles qui constituent des systèmes d'organisation politique et sociale. (Bouzar 2004: p. 148)

> (All the association leaders who were interviewed, whatever their relationship to the sacred texts, claim that if the Quran contains doctrinal elements that are related to the social question, it does not provide for the modalities of their implementation. A distinction is made between the moral principles designed to regulate human behaviour and the rules that constitute the systems of political and social organisation.)

So whilst Bouzar regards *laïcité* as an enabling framework that offers the possibility to distinguish religious ideals from the specific historical circumstances in which

Islam was established in Muslim societies, she argues that French society also needs to undertake a critical approach to its own collective national imaginary, particularly as it has evolved in recent years. It is only then that the image of 'Monsieur Islam' will recede in order to allow for the emergence of the notion of 'des musulmans sujets, dans une société qui saura composer son unité avec sa pluralité' (Bouzar 2004: p. 183) (Muslims as subjects, in a society that is able to reconcile its unity with its plurality). The main point Bouzar is making, then, is the need to articulate a vision of French national memory which incorporates Muslims as French, and Islam as part and parcel of that national imaginary. It is not surprising, therefore, that as in her later works on the question of radical Islam, Bouzar is also keen to dispel any myth that there is something specific about Islam as a religion that sets it apart from the other monotheistic religions. Here she compares the social engagement of Muslim association leaders to those of Christian Democrats:

> En prenant note de la distanciation que prennent ces leaders d'avec les autorités religieuses des pays musulmans sur la question de la laïcité, nous pensons notamment aux courants chrétiens-démocrates, qui se sont construits comme tentative de conciliation d'un idéal chrétien avec la modernité – et notamment avec la démocratie – à l'opposé d'un catholicisme intransigeant, traditionaliste et même réactionnaire. (Bouzar 2004: p. 50)
>
> (In acknowledging the distancing between these leaders and the religious authorities in Muslim countries around the question of secularism, we are reminded in particular of the Christian Democratic movements, which developed as an attempt to reconcile a Christian ideal with modernity – and democracy, in particular – in contrast to an intransigent, traditionalist and even reactionary Catholicism.)

Bouzar's focus on the processes by which Islam may be regarded as an integral, rather than a 'foreign' part of French society, is further developed in her 2005 essay entitled *Ça suffit!*, which was published in the wake of her resignation from the CFCM in 2005. Here, Bouzar explores the question of representation and self-representation of Muslims. The tone of this text is significantly different to *L'Une voilée, l'autre pas* and *Monsieur Islam n'existe pas*. This is a personal statement which directly addresses the French government and Sarkozy in particular as the *Ministre de l'Intérieur*, who Bouzar holds responsible for what she sees as the severe limitations of the CFCM. However, the critique is not solely directed at the Chirac government, which was in place at the time of writing and publication. It extends back to François Mitterrand and evokes the deep sense of disappointment amongst the *Marche pour l'égalité et contre le racisme* generation, who despite their faith in the Republic were denied any meaningful place in the *Parti socialiste* project and were regarded as foreigners in need of integration: 'Vous vous êtes mis à parler d'intégration: si les jeunes brûlaient des voitures ce n'était pas à cause de problèmes économiques et sociaux mais parce que leurs parents étaient de culture étrangère!' (Bouzar 2005: p. 21) (You started to talk about integration: if youths were burning cars it was not because of economic and social problems but because of their parents' foreign heritage!) This leads Bouzar on to bemoan the non-application of the Republican motto of *Liberté, égalité, fraternité*. Throughout the essay, Bouzar evokes the lack of space and opportunity available to French Muslims in general and French Muslim women in particular to express themselves in the public arena:

> Y a-t-il encore quelqu'un en France pour penser dès qu'il s'agit d'islam? Ce qui est certain, c'est qu'il y en a toujours un pour parler à la place de l'autre ... Se raconter sa propre histoire permet non seulement de la continuer mais surtout de décider qui on veut être ... Il faut se définir soi-même. Sortir des discours. (Bouzar 2005, pp. 7–8, 43)

> (Is there anybody left in France who is able to think when it comes to Islam? What is certain is that there is always someone who is able to speak for others ... Telling your own story allows you to develop it, but above all, to decide who you want to be ... One has to define oneself and move beyond existing discourses.)

Ca suffit! can therefore be regarded as an essay which denounces the tendency of politicians to view French Muslims through the prism of Islam, a tendency which she had already discussed at some length in her 2004 publication, *Monsieur Islam n'existe pas*. The Islamisation of debates is once again central to her critique:

> C'est toute la grille de lecture des comportements qui s'est islamisée. Fini la psychanalyse pour comprendre le rôle des parents dans le rapport à la loi, terminé la sociologie pour appréhender le conditionnement du milieu dans lequel on évolue! Tout ça, c'est parce qu'on grandit à l'ombre d'un minaret mental. (Bouzar 2005: p. 17)

> (It is the whole interpretative framework of behaviours that has become Islamised. Psychoanalysis is no longer pertinent in understanding the role of parents in the relationship to law, sociology is defunct as far as understanding the conditioning of the environment in which we grow up! Everything can be explained by the fact that they have grown up in the shadow of a mental minaret.)

Indeed, the main reason that she is critical of the CFCM is that its mission should have been conceived as being limited only to 'le culte musulman', i.e. to the religious affairs of French Muslims, rather than what it became in her view, namely an attempt to represent French Muslims in relation to social and political issues. In this, she articulates a very similar view to that of Leïla Babès (see Chapter 3):

> Car la seule légitimité du CFCM, c'était de mettre en place le culte. Point à la ligne. Hors de question que ce CFCM représente les musulmans! Il n'était pas là pour

faire de la politique mais pour donner les moyens aux musulmans de pratiquer leur religion … Nous sommes pour le dialogue interreligieux, mais attention à ne pas réduire les gens à leur religion. (Bouzar 2005: p. 23; p. 27).

(Because the sole legitimacy of the CFCM was to organise the religion. Full-stop. It is out of the question that the CFCM represents Muslims! It was not supposed to be involved in politics but rather to provide Muslims with the means to practise their religion … We are for inter-faith dialogue but we must take care to avoid reducing people to their religion.)

Bouzar therefore argues that it is incumbent on French Muslims and, in particular, French Muslim women to articulate those issues which concern them in a polyvocal manner, with no specific emphasis on their religious status, real or perceived, for according to her, 'Il n'y a pas de communauté musulmane en France, il y a des citoyens de confession musulmane' (Bouzar 2005: p. 29) (There is no Muslim community in France, there are citizens who are Muslim). That need for polyvocality is bound up with Bouzar's desire to give women's voices much more space in the realm of religious interpretation. Bouzar ends her essay by calling for the development of a new form of *discourse*, new images and new symbols that reflect the notion of gender *mixité* (diversity) within Islam:

Des hommes ont utilisé le Coran pour structurer le monde à leur image. Par son intermédiaire, ils ont décidé de nos vies sociales et personnelles. Les mots ne font pas qu'exprimer le monde, ils le façonnent … Il faut étirer le langage: fini les symboles uniquement masculins, et rajouter du féminin pour redonner de la profondeur au mystère divin. Nous voulons nommer les choses aussi. Mettre les mots en mixité. (Bouzar 2005: pp. 124–125)

(Men used the Quran to structure the world in their image. Using the Quran, they determined our social and personal lives. Words do not just reflect the world, they shape it. We must expand language: using solely masculine symbols will not work anymore, we must add feminine ones in order to give depth back to the mystery of the divine. We want to name things as well and to bring gender diversity into language.)

The introduction of the language of 'mixité' within Islam is of itself a further example of disruptive discourse: disruptive of patriarchal models prevalent within Islam and equally disruptive of representations of Islam as a religion that is in essence oppressive of women. A further way in which Bouzar can be seen to engage in the disruption of widely accepted discourse is in her analysis of the phenomenon of radicalisation. In *Désamorcer l'islam radical* (2014) and *Ils ont cherché le paradis, ils ont trouvé l'enfer* (2014), Bouzar maintains the position that the phenomenon of young people who practise an extreme form of Islam, some of whom then join terrorist organisations such as Al Jabhat al-Nusra or so-called Islamic State (or ISIS), is not due to some distortion of the message of the Quran. This process cannot, in effect, be regarded as radicalisation, since for Bouzar it is a process of indoctrination that is similar to a 'dérive sectaire' (Bouzar 2014a: p. 17) (cult-like spiral). According to Bouzar, such a 'dérive' operates in cults and new religious movements such as the *L'ordre du Temple solaire*, which became famous for the collective suicide-murders of its members, or certain evangelical Christian groups in the United States: 'Lorsque un discours religieux conduit l'individu à la rupture – sociale, sociétale, familiale etc. – on peut parler d'effet sectaire' (Bouzar 2014a: p. 17) (When religious discourse drives the individual towards social, societal and familial separation etc., it is possible to evoke a cult-like effect). So, for Bouzar, the alienation and social reclusion of young people who join organisations such as Islamic State (ISIS) represents a complete departure from the principles of Islam and results from a process of scriptural and interpersonal manipulation:

> Dès que les musulmans prennent la parole pour dénoncer le radicalisme, leurs propos sont utilisés non pas contre les radicaux mais contre … l'islam … C'est pour cette raison que j'ai voulu 'faire la différence' entre l'islam et le radicalisme. Il est temps d'arrêter de prendre les musulmans pratiquants pour des radicaux et il est temps d'arrêter de prendre les radicaux pour de simples musulmans trop pratiquants. (Bouzar 2014a: p. 14)
>
> (As soon as Muslims speak out to denounce radicalism, their words are used, not against the radicals, but against … Islam … It is for this reason that I wanted to 'make a distinction' between Islam and radicalism. It is time to stop portraying practising Muslims as radicals and radicals as simply over-pious Muslims.)

Bouzar's claim that radical Islam and terrorism committed in the name of Islam is somehow external to Islam itself and akin to a universal or psycho-social phenomenon of indoctrination marks a notable departure from the stances of other Muslim public intellectuals such as Meddeb and Bidar. Meddeb, for instance, consistently claimed that fundamentalism was somehow an inherent risk *internal* to Islam which arose mainly from literalist readings of the Quran (see, for instance, Meddeb's *La Maladie de l'islam* (2002) in Chapter 1). Bidar (see Chapter 5) recently argued that it is insufficient to simply claim that terrorist atrocities committed in the name of Islam have nothing to do with Islam and he calls for greater 'autocritique' (self-criticism) in order to understand how Islamist ideology can develop and spread from *within* Islam (Bidar 2015b). Such analyses as those developed by Meddeb and Bidar could be regarded as problematic in their refusal to take seriously the postcolonial legacies of discrimination and Islamophobia as a contemporary manifestation of anti-Maghrebi racism. It could even be argued that the theses of Meddeb and Bidar feed into a narrative of Islamophobia. Whether Bouzar is always successful in her attempts to speak out about Islamism whilst avoiding the stoking of Islamophobia is nevertheless open to debate. Indeed, some might argue that as a woman or *femme-alibi*, Bouzar occupies a much more fragile place in the public intellectual sphere than her male counterparts, as we shall see below.

The notion of *la femme-alibi*

The notion of *la femme-alibi* or the 'token' woman who is appointed to a visible public position in order to create the impression of gender equality is an issue that goes beyond gender and concerns a range of ethnic minorities and historically discriminated-against groups. It is a trope which is familiar to a feminist analysis of socio-political processes and has been explored in seminal feminist texts such as *Les Femmes s'entêtent* (Bernheim *et al.* 1975), edited by Simone de Beauvoir. Whilst Bouzar never explicitly refers to herself as 'une femme alibi', she does discuss in several of her texts the challenges she has faced from interlocutors who variously expected her to conform to certain expectations:

> La notoriété n'y change rien. Quand un haut membre d'une haute instance vous invite à faire part de vos recherches, il ne discute pas toujours vos résultats sur le fond ... Combien de fois me suis-je sentie bête, avec les dossiers de mes dernières enquêtes empilés sur les genoux. Je croyais être reçue en tant que chercheuse, et voilà que j'étais ramené à ... mes origines. (Bouzar 2005: p. 15)
>
> (Being well known does not change anything. When a high-ranking member of a high-status organisation invites you to share your research, he does not always discuss your results in depth ... I cannot count how many times I felt stupid, with the files from my latest fieldwork piled up on my lap. I thought I had been invited as a researcher and yet it was all brought back to my origins.)

It is certainly striking that Bouzar is one of only about two or three female Muslim intellectuals who are well known in France. The public intellectual landscape is one that remains dominated by men and this is even more pronounced for Muslim intellectuals. When Muslim women *do* intervene, they are often compartmentalised by the media, the political and academic fields into the less noble category of 'experts', as in Bouzar's case, or as witness-victims who are in possession of a 'lived experience' rather than knowledge (Grewal 2012: p. 572). In other words, such women are '"objects to be known" rather than the knower' (Grewal 2012: p. 587). This Orientalist paradigm would include prominent Muslim women who have become well known for their 'lived experience' as 'victims' of Islam, as in the case of high-profile ex-Muslims such as the French-Iranian Chahdortt Djavann in France or the Somali-born Dutch-American Ayaan Hirsi Ali in the Netherlands. Bouzar argues that this also feeds into a further problem, namely the ways in which Islam and Muslim 'questions' are still constructed as 'non-French'. That the head of the Stasi Commission on religious symbols in state schools, Bernard Stasi, claimed on the television station Canal+ that amongst the hearings which had taken place before the Commission, it was that of Chahdortt Djavann which had moved him the most is, according to Bouzar, indicative of this tendency to conflate the lived experiences of French Muslims with the lived experiences of Muslims in Muslim-majority societies such as in Iran or North Africa. Bouzar's frustration with regard to Stasi's statement is clear:

> Une musulmane prise dans un contexte islamiste, voilée de force. Pour comprendre des filles nées en France? ... J'avais enquêté auprès de deux cents jeunes filles pour *L'Une voilée, l'autre pas*, mais la Commission Stasi n'a pas jugé utile de m'entendre ... En revanche, les spécialistes du Maghreb ont défilé. (Bouzar 2005: pp. 32, 33)
>
> (A Muslim woman taken from an Islamist context, veiled against her will. In order to comprehend young women born in France? ... I had carried out interviews with two hundred young women for *L'Une voilée, l'autre pas*, but the Stasi Commission did not think it pertinent to hear from me ... On the other hand, specialists of the Maghreb streamed in.)

Of course, the categorisation of (postcolonial) women as 'experts' rather than intellectuals is not anodyne and reflects a certain taxonomy of legitimacy whereby the status of the generalist 'intellectual' is generally reserved for men. The prospect of postcolonial women being regarded as universal intellectuals is more elusive, as Kiran Grewal has shown in her work on the notion of voice or the 'reclaiming of voice' by the figure of the 'postcolonial woman' (Grewal 2012). The way in which Bouzar's nomination to the CFCM was reported in the media is also a telling sign of how Muslim intellectual women are constructed in public discourse. Bouzar writes about how the newspaper *Libération* described the event: 'Quand Nicolas Sarkozy m'a nommée, *Libé* a titré: "Sarkozy choisit sa Beurette"' (Bouzar 2005: p. 30) (When Sarkozy nominated me, *Libération* ran the headline: "Sarkozy chooses his Beurette"),[3] thus clearly reinforcing the notion of the *femme-alibi*. By using a contested term to refer to the descendants of North African immigrants (*beur*) and furthermore the diminutive, feminised form of the word, *beurette*, *Libération*'s headline trivialised Bouzar's appointment and contributed to the impression that she fulfilled the implicit requirements of appointing a token woman of North African origin. The reference to Bouzar as a *beurette* also overlooked the fact that she is of mixed French, Algerian, Moroccan and Italian heritage and focused only on a sort of domesticated and infantilised 'foreignness', which is part and parcel of the terms *beur* and *beurette*.[4]

Against this trend of viewing Islam and Muslims as 'un-French', as somehow in need of special treatment, Bouzar argues consistently for the 'droit à la similitude' (the right to be the same): 'Le problème, aujourd'hui, ce n'est plus le droit à la différence, c'est le droit à la similitude, tout en restant musulman!' (Bouzar 2005: p. 38) (The issue today, is no longer the right to be different, but the right to be the same, whilst remaining Muslim!). The call for a recognition of commonality would, of course, attenuate the 'femme alibi/musulman alibi' tokenism that Bouzar herself felt subjected to when she was nominated to the CFCM. The notion of 'le droit à la similitude' has broader legal implications and Bouzar often raises the question of how law and legislation should always apply to all groups in a given society, rather than to specific ones only. This is certainly the approach she develops in the book she co-authored with her daughter, Lylia Bouzar, *Allah a-t-il sa place dans l'entreprise?* (Bouzar and Bouzar 2009). This text, which is based on fieldwork on a range of private sector employers is presented as being of interest to workplace human resources departments. In it, Bouzar and her daughter state their preference for 'le droit à l'indifférence' (the right to be undifferentiated):

> Garantir une approche indifférenciée des individus et de leurs références constitue donc l'objectif à atteindre. Ce n'est pas le droit à la différence mais le droit à l'indifférence qui garantit l'égalité. Méfions-nous de tous les processus qui catégorisent et différencient, de la 'discrimination positive' à la 'laïcité positive'. (Bouzar and Bouzar 2009: p. 186).

> (The guarantee of an undifferentiated approach towards individuals and their reference points is therefore the objective to be attained. It is not the right to be different but the right to be undifferentiated which guarantees equality. We should be wary of any processes that categorise and differentiate, from 'positive discrimination' to 'positive secularism').

Allah a-t-il sa place dans l'entreprise? and Bouzar's subsequent single-authored *Laïcité mode d'emploi – cadre légal et solutions pratiques: 42 études de cas* (Bouzar 2011) certainly suggest that Bouzar in fact positions *herself* as an 'expert' rather than as an intellectual (indeed, she is quite critical and disparaging of what she constructs as theoretical and overly abstract debates in *Ça suffit!*). She also seeks to present her expertise as stemming from her status as 'une femme du terrain', as it were, coming back with almost obsessive frequency to her formative years as an *éducatrice spécialisée* (specialist youth worker) with the *Ministère de la Justice*. Yet, Bouzar holds a doctorate in Anthropology of Religions from Université Paris 8, and although she does not work in academia, her aversion to intellectualism is arguably symptomatic of what we might call the internalisation of Bourdieu's notion of symbolic violence within the intellectual field. That is, it would seem that Bouzar – as a Muslim woman – constructs a niche for herself to intervene as a woman of *action* – an *expert* on how *laïcité* should be applied in the workplace, an *expert* on how to deal with the indoctrination and radicalisation of young Muslims via the CPDSI; in doing so, she distances herself from the sphere of public intellectuals that includes figures such as Bidar, Meddeb, Chebel and

Babès. Of course, some detractors might argue that the depth of her scholarship is not comparable to such authors; however, it would seem that on some levels, Bouzar's strategy is self-limiting and arises from what Grewal calls the postcolonial habitus that 'reflects the depth of internalisation of colonial regimes of control' (Grewal 2012: p. 585). Such a regime did not accord women, let alone (post)colonial women, voice and legitimacy on a par with male subjects, so when those women *do* speak and participate in the production of knowledge, they do so within self-limiting paradigms. Bouzar has certainly faced public criticism from the media for her work on radicalisation and de-radicalisation whereby she has argued that radicalisation is not linked to Islam per se but can be regarded as a psycho-social phenomenon. Her integrity as a researcher and expert is frequently attacked by journalists from both sides of the political spectrum, with some questioning her methodology and others questioning her links with so-called ex-jihadists in her de-radicalisation work.[5] On the other hand, Bouzar would presumably argue that her integrity and independence as a researcher are central to her work and indeed explain her decision to end the partnership between the CPDSI and the *Ministère de l'Intérieur* in February 2016 in response to the bill to introduce *la déchéance de nationalité*, the stripping of French nationality for those of dual nationality convicted of terrorism offences (CPDSI 2016). Such a decision would suggest that Bouzar is in some ways attempting to move beyond the self-limiting practices of the 'expert' in the service of the State's short-term goals.

Feminism and anti-racism

A further way in which Bouzar goes beyond such self-limiting forms of self-presentation is in her simultaneous engagement with anti-racist and feminist struggles. Unlike women such as Ayaan Hirsi Ali or Chahdortt Djavann, who present themselves as authentic representatives of victims of a patriarchal Islam, Bouzar sees no conflict between the notions of being a Muslim and a feminist. Neither is she a cultural relativist, and indeed she is extremely critical of the risks of cultural relativism in the name of cultural tolerance, denouncing, for example, what she calls the 'permissiveness' of those who accept the *niqab* or *burqa* because it supposedly represents freedom of religious conscience rather than a practice that is oppressive of women and not even derived from the Quran. In this sense, then, we can view Bouzar's work as extending secular feminist paradigms by integrating an anti-racist and feminist logic into a context where what she calls 'Muslimphobia' (as opposed to Islamophobia) has become one of the major forms of cultural racism today. Whilst mainstream French feminist movements have historically struggled with the dilemma of how to reconcile anti-racist and feminist struggles, Bouzar's work seems to explicitly seek to take on both these issues simultaneously. Indeed, Bouzar consistently explores the issue of how women are constructed within Islam in general and within extreme forms of

Islam in particular. As such, despite her apparent reticence to engage with certain forms of knowledge production, distancing herself from the figure of the public 'intellectual' and taking on the persona of the policy 'expert', Bouzar's writing and public interventions do seek to carve out a space for a critical Muslim feminism which does not place the struggle against Islamphobia/Muslimphobia on a higher plane than the struggle against women's oppression in the name of Islam. In the latter part of her essay *Ça suffit!*, Bouzar recounts a meeting she had with two Muslim women who had set up an association working against religious fundamentalism, stating: ' "Les religions sont ce que les hommes en font" … "Et vu ce que les hommes en ont fait, on pourrait réfléchir à ce que les femmes peuvent en faire" ' (Bouzar 2005: p. 100) ('Religions are what men make of them' … 'And given what men have made of them, we could reflect on what women might make of them'). Bouzar's Muslim feminism is illustrated by her insistence on the importance of the individual and individual subjectivities in relation to the interpretation of the Quran and Islamic practice. Some aspects of her stance resonate with Abdennour Bidar's notion of self Islam (see Chapter 5):

> *Je* donne une signification au sens du texte. *Je* démêle le message divin des formes historiques dans lesquelles il a été mis en œuvre. *Je* repense aux faits locaux dans lesquels Dieu a parlé … Il faut restituer au texte son contexte sémantique et historique. Ne pas donner une valeur définitive à une phrase destinée à une étape particulière de la Révélation. (Bouzar 2005: p. 114; emphasis in the original)
>
> (*I* give meaning to the text. *I* untangle the divine message from the historic context in which it was constructed. *I* think over the local circumstances in which God spoke … One must return the semantic and historical context to the text and not give a definitive value to a sentence that was designed at a particular stage of the revelation.)

But although Bidar's work does not focus on women or the notion of feminism within Islam, Bouzar is clearly interested in overcoming the historical boundaries between feminist and religious discourse, where in France, feminist movements have been not only secular but have gone further and often rejected religion as a patriarchal construct to be overcome in the struggle for women's liberation. There are several notable Muslim feminist scholars around the world (such as Asma Lamrabet, Fatema Mernissi and Amina Wadud) but their numbers are relatively small and, besides Zahra Ali and Malika Hamidi in France, there are very few audible or visible Muslim feminist voices in the public sphere. So it is significant then that Bouzar invokes Amina Wadud, the American Muslim imam, focusing in particular on her experience of becoming Islam's first female imam to lead mixed prayers in a New York Anglican church in March 2005: 'C'est drôle, elle n'a pas compris la même chose que ses frères … Elle leur prouve que le Prophète encourage les femmes à devenir chefs spirituels.' (Bouzar 2005: p. 122)

(It is funny; she did not come to the same conclusions as her brothers … She proves to them that the Prophet encourages women to become spiritual leaders). Bouzar ends *Ça suffit!* with a homage to Amina Wadud, who comes to symbolise a notion of Muslim feminine resistance and hope, as well as a powerful example of the ways in which the legacy of a secular feminism is being extended through Bouzar's engagement with a Muslim feminism and a simultaneous espousal of critical anti-racist and anti-feminist struggles:

> Amina est devant. Elle rythme la prière. Quand nous, les femmes, comprenons les causes de notre souffrance, nous nous redressons d'un seul bloc. Alors il y a résistance et espoir … Nous regardons devant. Nous habitons le monde. Nous devenons enfin les artisans de notre histoire. (Bouzar 2005: p. 125)

> (Amina is at the front. She paces the prayer. When we, women, understand the causes of our suffering, we will rise up as one. So there is resistance and hope … We are looking forwards. We inhabit the world. We will finally become the artisans of our story.)

Notes

1 On the question of the veil and identity politics, see Renaut and Touraine (2005) or Touraine and Khosrokhavar (2000) for examples of such debates between high-profile thinkers.
2 For a detailed discussion of the concept of the superaddressee, see the Introduction to this volume or Bakhtin (2006: p. 126 cited in Buden *et al.* 2009: p. 205).
3 *Beurette* is the feminised form of *beur* and is used to refer to French-North Africans. Whilst the term was popular in the 1980s when the second generation emerged on a large scale, it has since been increasingly marginalised, regarded by many as problematic and possibly even pejorative by some.
4 On the question of *beurettes*, see Guénif Souilamas (2000).
5 See, for example, Perrotin (2015), Bastié (2016) and Jouan and Leclerc (2017).

5

Abdennour Bidar: existentialist Islam as intercultural translation

Abdennour Bidar is a French philosopher, a member of *L'Observatoire de la laïcité* and *chargé de mission sur la laïcité* for the *Ministère de l'Éducation nationale*. He also recently directed a working group tasked by the government to establish *une pédagogie de la laïcité* (Bidar and HCI 2013). Through his publications, scholarly articles and radio programmes on Radio France Inter and Radio France Culture (*France Islam: questions croisées, Cause commune, tu m'intéresses* and, since Abdelwahab Meddeb's death, *Cultures d'islam*), Bidar attempts to sketch out the contours of what he calls a twenty-first century Muslim existentialism (Bidar 2008/2012a).[1] Muslim existentialism emerges from what Bidar calls *un islam sans soumission*. Islam or Islamic belief without submission is premised on a profound desire for freedom of conscience, expression and dissent. Bidar argues that the roots of such a notion of freedom can be found in the Quran itself, which he describes as an 'instrument of liberation' (Bidar 2008/2012a: p. 17) through which human beings can become conscious of their abilities. Prior to his work on the notion of Islam without submission, Bidar also developed the term self Islam in reference to Europe's citizens of Muslim heritage, the majority of whom choose to define their own diverse relationships with Islam on their own terms. According to Bidar, self Islam should not be understood as a selfish or individualist undertaking, but rather one that is premised on the notion of autonomy and personal responsibility. His work, which places him at the intersections of the academic world, the media and the political arena, makes him a particularly interesting figure through which to investigate the circulation of narratives concerning French Muslims and their diverse relationships with political and social secularism.

Bidar was born in 1971 in France to a French mother who had converted to Islam before his birth and who raised him as a Muslim. Bidar grew up in the Auvergne region before leaving at the age of eighteen to attend the Lycée Henri-IV in Paris in order to prepare for the entrance examinations for the prestigious *École Normale Supérieure*. As a former student of the *École Normale Supérieure* and an *agregé de philosophie* (a qualified Philosophy teacher), Bidar has taught philosophy both in post-high school *classes préparatoires* and at the University of Nice. Although Bidar has only been publishing since 2004, it is clear that his reflections about a European Islam have developed quite rapidly over the space of about twelve years. The discussion in this chapter will focus on eight of Bidar's books and essays, all of which were published between 2004 and 2016: *Un islam pour notre temps* (2004), *Self islam: histoire d'un islam personnel* (2006), *L'Islam sans soumission: pour un existentialisme musulman* (2008/2012), *L'Islam face à la mort de Dieu: actualité de Mohammed Iqbal* (2010), *Comment sortir de la religion* (2012), *Plaidoyer pour la fraternité* (2015), *Lettre ouverte au monde musulman* (2015) and *Quelles valeurs partager et transmettre aujourd'hui?* (2016). The discussion that follows will show how it is possible to identify certain key points in Bidar's own trajectory from focusing initially on the reform of Islam (Bidar 2004) towards notions of individualised practice and spirituality (Bidar 2006) and then on to the more audacious intellectual movements which are first premised on the notion of Man as the heir (*héritier*) of God (Bidar 2008/2012a) and finally via a discussion of Mohammed Iqbal's legacy (Bidar 2010a) towards the notion of overcoming religion (Bidar 2012b).[2]

Despite the rapid development of Bidar's thought, it is possible to detect a consistent approach that characterises his work. This approach can be described as a project of cultural translation, where Bidar as philosopher can be regarded as a cultural mediator who seeks to productively confront non-Western and Western concepts of religion, spirituality, modernity and humanism. However, his work goes well beyond a limiting notion of intercultural dialogue based on a concept of cultures as bounded entities and indeed, changes over the course of several years. So, at the start of his career, Bidar's work seems to resonate with the German Romantic approach to translation as developed by Wilhelm von Humboldt (1816–1909) whereby, according to Buden *et al.*, 'the translator should be faithful to the "foreign" (*das Fremde*) of the source text, for it is a new quality which is added to his or her patriotic language, thereby building its spirit, the spirit of the nation' (Buden *et al.* 2009: p. 199). For Bidar, the source text here can be regarded as Islam/the Quran and the patriotic language and the nation as the Republican principles of *liberté, égalité, fraternité, laïcité* and *universalisme*. However, several years later, Bidar's intellectual project seems, in some ways, to correspond more to Walter Benjamin's critical or deconstructionist approach to 'the task of the translator' whereby, as Buden *et al.* claim,

> translation is like a tangent which touches the circle (i.e. the original) at one single point only, thereafter to follow its own way. Neither the original nor the translation, neither the language of the original nor the language of the translation are fixed and enduring categories. They do not have an essential quality and are constantly transformed in space and time. (Buden *et al.* 2009: pp. 199, 200)

So Bidar's work, which embraces a dual-pronged critique of both Islam and post-Enlightenment modernity and which is constructed around the need for a renewal of humanism in order to articulate what he calls 'un universel partagé' (Bidar 2010a: p. 166) (a shared universal), in some ways resonates with Benjamin's understanding of translation, and subsequently with Homi Bhabha's notion of cultural translation or negotiation, although he does not make explicit reference to these thinkers (see Buden 2006). At the time of writing in 2019, it should be pointed out that as French political and social life has become increasingly affected by the wave of terror attacks perpetrated in the name of Islam, we see a slightly different type of intellectual and civic engagement by Bidar whereby his work appears to have moved once again towards a stance founded on cultural translation in the service of bolstering the French Republic (in particular, the value of *fraternité* – or *le vivre ensemble*). In doing so, he seems to be placing greater emphasis on the nation-building approach. This raises broader questions about the role of the public intellectual during times of crisis, to which I will return in the conclusion to this chapter.

Bidar the reformist

In *Un islam pour notre temps* (2004), Bidar begins by posing the question of whether the notion of reform of Islam is a legitimate one; in doing so, he clearly positions himself as a Muslim thinker: 'Nous, musulmans, en avons-nous réellement besoin?' (Bidar 2004: p. 11) (Do we Muslims really need this?). It quickly becomes clear that Bidar's opening question is a rhetorical device which allows him to make the case for reform of a religion that governs the lives of Muslims who, according to Bidar, have already become modern citizens of the world but who have still to explicitly acknowledge that transformation: 'nous, musulmans, sommes devenus des citoyens du monde et nous ne pouvons plus aujourd'hui faire semblant d'ignorer cette modernité qui imprègne et transforme chaque jour un peu plus notre vision du monde et nos conditions de vie matérielles' (Bidar 2004: p. 13) (we Muslims have become citizens of the world and today we can no longer pretend to ignore this modernity which everyday saturates and increasingly transforms our vision of the world and the material conditions of our lives). Bidar argues that despite the diversity of circumstances affecting and characterising Islam and the Muslim world today, a constant problem afflicts it, namely an antagonistic relationship with modernity. Bidar's main claim is that 'le monde musulman' (the Muslim world) has in actual fact been changing for a long time and has been adopting aspects of modernity associated with more secular societies in Europe. Yet in spite of these piecemeal changes, Bidar argues that the Muslim world as a whole does not want to consciously acknowledge its own modernity and changing relationship with Islam (Bidar 2004: p. 15). This inability or unwillingness of Muslim-majority societies to acknowledge their own modernity allows Bidar to turn the 'clash of civilisations' debate on its head, arguing that Samuel Huntington's well-known thesis (Huntington 1998) on the cultural incompatibility of the West and the Muslim world is a paradigm that is largely unchallenged in many Muslim-majority societies:

> C'est bien sous le visage de la domination, de la destruction de l'ordre ancien, du mépris des croyances, que l'Occident a autrefois envahi le monde musulman. Mais comment expliquer que l'islam ne se soit toujours pas remis de ce choc et en soit resté à ce sentiment premier d'incompréhension, de rejet et de condamnation? Il aurait dû, depuis longtemps, s'interroger plus en profondeur sur cette modernité qui certes le déstabilisait violemment, mais portait tout de même dans son bagage autre chose que des armes. (Bidar 2004, p. 39)
>
> (It is certainly in the guise of domination, destruction of the old order, and disdain for beliefs, that the West invaded the Muslim world. But how is it that Islam has still not recovered from this trauma and remains within this preliminary affective space of incomprehension, rejection and condemnation? It should have examined this modernity in more depth a long time ago, a modernity which, to be sure, violently destabilised it, but which nonetheless brought something else beyond conflict.)

Like Abdelwahab Meddeb (see Chapter 1), Bidar thus argues for the need to move beyond a colonial and postcolonial framework of analysis in order to liberate the West from a form of post-imperial guilt and in order to challenge the perpetrator–victim dichotomy that continues to inform cultural, political and symbolic relationships between the West and a number of Muslim countries (Bidar 2004: p. 22). Just as Bidar is committed to challenging the notion that Islam and modernity are somehow at loggerheads, he similarly makes the case for moving beyond facile oppositions between modernity and tradition, thus evoking the need to create 'modern tradition' within Islamic thought (Bidar 2004: p. 32). This modern intellectual and theological tradition would break open what Mohammed Arkoun referred to as 'la clôture idéologique' (Arkoun, cited by Bidar 2004: p. 33) (ideological closure) which has historically blocked any serious notion of Islamic reform. Of particular significance is the fact that Bidar's understanding of modernity is not a post-Enlightenment rationalist one, which has been the dominant variant in the West. Indeed, Bidar rejects what he later comes to call 'primitive modernity' (Bidar 2012b), which is characterised by the death of God and the ensuing absurdist ethic of the human condition as being defined by its finitude. Instead of this 'primitive modernity' which dominated the West in the nineteenth and twentieth centuries, the challenge thrown down by Bidar is how to develop a concept of the modern which is reconciled with the notion of *le sacré* or spirituality (Bidar 2004: p. 37). The challenge to conceptualise modernity as 'un événement spirituel' (Bidar 2004: p. 38) (a spiritual event) rather than as a purely scientific or technological notion of progress allows Bidar to make the case for the reform of Islam, whereby it is 'la modernité comme événement spirituel' (modernity as a spiritual event) that facilitates a rethinking or reformist movement within Islam (Bidar 2004: p. 38).

Before articulating how Islam should be reformed, Bidar makes a point of distinguishing his approach from other well-known reformist voices. In particular, Bidar is very critical here (and also later in Bidar 2010a) of the notion of reform as outlined by Tariq Ramadan in his book *Les Musulmans d'Occident et l'avenir de l'islam* (2003), because he is fundamentally opposed to Ramadan's claim that reform must come from within Islam. In *L'Islam face à la mort de Dieu*, Bidar develops his criticism of Ramadan's position further by arguing that the fundamental problem of Ramadan's approach to Islamic reform is that it does not challenge a juridical paradigm of Islam and *islamité*. So Ramadan speaks of the adaptation of sharia law rather than dismantling the notion of theologically derived laws altogether. Bidar, on the other hand, is in favour of a spiritual Islam (in a similar manner to Babès; see Chapter 3) as opposed to a juridical one and argues that the very notion of sharia law should be abandoned.

Bidar's understanding of reform is one that is firmly premised on the principles of human rights, understood as *liberté*, *égalité* and *fraternité* (liberty, equality and fraternity), and in this move Bidar seems to most clearly take on the role of the intellectual as cultural mediator or cultural translator. Bidar's starting point is the first article of the Universal Declaration of Human Rights, citing it as: 'Tous les êtres humains naissent *libres* et *égaux* en dignité et en droits. Ils sont doués de conscience et de raison et doivent agir les uns envers les autres dans un esprit de *fraternité*.' (Bidar 2004: p. 43; Bidar's emphasis) (All human beings are born *free* and *equal* in terms of dignity and rights. They are conscious, rational beings and must interact with one another in a spirit of *fraternity*.) In light of this article and these principles, Bidar proposes that Islam be refounded according to these three principles: 'l'affirmation de la *liberté* de choix spirituel pour toutes les pratiques et croyances, *l'égalité* stricte en valeur de tous ces choix, la création d'une *communauté* accueillant leur différence' (Bidar 2004: p. 43; emphasis added) (the claim to *freedom* of spiritual choice for all practices and beliefs, strict *equality* of value of all these choices, and the establishment of a *community* which welcomes their difference). At the centre of Bidar's approach to Islamic reform, then, is the notion of Islamic or spiritual humanism. The principles of liberty, equality and fraternity have a spiritual value beyond their socio-political value. And since Bidar's understanding of the notion of Islamic reform is based on such humanist ideals, it follows that the notion of the individual is central to his simultaneous re-thinking of both Islam and Western modernity:

> Voilà le geste fondamental de la modernité, celui qui la caractérise de la façon la plus essentielle et en fait un mouvement de civilisation sans précédent: *elle déplace le lieu du sacré*, le faisant descendre du ciel sur la terre et passer d'un au-delà lointain

au cœur de nous-mêmes. Dieu nous a rejoints et ne fait plus qu'un avec chacune de nos vies. (Bidar 2004: p. 45)

(Such is the fundamental gesture of modernity, which in essential terms characterises a civilisational shift without precedent: *it displaces the realm of the sacred*, bringing it down to earth and moving from a far-off beyond towards the core of our very being. God has joined us and is entwined in each of our lives.)

So Bidar's reading of modernity as being a process by which the sacred is located in human individuals rather than in God allows him to fundamentally challenge the Nietzschean understanding of modernity expressed in the notion of God-as-dead: 'Elle [la modernité] n'est donc pas la mort de Dieu, comme le croyait Nietzsche ... notre civilisation n'a pas tué Dieu, elle l'a donné à chacun de nous' (Bidar 2004: p. 48) (Modernity is therefore not the death of God, as Nietzsche believed ... our civilisation did not kill God; rather it bestowed God on to each of us).[3] The cultural or intellectual mediation that Bidar is undertaking here, then, is to invite readers to re-think their understandings of post-Enlightenment modernity, since he argues that modernity has been misrecognised or misidentified as being a phenomenon that wholeheartedly eliminates the 'divine' and spiritual aspects of human existence. In response to this misreading of post-Enlightenment modernity, Bidar proposes that we understand the birth of modern European democracies from the eighteenth century onwards as being a process characterised by 'la divinisation de l'individu, puisque désormais le chef politique n'est plus le représentant de Dieu – comme l'étaient les rois – mais celui du peuple' (Bidar 2004: p. 49) (the sacralisation of the individual, since from then on political leaders are not the representatives of God – as kings once were – but of the people).

Bidar's emphasis on the importance of the individual in Islam should not be interpreted as a move that is founded on individualism in a selfish sense. Indeed, Bidar places considerable emphasis on the principle of discussion and exchange of different views or reflections on specific aspects of Islam. Rather, his focus on the individual and what he calls the 'divinisation' of the individual lays a foundation for him to articulate his vision of an Islamic humanism, couched in the principles of *liberté, égalité* and *fraternité*. Bidar uses the Quran itself to argue for what he calls 'le principe de liberté spirituelle' (Bidar 2004: p. 52) and its claim that 'Dieu marche avec vous où que vous soyez' (*The Qur'an*, sura 2, v. 148; OUP 2004 translation, p. 17) (and wherever you are, God will bring you together).[4] Bidar interprets this verse to mean that the Quran is suggesting that there is not just one way of being Muslim, but many:

Je propose donc que désormais prévale en islam le principe suivant: *Il y a en islam autant de voies droites, vraies et justes qu'il y a des choix spirituels réfléchis et sincères, chacun étant maître de déterminer, parmi toutes les croyances et pratiques de l'islam, celles qui lui sont utiles. Tous ces choix sont égaux, et nul n'a le droit d'imposer à un autre croyant sa propre démarche.* (Bidar 2004: p. 52; emphasis in the original)

(I therefore suggest that the following principle apply to Islam: *There are within Islam as many right, true and just paths as there are considered and sincere spiritual choices, with everyone in a position to determine, amongst all Islamic beliefs and practices, those that are useful to them. All these choices are equal, and nobody has the right to impose their own approach on another believer.*)

Bidar builds his case for a move towards individuation in Islam via the Quranic text, citing further suras: 'Dieu n'impose à chaque homme ce qu'il peut porter' (Bidar 2004: p. 53 cites *The Qur'an*, sura 2, v. 286; OUP 2004 translation, p. 33) (God does not burden any soul with more than it can bear) or 'Il y a pour chacun une direction vers laquelle il se tourne' (Bidar 2004: p. 54 cites *The Qur'an*, sura 2, v. 148; OUP 2004 translation, p. 33) (Each community has its own direction to which it turns). Bidar thus takes these suras as evidence that we can see in the Quran a move towards individuation, equality of personal choices and responsibility for all Muslims to choose their own path in Islam. By according the notion of individual liberty within Islam a central place, Bidar argues that the principle of sharia is fundamentally transformed because it becomes internalised: 'Elle ne disparaît pas, elle n'est pas abolie. Elle s'intériorise, c'est-à-dire qu'elle ne commande plus du dehors mais du dedans. Elle n'est plus une loi collective … elle devient une *loi personnelle*.' (Bidar 2004: p. 62; emphasis in the original) (It does not disappear; it is not abolished. It is internalised, that is to say it no longer rules from without but from within. It is no longer a collective law … it becomes a *personal law*.) It is significant to note that Bidar's position on the question of sharia seems to develop in later publications beyond the notion of internalising sharia towards an abandonment of any normative or juridical principle of religiosity altogether. However, in 2004, Bidar remains fairly guarded in his discussion of sharia and Islamic reform, choosing instead to make a qualitative distinction between the notion of 'contrainte' (constraint) and 'obligation' (duty), arguing that whereas constraint stems from external forces that coerce action from believers, obligation stems from internally derived sources or objectives that individuals set for themselves.

Having explored the question of how liberty can be used as a principle to reform Islam, Bidar moves his attention to the principle of equality amongst Muslims and the need to discredit the domination of imams. Bidar's call for a reassessment of the role and influence of imams does not imply an abandonment of the principle of training imams in France, so Bidar's position is markedly less far-reaching than his later interventions on this topic as found, for example, in *L'islam face à la mort de Dieu* (2010), in which he argues against the expenditure of public funds to train imams in France. The call to completely abandon the training of imams shows not only the rapid development of Bidar's thought but also his quite radical stance in relation to some of the other thinkers discussed in this book. Even Meddeb, who described himself as an atheist Muslim, still called for the public financing of French-trained imams specifically so as to avoid the influence of certain foreign states and Wahhabi Islam in particular. The importance that Bidar attaches to the principle of equality within a reformed vision of Islam is explored in relation to the place of women in the Quran and in Islam and he argues that any suras within the Quran that are deemed to be incompatible with modern principles of liberty, equality and fraternity should be discredited and disregarded. In making this move, Bidar draws on the tradition of the Mutazilite movement to argue that the Quran is expressed in human language and therefore must be distinguished from the divine wisdoms that can be found within them. Once again, Bidar uses the Quran to defend his position, citing the sura in which the notion of change and substitution is mentioned: 'Dès que nous abrogeons un verset ou le faisons oublier, nous en apportions un meilleur ou un égal' (Bidar 2004: p. 66 cites *The Qur'an*, sura 2, v. 106; OUP 2004 translation, p. 13) (Any revelation We cause to be superseded or forgotten, We replace with something better or similar).

Finally, Bidar moves on to the third principle necessary for a humanist Islam: fraternity. Whilst Bidar recognises that the notion of fraternity is fairly well developed in Islam, notably via the requirement of *zakat* (alms-giving; one of the five pillars of Islam), he argues that fraternity without spiritual liberty is self-defeating. The current lack of spiritual liberty in effect undermines any notion of Islamic fraternity, since those Muslims who do not conform to accepted or orthodox images of the 'Good Muslim' are ostracised by the 'community' when that model of community is closed, rather than being 'un modèle de communauté ouverte' (Bidar 2004: p. 69) (a model of open community) whereby members are free to enter and leave as they please. In what is arguably one of the less-developed sections of the book, Bidar states that the risk of *communautarisme* (cultural fragmentation) is one of the biggest challenges facing Islam and Muslims today. Indeed, Bidar's discussion of *communautarisme* does not take into account socio-economic factors or the impact of postcolonial legacies linked to systemic discrimination and inter-generational reproduction of educational and economic inequalities amongst European Muslim populations. So Bidar's concerns about *repli communautaire* (community segregation) at work within some sections of Europe's Muslim populations do not take account of *le vivre ensemble* as a multi-directional process mediated by questions of social, economic, political and symbolic power.

Bidar's exploration of the potential dangers posed by *communautarisme* are a way into his discussion on the theme of *laïcité*, which surprisingly, given its key status in debates about religion in general and Islam in particular, is not introduced until about two thirds of the way through the book. Bidar's position on *laïcité* is straightforward: State and religion should be separate and Muslim countries should adapt their constitutions to introduce state neutrality vis-à-vis all religions. Bidar draws on the Egyptian theologian Ali Abderraziq, who in the first half of the twentieth century argued for separation between State and religion, claiming that, from a historical perspective, the State did not really exist during the Prophet's lifetime (Bidar 2004: p. 72). Bidar's suggestion that universities and higher education institutions in Muslim countries should include curricula on the reform of Islam so as to bring about 'une révolution culturelle de la conscience musulmane' (Bidar 2004: p. 80) (a cultural revolution in the Muslim conscience) is constitutive of his understanding of *laïcité* and is bound up with his desire to articulate a new vision of modernity based on both Western and Islamic cultural knowledge.

So the third and final chapter of Bidar's short book focuses more closely on not only how Islam might reform itself according to modern principles of humanism but also how to think through how modernity can be enriched or enhanced through sustained engagement with Islam. This intercultural mediation approach is summed up by Bidar in the following question: 'En particulier, quelle peut-être la contribution propre de l'islam à l'humanisme moderne?' (Bidar 2004, p. 81) (In particular, what might be the specific contribution of Islam to modern humanism?). Bidar sees that contribution as being particularly pertinent in the face of what he calls a crisis of humanism, which plays out in neo-liberal systems of worker exploitation and the alienating forces of the culture industry (as understood and analysed by thinkers such as Adorno and Horkheimer (2016) in *Dialectic of Enlightenment*; Bidar 2004: p. 82). In particular, Bidar regards the crisis of humanism as the result of a sustained attack on the dignity of Man (*l'homme* is the term used by Bidar most of the time, with a few exceptions when he uses the more gender-neutral *être humain*). Such an attack arises out of a Western modernity, defined by the notion of human finitude and the absurdity of the human condition, itself a consequence of the death-of-God meta-narrative. Bidar argues that given the meta-narrative of human finitude and the absurdist ethic, it is no wonder that humanity has not over-exerted itself in the struggle for greater liberty, equality and fraternity, for what is the point of an existence defined by being-towards-death? Bidar proposes rehabilitating the principles of humanism by using religious heritage as a tool. The rationale for using religious heritage as a way to renew modernity's rather worn-out humanism is that according to Bidar it will allow us to *sacralise* human beings rather than denying them dignity, as a consequence of a post-Enlightenment European modernity that was predominantly defined and structured by the idea of the death of God and human finitude. He makes a strong claim in defence of the capacity of religious texts and rituals to purvey what he calls 'une énergie spirituelle sans équivalent, qui seule peut rendre à notre existence son caractère sublime' (Bidar 2004: p. 85) (a spiritual energy without equivalent, which alone can give to our existence its sublime character). Bidar's stance suggesting a turn to religion and religious texts in order to reinvigorate or re-sacralise human existence is markedly different to the stance he takes just four years later in *L'Islam sans soumission* (2008/2012) where he advocates turning to religion and to the Quran in particular in order to develop the notion of human beings as the heirs of God. This is different yet again from his stance in *Comment sortir de la religion* (2012) in which he advocates a turn to religion to overcome religion, thus mapping out a post-theological engagement with religion in particular, similar to the approach adopted by someone like Quentin Meillassoux, for example (Watkin 2011). Indeed, in his later books (Bidar 2008/2012a, 2010a, 2012b) Bidar is dismissive of the notion of religious ritual, which he criticises for its lack of interiority and the associated risk of a dogmatic approach to religion as ritual. So, in *Un islam pour notre temps*, Bidar adopts what we might see as a first 'stage' of the stance of intercultural mediator when he states that 'il [l'islam] peut offrir à la modernité ... ce qu j'appellerais volontiers *le sanctuaire de la vie humaine*' (Bidar 2004: p. 85; emphasis in the original) (it [Islam] can bring to modernity ... what I would willingly call *the sanctuary of human life*).

Furthermore, Bidar attempts to use Quranic scripture as a metaphor for the current 'crisis of modernity', arguing that the non-linear, non-chronological aspects of the Quran are reflective of the chaos of modernity: '*Pour éclairer le désordre du monde contemporain, il nous faut méditer sur ce modèle de désordre que nous offre le Coran*' (Bidar 2004: p. 87; emphasis in the original) (*In order to explain the disorder of the contemporary world, we must meditate on the model of disorder that is offered to us by the Quran*). Bidar also uses the Quran to argue that when human civilisation appears to be desolate, the Quran does not evoke any sort of divine retribution or punishment but rather the emergence of a time when human beings will take destiny into their own hands following an encounter with God:

> Lorsque le ciel se déchirera, il écoutera son seigneur et il fera ce qu'il doit faire. Lorsque la terre sera nivelée, qu'elle rejettera son contenu, qu'elle se videra, elle écoutera son seigneur et elle fera ce qu'elle doit faire. Alors toi, l'homme qui te tournes vers ton seigneur, tu le rencontreras. (Bidar 2004: p. 95 cites *The Qur'an*, sura 84, v. 1–6; OUP 2004 translation, p. 415)

> (When the sky is ripped apart, in rightful obedience to its Lord's command; when the earth is levelled out, casts out its contents, and becomes empty, in rightful obedience to its Lord's command, you humans, toiling laboriously towards your Lord, will meet Him.)

Bidar then elaborates on how the encounter with God engenders the concept of the end of time and the emergence of an eternal present before moving on to a discussion of the need to abrogate the notion of *jihad* (Bidar 2004: p. 97). But before he gets to that stage, he tackles the question of the retreat or end of religions as being symptomatic or illustrative of the achievement of their objectives:

> L'homme ayant comblé la distance qui le séparait de cet absolu, qu'il trouve désormais en lui-même, grâce à la sacralité de ses droits spirituels (déterminer soi-même le contenu de sa pratique), leur fonction plurimillénaire de véhicules vers la présence divine est terminée. (Bidar 2004: p. 98)

> (Having closed the gap between himself and this absolute, which, thanks to the sacred nature of his spiritual rights (self-determined practice), he now finds within himself, the multi-millennial function of religions as pathways towards divine presence is surpassed.)

Bidar argues that the 'new (hu)man' who emerges after religion has achieved its objectives allows us to think through a reversal of the Fall narrative (Bidar 2004: p. 98). This tendency of Bidar to systematically assign meaning to life and to religion and to assign objectives (*fins*) on to religions has something very religious about it. It is deterministic and thus depicts all human existence as moving towards one thing: the realisation of l'homme (in later Bidar texts, this new (hu)man is described as 'l'homme créateur' (Man as creator) as opposed to 'Dieu créateur' (God as creator). So, in a sense, although Bidar is moving towards the articulation of a post-theological engagement with Islam and religion in general, at this stage in his intellectual project he seems to articulate what Watkin describes as an 'imitative atheism', that 'merely replaces "God" with a supposedly atheistic placeholder such as "Man" or "Reason", explicitly rejecting but implicitly imitating theology's categories of thinking, changing merely the terms in which those categories are articulated' (Watkin 2011: pp. 1–2).

Regardless of the apparent 'imitative atheism' of Bidar's argument in *Un islam pour notre temps*, his work is notable for its categorical rejection of *jihad*, both in its conventionally understood form (war on unbelievers) and in terms of the notion of striving to improve or enhance the self, and he maintains a consistent position on this matter in *Self islam: histoire d'un islam personnel* (2006). For the very notion of self-improvement of Man loses its potency in a scenario where God has met Man:

> L'enjeu de cette apparition de Dieu en nous-mêmes – non plus dans le secret du cœur comme autrefois mais à la surface même de notre moi – est considérable: le Coran vient ici nous délivrer de l'obsession qui a toujours été la nôtre de nous élever au-dessus de nous-mêmes. (Bidar 2004: p. 100)

> (The stakes of this emergence of God in ourselves – no longer in the secrecy of the heart but at the very surface of our being – are significant: the Quran therein delivers us from our perennial obsession of surpassing ourselves.)

In the place of the 'Fall' narrative, Bidar develops what we might call a 'Descent' narrative, in the sense that in his articulation of a modernity invigorated by the encounter of Man and God, the very notion of struggle within or beyond the self via the principle of *jihad* becomes redundant:

> Plus rien n'est à conquérir ni à vaincre. Tout est offert. Et par conséquent tous ceux qui associent l'islam à un combat, contre autrui ou contre eux-mêmes, sont en dehors du temps présent: en prétendant instaurer par la force le règne de Dieu, ils se montrent aveugles à la descente spontanée de sa grâce. (Bidar 2004: p. 101).

> (There is no longer anything to conquer or vanquish. Everything is given. And as a result all those who associate Islam with conflict, against the other or against themselves, are out of step with the present: by claiming to instil the reign of God by force, they show themselves to be blind to the spontaneous descent of his grace.)

In the conclusion to this short book, Bidar ends with a consideration of the life of Mohammed, whose divinity, according to Bidar, should be regarded as his humanity, as expressed in sura 41 of the Quran in which he claims: 'Je ne suis qu'une créature comme vous' (Bidar 2004: p. 106 cites *The Qur'an*, sura 41, v. 6; OUP 2004 translation, p. 307) (I am only a mortal like you). Bidar takes this as his cue to argue that Mohammed was, in a sense, the first of men of this new era that he is attempting to describe. And then, quite audaciously, Bidar ends his essay with the following final statement: 'Le temps vient où *Mohammad* sera le nom de tout homme' (Bidar 2004: p. 107) (The time when *Mohammad* will be the name of all men is near), indicating that for Bidar the Prophet Mohammed should be regarded as a universally humanist figure of civilisation.

Bidar's self Islam

In *Self islam: histoire d'un islam personnel* (Bidar 2006), Bidar develops many of the themes already introduced in *Un islam pour notre temps*, but whilst *Un islam pour notre temps* can be read as an outward-looking text (albeit only partially, since it seems to mainly be addressing Muslims with formulations such as 'Nous musulmans...'), *Self islam* can be regarded as an autobiographical text that explains how Bidar came to where he is currently in his reflections and practices of Islam, but also as a normative essay that sets out how he thinks Islam in France and in the 'Muslim world' should develop. The notion of cultural translation is perhaps even more emphasised in this text than in *Un islam pour notre temps* because it focuses mainly on Bidar's own personal struggles to reconcile his Muslim and French identities. Nevertheless, despite its personal focus, *Self islam* does provide a more general reflection on Islam and its relationship with European modernities; as such, we find a number of themes which have already been introduced in *Un islam pour notre temps*, namely Islamic humanism, spirituality, new forms of universalism and a critique of finitude. The book charts Bidar's own 'exit' from Islam, not in the sense of making him an 'ex-Muslim', but in much broader terms of a personal 'overcoming' of Islam. So *Self islam* goes further than *Un islam pour notre temps* but certainly does not articulate a general notion of overcoming religion, which is explored most fully in *Comment sortir de la religion* (Bidar 2012b).

The main thread connecting the autobiographical narrative in *Self islam* is the idea of evolution – a process of unfolding that concerns, on one level, the author's personal story and, on the other, that of humanity in its entirety. It is no coincidence, then, that Bidar begins *Self islam* with an epigraph, citing Jesuit philosopher and palaeontologist Pierre Teilhard de Chardin about the universality and similarity of all human beings: 'L'homme est essentiellement le même en tous; et il suffit de descendre assez profondément en soi-même pour trouver un fond commun d'aspirations et de la lumière' (Bidar 2006 cites Teilhard de Chardin 1969: p. 118) (Human beings are essentially the same; it suffices to delve deep enough down into ourselves to find a common core of aspirations and light). The theme of evolution is developed much more explicitly and in a more generalist sense in Bidar's later work, particularly in *L'Islam sans soumission* (2008/2012) and in *L'islam face à la mort de Dieu* (2010), but in *Self islam* the notion of unfolding is mainly premised on Bidar's own personal journey to a complexified sense of cultural, religious and spiritual consciousness. That journey begins in his childhood, about which he explains that the unusual circumstances of having a French Muslim convert mother but also a close and formative relationship with an atheist maternal grandfather did not initially pose a problem for him. Indeed, the first chapter of *Self islam* is entitled 'Entre les vignes et la mosquée' (Between the vines and the mosque) and deals in particular with Bidar's mother's family, a non-immigrant French family who were winegrowers from the Auvergne region of France. In this chapter, Bidar discusses how contradictions of his childhood did not pose any real problems for him: 'Pendant longtemps, tout au moins jusqu'à l'âge de huit ou neuf ans, j'ai vécu le fait d'être musulman le vendredi et vigneron le samedi sans trop souffrir de la contradiction' (Bidar 2006: p. 29) (For a long time, until at least the age of eight or nine, I experienced being a Muslim on Fridays and a winegrower on Saturdays without suffering too much as a result of the contradiction). Regarding the atheism of his grandfather Jean, for example, Bidar argues that it was not a dogmatic or intolerant form of atheism but a more spiritual one: 'Son athéisme était bien plus spirituel que la superstition des fanatiques, qui se précipitait vers la mort avec des images puériles et stupides de "super-Paradis"' (Bidar 2006: p. 18) (His atheism was much more spiritual than the superstition of fanatics, who rushed towards death with childish and stupid ideas of a 'super-Heaven'). In his dismissal of religious fanaticism, Bidar argues that, thanks to his maternal grandfather, 'j'ai compris qu'il pouvait y avoir une grandeur de l'athéisme, aussi respectable que celle de la foi' (Bidar 2006: p. 19) (I understood that there could be a greatness in atheism, just as respectable as that associated with faith). The duality which characterised Bidar's childhood is painted as unproblematic, and although he mentions that his mother subsequently married a Moroccan Muslim who was an active member of the extremely devout *Tablighi Jamaat* movement, Bidar seems at pains to point out to the reader that he was never an ordinary Muslim. In fact, he spends several pages discussing how although he grew up as a Muslim, he should not be regarded as Arab in any way:

> Ni minaret, ni école coranique, ni "communauté" ... Mes ancêtres les Arvernes sans une seule goutte d'arabité. Le décor était planté pour ce qui allait devenir le singulier itinéraire d'un drôle de musulman ... C'est la petite église Notre-Dame-du-Port, chef-d'œuvre de l'art roman au centre de la ville, qui m'a toujours servi de référence en matière d'édifice religieux ... La Mosquée bleue d'Istanbul n'aura jamais pour moi la même chaleur spirituelle que cette chapelle chrétienne. (Bidar 2006: pp. 20–21)

> (Neither minaret nor Quran school nor 'community' for me ... My Arverne ancestors were without a trace of Arabness. The stage was set for what was to become the singular itinerary of an odd Muslim ... The small church of Notre-Dame-du-Port, masterpiece of Norman art in the town's centre, was always my reference in terms of religious buildings ... The Blue Mosque of Istanbul will never have the same spiritual warmth for me as that Christian chapel.)

Once Bidar has discussed his rather atypical childhood, he goes on to explore his cultural duality further, and this allows him to develop his role as cultural translator to what seems to be an intended French readership or Bakhtinian 'superaddressee' (unlike in *Un islam pour notre temps*, where the apparent intended readership was fellow Muslims). We can read his critical stance on French Muslims who are, in his view, too assertive in their minority religious demands, and his dismissal of the 'incivility' of immigrant-origin youths (Bidar 2006: p. 27) as part of this attempt to reach out to an intended French/non-Muslim readership. This rather protracted section on his duality is not just self-indulgent narcissism, however, and is quite clearly linked to Bidar's intention to present himself to the reader as a cultural mediator: 'Était-ce là le sens de ma vie? De faire communiquer ces deux mers qui se touchent sans mêler leurs eaux, cet Orient et cet Occident qui se côtoient sans vouloir se reconnaître?' (Bidar 2006: p. 30) (Was this my purpose in life? To make these two parallel universes, this 'East' and 'West' – which frequent yet do not recognise each other – communicate?):

> Du point de vue social et politique, je suis 'français musulman': mon attachement à la nation française, à ses valeurs de liberté, égalité, fraternité, m'impose de faire passer mon islam au second plan ... Sur le plan spirituel et privé, je suis 'musulman français', c'est-à-dire homme de foi nourri au centre de mon être par le Témoignage

de foi et le Coran, mais aussi par la culture française qui, à travers ses penseurs, ses écrivains, ses artistes, a donné à ma spiritualité musulmane une couleur toute à fait spéciale. (Bidar 2006: pp. 32–34)

(From a social and political perspective, I am a 'Muslim Frenchman': my attachment to the French nation, to its values of liberty, equality and fraternity, require that my Islamic identity remains in the background ... In spiritual and private terms, I am a 'French Muslim', that is to say, a man of faith fundamentally sustained by the Testimony of faith and the Quran, but also by French culture, which, via its thinkers, writers and artists has given my Muslim spirituality a distinctive character.)

So this rather lengthy section on how Bidar positions himself in relation to his faith and to French society and politics seems to reflect an effort of Bidar to legitimise his position as being a good or exemplary French citizen (in terms similar to those discussed by Mas 2006, Fernando 2009 and Kiwan 2013) by virtue of respecting the strict dividing line between the public and private spheres and by separating the spiritual and socio-political dimensions of his identity. Part of being a good French citizen seems, as a consequence, to entail an almost apolitical engagement with some of the challenges and legacies of postcolonial migration in contemporary France. In effect, Bidar does not engage in the debates about the place of Muslims in France, or about the problematic lack of cultural capital and symbolic power experienced by French Muslims who are also mainly descendants of North African immigrants. On the contrary, Bidar is at pains to point out to the reader his non-connection with immigration and his French 'de souche' ('ethnic French') origins; this seems to allow him to in some way divest of any meaningful exploration of the domestic socio-economic, socio-cultural and socio-political contexts which frame discussions of the place of Islam and Muslims in France. So Bidar's act of strategic positioning in relation to his location within the context of a Muslim and French atheist family also enables a strategic avoidance of the domestic and political issues concerning Islam and French Muslims. As such, Bidar limits himself to the dominant discursive framework of the secular Muslim.

Whilst in *Un islam pour notre temps* (2004) Bidar is very critical of the notion of a clash of civilisations, in *Self islam* he claims that he was defined by it and even 'torn apart' by it as well. Once again, the notion of translating cultures comes into play and the difficulty or perhaps even untranslatability of the double cultures is foregrounded:

'Ce choc a eu lieu dans mon cœur et mon histoire, et pas entre des mondes abstraits. Je n'en suis pas mort, même si j'ai eu le plus grand mal à lui survivre. Je suis l'un des enfants que l'Occident et l'islam ont eus ensemble, bâtards des deux côtés sans doute, mais qui veulent une place dans le monde, et qui portent peut-être en eux-mêmes la civilisation de la réconciliation à venir.' (Bidar 2006: p. 62)

('This clash took place in my heart and in my own story and not between abstract worlds. I did not die as a result of it, but I found it extremely difficult to overcome. I am one of the children that the West and Islam had together, bastards on both sides without doubt, but that seek a place in the world, and perhaps carry within them the culture of reconciliation to come.')

Bidar places the above passage within quotation marks, thus creating the impression that he is presenting a sort of speech to an imagined reader/superaddressee, to whom he presents his personal story as une 'offrande' (Bidar 2006: p. 62) (gift). The process of reconciliation which is 'à venir' (to come) reflects Bidar's future-oriented philosophy, which structures not only the self-introspection regarding his personal journey to consciousness but his discussion of a renewed modernity and a renewed understanding of the human and humanism which is also yet to come. Indeed, Bidar once again makes a strong link between humanism and Islam, pointing out that it was the Sufi spiritual education provided by his mother during his childhood that led to this conviction:

Ce que ma mère m'a transmis, en puisant au centre de l'héritage islamique, c'est l'image d'un homme *relié*, aux autres, à la nature, à la vie ... J'ai compris grâce à elle que l'islam était avant tout un humanisme, c'est-à-dire une parole sur l'homme qui nous apprend ce qui en fait sa dignité. (Bidar 2006: p. 73)

(What my mother passed on to me, by drawing from the foundations of Islamic heritage, is the image of a man who is *linked* to others, to nature, to life ... Thanks to her, I understood that Islam is above all a humanism, that is to say a claim about Man which teaches us about his dignity.)

At the end of Part I, Bidar finally provides an explicit definition of the title's key phrase, self Islam, as follows: 'la responsabilité spirituelle de chaque musulman est de trouver sa voie, *son* islam – ce que je nomme le *self islam*, l'islam personnel, c'est-à-dire la façon propre à chacun de se rattacher à l'islam et, même au-delà, à la culture musulmane' (Bidar 2006: p. 82) (the spiritual responsibility of each Muslim is to find their path, *their* Islam – what I call *self Islam*, personal Islam, that is, each individual's specific way of investing in Islam, and even beyond it, in Muslim culture). The notion of religiosity as interiority which is quite frequent in Leïla Babès' work (see Chapter 3) is frequently referenced by Bidar and can be regarded as a sort of axis upon which his concept of self Islam can develop: 'Le musulman est celui qui, étant toujours à l'écoute de ses besoins spirituels, obéit à une voix intérieure qui parfois lui demande de prier, de jeûner, de faire l'aumône – et qui parfois se tait' (Bidar 2006: p. 83) (A Muslim is someone who is always aware of their spiritual needs, who listens to an internal voice that sometimes requires them to pray, to fast, to give alms, and sometimes remains silent).

Bidar explains that after a long battle between the Western and Muslim dimensions of his identity, which culminated in him dropping out of the *École*

Normale Supérieure and joining a Moroccan Sufi brotherhood for seven years, he came to realise that it was possible to reconcile both sides of his cultural heritage. Arguing that he eventually realised that the Sufi brotherhood operated more like a hierarchical cult than a democratic space for spiritual exploration and growth, he describes this as a major turning point in the process of intercultural reconciliation: 'C'est l'occident qui s'est reveillé en moi: mon esprit critique, mon désir de liberté, et peut-être aussi le caractère français fait d'indépendance et d'insubordination' (Bidar 2006: p. 154) (The West within me was awoken: my critical thinking, my desire for freedom, and maybe also those French traits of independence and insubordination). However, this moment of awakening should not be regarded as a wholehearted or uncritical acceptance of Western models of modernity, and Bidar once again embarks on a critique of Western modernity as predominantly defined by human finitude:

> Nos poètes, nos philosophes, nos romanciers, nos peintres, nos musiciens, nos chorégraphes, presque tous ceux qui ont pris la parole en ce siècle pour nous parler de notre condition n'ont fait que mettre en scène un homme souffrant, désespérant, errant, agonisant, mourant. (Bidar 2006: p. 180)

> (Our poets, philosophers, novelists, painters, musicians and choreographers, nearly all those who have spoken about our condition this century, have only foregrounded a suffering, hopeless, aimless, agonised and dying human.)

Bidar's critique of the notion of human finitude and human suffering allows him to take his reflection on a future-oriented humanism further, arguing that one can find inspiration or evidence of such a human condition 'to come' within Quranic scripture: 'le Coran ne présente jamais cette Apocalypse comme une catastrophe, mais au contraire comme une Heure de clarté absolue, ou, dit-il, "toute âme saura ce qu'elle a fait de bien et de mal"' (Bidar 2006: p. 185 cites *The Quran*, sura 82, v. 5; OUP 2004 translation, p. 412) (The Quran never presents this Apocalypse as a catastrophe but rather as a moment of absolute clarity, where, it says, 'each soul will know what it has done well and what it has left undone'). By the end of *Self islam*, Bidar appears to have reached his 'hour of absolute clarity', declaring that his sense of being a Muslim is no longer linked to the notion of religious ritual or doctrine: 'que je prie ou non, que je mange du porc ou non, n'a strictement aucune importance. Mon islam n'a plus rien de religieux' (Bidar 2006: p. 191) (whether I pray or not, whether I eat pork or not, is of no importance at all. My Islam has nothing religious about it). Bidar's personal journey of intercultural reconciliation takes on a confessional quality. Indeed, Andrea Teti's work on Orientalism as a form of confession is relevant here, in which he shows that Michel Foucault's analysis of confessional discourse shares some features with Orientalist discourse (Teti 2014). In some ways, it is as though *Self islam* is a sort of 'coming out' narrative, aimed at a French or secular readership who is imagined to be waiting to congratulate Bidar's on his moment of awakening: 'je retrouvais en même temps que l'islam essentiel selon lequel j'avais été éduqué ... les valeurs de la France et de la modernité: liberté, égalité, fraternité' (Bidar 2006: p. 192) (I simultaneously rediscovered the main aspects of Islam which I had been brought up in ... and the values of France and modernity: liberty, equality, fraternity). Once again Watkin's notion of 'imitative atheism' (Watkin 2011) is relevant to Bidar's discussion of his 'eureka moment': 'Ces sociétés, ces peuples, ces foules qui soulèvent aujourd'hui l'étendard de l'islam comme "vérité unique" seront convertis bientôt par l'esprit du temps' (Bidar 2006: p. 203) (Those societies, peoples and masses that raise the sword of Islam as 'unique truth' will soon be converted by the spirit of the times). Even the vocabulary, with the use of the verb 'convert', indicates a struggle for Bidar to fully map out a post-theological engagement with Islam.

So *Self islam* could be described as the most personal of Bidar's books to date. It does not really engage with politics or the political nature of its own narrative and approach. The only discussion of politics comes at the very end, where Bidar tries to counter what he imagines might be a criticism of his stance, namely that he says what he says simply to please the political establishment in France. His response to this imagined critique is that his duality, his non-orthodox take on *islamité*, is not something that politicians necessarily want to hear: 'je ne suis pas sûr que cet islam de l'avenir que je vois dessiner et auquel j'essaie de donner un visage plaise aux politiques' (Bidar 2006: p. 222) (I am not sure that this future Islam which I see being designed and to which I try to give a face is looked upon favourably by politicians). His justification for this is the CFCM (*Conseil français du culte musulman*) project which, he argues, can be taken as evidence that the French state seems to prefer to deal with a reactionary Islam in a fairly tightly controlled or corporatist (Laurence 2005) process which does not account for the prospect that Islam will change and evolve into something else. Bidar's criticism of the CFCM and the proposal to establish an *Institut de formation des imams* lies in his rejection of the principle of facilitating an official Islamic clergy. Instead, Bidar calls for the training of a new Islamic intellectual elite. It is not clear whether Bidar sees himself as a sort of prototype for a new kind of Muslim intellectual, but he is clearly positioning himself to a Bakhtinian 'third party' or 'superaddressee' (Buden *et al.* 2009: p. 205 cites Bakhtin 2006: p. 126). In other words, he seems to be addressing an imaginary French reader who is somehow imagined to be representative of the Republican state and Republican values.

Islam without submission

Bidar's construction of his intellectual project in terms of multi-directional cultural translation – inviting Islam to translate itself into the Western modern principles of liberty, equality and fraternity – whilst simultaneously inviting

Western modernity to translate itself away from a modernity truncated by the notion of human finitude intensifies in his next book, *L'Islam sans soumission: pour un existentialisme musulman* (2008/2012). The striking title of Bidar's book indicates that the author has moved from an approach that is focused on the notion of reform from within Islam to one that is designed to radically overhaul some the most basic assumptions of Islamic belief and practice, namely that Islam itself requires submission to God, i.e. to a non-human divine will and order. Despite the apparent audacity suggested by the book's title, Bidar is in fact returning to many similar themes which he introduced in *Un islam pour notre temps* and *Self islam*. In particular, Bidar develops (1) his discussion of a re-thinking of Islam through humanistic principles of liberty, equality and fraternity; (2) a critique of the notion of human finitude; and (3) a future-oriented philosophy of humanity in which emphasis is placed on the progression of the human condition facilitated by the realisation and acknowledgement of the Quran and Islam as heralding a moment in human history where Man is conceived as the *heir* (*héritier*) of God. Bidar evokes Charles Darwin's theory of evolution, arguing that it is possible to imagine a spiritual Darwinism in his vision of a humanity-heir-of-God-to-come.

On the question of Islamic humanism, Bidar opens the second edition of this 2008 text by reflecting on the events of the Arab Spring, arguing that the uprisings are testimony to the emergence of a new generation of Muslims who want to have more freedom, both in France and elsewhere: '*Ils veulent se sentir libres de vivre leur islam*. Ils veulent *un islam de liberté* et *une liberté dans l'islam*' (Bidar 2008/2012a: p. 11; emphasis in the original) (*They want to feel free to live their Islam. They want an Islam of liberty and liberty within Islam*). He calls this profound desire for freedom 'un existentialisme musulman' (Bidar 2008/2012a: p. 11) (Muslim existentialism).

Bidar then shifts from an observational perspective to a prescriptive or normative one, arguing that a human rights paradigm should be the basis for Islam's development:

> Le monde musulman est sommé aujourd'hui d'intégrer ce que déclare l'article 18 de la Déclaration universelle: 'Toute personne a droit à la liberté de pensée, de conscience et de religion; ce droit implique la liberté de changer de religion ou de conviction ainsi que la liberté de manifester sa religion ou sa conviction seule ou en commun, tant en public qu'en privé, par l'enseignement, les pratiques, le culte et l'accomplissement des rites'. (Bidar 2008/2012a: p. 42)[5]

> (The Muslim world is today summoned to integrate article 18 of the Universal Declaration: 'Everyone has the right to freedom of thought, conscience and religion; this right includes freedom to change his religion or belief, and freedom, either alone or in community with others and in public or private, to manifest his religion or belief in teaching, practice, worship and observance'.)

Bidar criticises what he sees as a disjuncture between the emphasis placed on the principle of equality within Islamic humanism and the simultaneous lack of engagement with the principle of liberty, which leads him to refer to the notion of 'une égalité, mais d'esclaves' (Bidar 2008/2012a: p. 44) (a slave-like equality). He therefore poses the following question: 'Mais que vaut l'égalité sans liberté?' (But what is equality worth, without liberty?). The lack of freedom stems from what Bidar sees as 'une culture de la soumission' (Bidar 2008/2012a: p. 44) (a culture of submission) in Islam, which plays out in not only religious but also socio-political terms (Bidar 2008/2012a: p. 44). Bidar thus draws a direct link between the notions of metaphysical and socio-political submissiveness or oppression: 'Un Dieu qui écrase l'homme produit des sociétés où l'homme écrase l'homme' (Bidar 2008/2012a: p. 46) (A God that overpowers Man produces societies where people overpower people).

However, Bidar claims that today it is possible to re-read and reinterpret the Quran against the theological passivity which has come to define Islam or what he refers to as 'la conscience islamique' (Bidar 2008/2012a: p. 48). He argues that he intends to go beyond the critiques of the Mutazilite movement, which, according to him, remained limited by the paradox of proclaiming the liberty of Man in conjunction with his simultaneous and necessary submission to God (Bidar 2008/2012a: pp. 52–53). This allows him to introduce his main argument for the book as a whole, namely that the Quran and Islam can be interpreted as an invitation to move from a theocentric humanism to a human-centric humanism via the notion of humankind as inheritor or heir to God. Bidar argues that the notion of humanity as heir to God can be located in a key sura of the Quran, *Al-Baqara* (The Cow), in which verses 30–34 deal with the concept of the *khalifat* as follows: 'Lorsque ton Seigneur dit aux anges: "*Je vais établir un* khalif *sur la terre*"' (Bidar 2008/2012a: p. 67 cites sura 2, v. 30–34, *The Qur'an*; OUP 2004 translation, p. 7) (When your Lord told the angels, 'I am putting a successor on earth'). *Khalifat* is generally understood as meaning lieutenancy ('l'homme ministre de Dieu sur terre'; Bidar 2008/2012a: p. 98 (Man as minister on earth)) and in these verses the lieutenancy is assigned to Adam by God. However, Bidar argues that the notion of lieutenancy is inadequate: 'l'idée de lieutenance est *inadéquate* au sens arabe du mot *khalifat* et de sa racine *kha-la-fa* (composée des lettres arabes: *kha, lam, fa* [here Bidar uses Arabic script for the letters concerned]) parce qu'elle est très loin d'en recouvrir toute la signification' (Bidar 2008/2012a: p. 70; emphasis in the original) (the idea of lieutenancy is *inadequate* in the Arabic sense of the word *khalifat* and its root *kha-la-fa* (composed of the Arabic letters *kha, lam, fa*) because it does not capture its full signification). Bidar instead argues that *khalifat* should in fact be understood as 'successor' ('"suppléant", "remplacant", "successeur"'; Bidar 2008/2012a: p. 70 ('deputy', 'substitute', 'successor')) in accordance with how the term is generally translated elsewhere in the Quran. Bidar argues that if we give due weight to this sura as God establishing a successor on earth in the form of human beings, his earlier notion of *Self islam* is given further legitimacy:

> L'homme héritier de Dieu pourrait-il en effet continuer de recevoir le qualificatif même de 'créature'? De définir sa nature comme mortelle? De considérer sa condition comme faible et dérisoire? Au contraire, l'idée d'héritage nous propose une nouvelle image de l'homme, laissé totalement libre de son destin par la volonté même d'un Dieu qui lui a remis toutes ses puissances et toute la responsabilité de l'univers. (Bidar 2008/2012a: p. 118; emphasis in the original)
>
> (Could Man as heir to God still be referred to as a 'creature'? Could he be defined as mortal? Could his condition be regarded as fragile and derisory? On the contrary, the notion of inheritance gives us a new image of Man, one who is liberated from his destiny by the will of a God who has bestowed on him all the powers and responsibility of the universe.)

By redefining our understanding of the term *khalifat* in the Quran to signify Man as successor to God rather than Man as God's lieutenant, Bidar seeks to articulate a vision of Islam without submission and an understanding of the notion of transcendence which is liberating rather than restraining. This move allows Bidar to develop his broader point about the mutual benefit that Islam and modernity can offer each other:

> Si nous trouvons dans notre texte fondamental de quoi libérer l'homme de la tutelle théologique et produire la représentation d'un homme ontologiquement libre, alors nous ferons entrer l'islam dans une modernité dont le principe est justement l'affirmation de la liberté de choix de la personne humaine. (Bidar 2008/ 2012a: p. 74)
>
> (If we find within our foundational text a means of liberating Man from theological tutelage and producing a representation of a human who is ontologically free, then we will have succeeded in introducing Islam into a modernity whose principle is precisely the assertion of human freedom of choice.)

The argument that Bidar makes with regard to the verses contained within the *Al-Baqara* sura, namely that Man is designated by God as God's successor on earth (*khalifat*), is crucial to his overarching endeavour to position himself as a public intellectual whose work is centrally concerned with cultural translation. Bidar's attempts at cultural translation become particularly apparent if we consider the ways in which he is presenting his argument to a 'superaddressee' – the French state:

> C'est pourquoi il s'agit de faire ici l'effort constant d'articuler ces deux univers de référence, de telle façon que l'anthropologie coranique qui émergera de cette réflexion soit le résultat d'une lecture à la fois intérieure et extérieure à l'islam, intérieure et extérieure à l'Occident, produite par les deux et débordant les deux,

pour produire une idée de l'homme que les deux puissent partager en revendiquant légitimement son enfantement commun. (Bidar 2008/2012a: p. 79)

(This is why it is a question of making a constant effort to articulate both these reference points, in such a way that the Quranic anthropology which will emerge from this process will be the result of a simultaneously internal and external reading of Islam, internal and external to the West, produced by both and going beyond both in order to produce an idea of the human that the two may share in legitimately claiming its mutual creation.)

The communal 'enfantement' (creation) is in fact the staging of a new universalism which can be 'extracted' from Islam and Quranic scripture. Bidar's attempts to break open new understandings of the Quran and Islam rely heavily on the notion of an untapped 'truth' or 'meaning' within the scripture (the *Al-Baqara* sura) (Bidar 2008/2012a: p. 81). However, once the process of exploration and extraction of meaning has taken place, Bidar is able to articulate the notion of a 'dynamic anthropology' which becomes the basis for what we might call his future-oriented philosophy of humanity whereby emphasis is placed on the notion of an unfolding progression in the human condition, facilitated by the realisation and acknowledgement of the Quran and Islam as heralding a moment in human history where Man is conceived as the *heir* (*héritier*) of God.

The notion of dynamic anthropology is bound up with Bidar's interest in Darwin's theory of evolution and how it may be applied to Islam:

Ce qui a été découvert et théorisé scientifiquement en Europe aux XIXe et XXe siècles par les réélaborations successives de la théorie de l'évolution paraît relever du même paradigme que le texte coranique et comme anticipé symboliquement dans la révélation de Mohammed. (Bidar 2008/2012a: p. 84)

(What was discovered and scientifically theorised in Europe in the nineteenth and twentieth centuries by the re-elaborations of the theory of evolution seems to emerge from the same paradigm as the Quranic text, as though symbolically anticipated in the revelation of Mohammed.)

Bidar emphasises how humanity as heir to God is in a state of perpetual development and improvement ('perfectionnement'; Bidar 2008/2012a: p. 83) which ultimately will enable the emergence of what he refers to as '[d']un être humain libéré de ses limites, [d']un homme infini' (Bidar 2008/2012a: p. 85) (a human being freed from their limitations, an infinite being). This new human to come and the one God seems to instruct the angels to worship in the *Al-Baqara* sura ('Alors nous avons dit aux anges: Prosternez-vous devant Adam!, et ils se prosternèrent'; Bidar 2008/2012a: p. 91 cites sura 2, v. 34; OUP 2004 translation, p. 7 (When we told the angels, 'Bow down before Adam', they all bowed)) is thrust out into the world by a God who is conceptualised by Bidar as a feminine matrical figure.

Drawing on the work of Mohamed Talbi and his claim that the words Rahman and Rahim, which are both references to God in the Quran, derive from the stem R-H-M, which evokes the concept of the mother/maternal, Bidar argues that the act of a mother giving birth to her child could be regarded as one which delivers their offspring to their own autonomy: 'Contrairement au père qui symbolise la tutelle, l'autorité contraignante, la mère nous "expulse", nous "libère", après nous avoir "portés en elle"' (Bidar 2008/2012a: p. 163) (Unlike the father who symbolises tutelage and constraining authority, the mother 'expels' us, 'frees' us after having 'carried us within her'). So the feminine figure of God gives birth to a 'new man' (humanity), who as heir to God will evolve by developing an infinite capacity to create and to act upon the world. There is of course a paradox between Bidar's emphasis on a human condition defined in opposition to the modern narrative of finitude, that is, defined by 'une infinie puissance d'agir' (Bidar 2008/2012a: p. 175) (an infinite power to act) and the notion that this capacity for action is somehow a teleological destiny:

> A travers cette idée de puissance infinie d'agir, nous commençons à comprendre à quel point l'héritage que nous propose le Coran nous offre une vision inhabituelle de notre nature humaine, et nous invite à un considérable effort d'imagination qui est en même temps un effort d'anticipation et de *mise en tension* de nous-mêmes vers cette fin supérieure. (Bidar 2008/2012a: p. 178, emphasis in the original)

> (Through this idea of an infinite power to act, we begin to understand to what extent the heritage offered to us by the Quran provides an unusual vision of our human nature, and invites us to make a considerable imaginative effort which is simultaneously an effort of anticipation and bracing of ourselves towards this higher outcome.)

Bidar does fleetingly acknowledge this paradox when he points out that critics may argue that his emphasis on a deterministic reading of the Quran diminishes his otherwise consistent commitment to the notion of human freedom and agency. His response to such hypothetical detractors is that human agency can itself be regarded as having been a driving force or a predetermining factor which has characterised human endeavours for millennia (Bidar 2008/2012a: p. 188).

The notion of an infinite creative capacity that will define humans as heirs to God is clearly linked to Bidar's critique of the idea of the human condition being limited by its finitude. Throughout his work, Bidar is consistently critical of modern post-Enlightenment preoccupations with human finitude, and in *L'Islam sans soumission* he takes up the representation of the life and death of Jesus in the Quran as a means of challenging the notion of human mortality. Bidar refers to the fact that the Quran refutes the idea of Christ dying on the cross and cites the sura entitled *An-Nisa* (The Women), as follows: 'Mais ils l'ont pas tué; ils ne l'ont pas crucifié, cela leur est seulement apparu ainsi ... mais Dieu l'a élevé vers lui' (Bidar 2008/2012a: pp. 212–213 cites *The Qur'an*, sura 4, v. 157–158; OUP 2004 translation, p. 65) (They did not kill him, nor did they crucify him, though it was made to appear like that to them). Bidar concludes that this sura presents Jesus as the first representative of the humanity to come because he surpasses death and his immortality is not a supernatural post-death event but rather an earthly immortality. Bidar refers to the expression in the Quran of a 'paradis rapproché' (*The Qur'an*, sura 81, v. 13; OUP 2004 translation, p. 411) (Paradise brought near) in the sura *Al-Takwir* (Shrouded in Darkness) as further indication that human immortality will be achieved in this world, 'ici-bas', as it were. It is never really made clear *why* the avoidance of death or the overcoming of human finitude is a cause worth fighting for, if only to go beyond certain levels of human suffering and a debilitating absurdist ethic:

> Le Coran porte ainsi de bout en bout l'intuition centrale que l'espèce humaine n'est pas du tout une forme de vie comme les autres, mais que parvenue à un stade très avancé de son évolution, elle est susceptible de déclencher dans l'univers un retournement de situation qui verra la victoire définitive de la vie. (Bidar 2008/2012a: p. 182)

> (The Quran therefore includes from start to finish the central intuition that the human species is unlike any other life-form, but that at an advanced stage of its development, it is likely to unleash a paradigm shift which will see the definitive victory of life.)

However, the definitive victory of life, or human immortality over human finitude, should not be seen as the advent of an ethically questionable prototype humanity. Indeed, Bidar is aware of the potential risks that could arise from the emergence of a highly evolved 'homme nouveau' and he calls for an equal distribution of creative capacities ('puissances d'agir'; Bidar 2008/2012a: p. 197).

The final part of *L'Islam sans soumission* is entitled 'Un autre modèle de sortie de la religion' and can be read as a precursor to Bidar's 2012 book *Comment sortir de la religion* in that it deals with the process of overcoming religion. Once again, Bidar positions himself most explicitly in the role of cultural translator. He begins this section with the following overarching question:

> En quoi l'Occident peut-il aider l'islam à se saisir de cette idée d'héritage divin qu'il porte en lui dès l'origine – au cœur de la source coranique elle-même – mais dont il n'a jamais su s'emparer? En quoi l'islam peut-il apporter un second souffle à l'humanisme occidental épuisé, pour qu'ils constituent ensemble – par l'addition de leurs génies – une nouvelle 'grande image' possible de l'homme? (Bidar 2008/2012a: p. 223)

> (How can the West help Islam to seize upon this idea of divine heritage which it carries within in from the outset – at the heart of the Quranic source itself – but which it has never known how to take possession of? How can Islam revive an

exhausted Western humanism, so that they may together constitute – via the combination of their wisdom – a new possible 'grand image' of the human?)

Bidar evokes the unwillingness of Muslim scholars to acknowledge the Quran and Islam as ushering in the concept of Man as heir to God and thus argues that the West could now come to the 'aid' of the Muslim world because of the historical contribution of Western philosophy to the notion of inheritance. Here he evokes the works of Hegel and Feuerbach, in particular Hegel's *Leçons sur l'histoire de la philosophie*, where Bidar draws attention to Hegel's claims that the gods corresponded to idealised and objectified images that humans projected of themselves, thus transforming those idealised images into deities or the image or notion of a God. Indeed, he states that it is perhaps no coincidence that a Muslim living in the West such as himself has been able to recognise the notion of *l'homme héritier de Dieu*. So Bidar's strategic position as a Western Muslim means that he is able to act as interpreter of the Islamic tradition because, he implies, Muslims located in the Muslim world itself are unable or unwilling to do so themselves:

> L'éloignement géographique et mental qui est le mien vis-à-vis du monde musulman et de la tradition islamique (tout en constituant à d'autres égards des handicaps ou des déficits) est ainsi la condition d'une proximité nouvelle avec le texte même – comme si le *khalîfat* héritage promis à l'homme avait attendu, scellé dans le texte, que le découvre le regard d'un musulman nourri par l'Europe. (Bidar 2008/2012a: p. 225)

> (The geographical and mental distance which is mine vis-à-vis the Muslim world and the Islamic tradition (which in other ways constitutes a handicap or deficit) is thereby the condition of a new proximity with the text itself – as though the *khalîfat* heritage which was promised to humanity had waited, sealed within the text, to be discovered by a European Muslim.)

Such a stance is reminiscent of Edward Said's critique of Orientalist scholars who strategically position themselves as being outside of the Orient, their external location supposedly allowing them to somehow better decipher the 'mysteries' of the Orient for their fellow Westerners. Apart from the Orientalism of the above statement, it seems as though Bidar is almost presenting himself as a kind of community- or nation-builder in the sense that he sees his act of translating the meaning of the text as serving to unveil some hidden or at least unrecognised significance in the Quran. So it would seem, then, that Bidar's self-understanding as cultural translator is premised on a normative model of cultural translation. Indeed, as Buden *et al.* emphasise, according to the German Romantic theory of cultural translation: 'translation was understood in terms of its positive effects on German language and culture; its role was to improve both' (Buden *et al.* 2009: p. 199). Bidar seems to be suggesting that by revealing the Quranic concept of Man as inheritor of God, he is not only developing Islamic thought but also providing an alternative to the narrative of the modern human condition as being defined by the death of God and the subsequent post-theological void of human finitude. Indeed, Bidar's notion of Man as heir to God allows him to offer an alternative post-theological narrative to the dominant European post-Enlightenment frame. This implies not only an overcoming of religion but also an overcoming of atheism:

> La voie s'ouvre aussi vers un dépassement même de l'athéisme ... Notre vue d'héritiers sera bien d'une certaine façon une vie sans Dieu, mais plus du tout au sens qu'implique justement l'athéisme, qui est la négation de l'existence de Dieu ... Loin donc de le nier, il lui vouera une gratitude éternelle ... Cet être dont il a reçu sa dignité suprême. (Bidar 2008/2012a: p. 261)

(The path even opens towards an overcoming of atheism as well ... Our worldview as successors will certainly be in some sense a life without God, but no longer at all in the sense implied by atheism, which is the negation of the existence of God ... Far from denying God, it will express an eternal gratitude towards God ... This being from whom they have received their supreme dignity.

Overcoming religion?

This performative stance of a Muslim who stands apart from the Muslim world but who is profoundly concerned by it seems to be fairly recurrent with Bidar. Indeed, it is perhaps in *Comment sortir de la religion?* (2012) that Bidar most actively stands apart from the Muslim world and Islam itself, since his ideas about the overcoming of religion that are developed here do not solely concern Islam but are applied generally to all religions.

It is worth noting that in between *L'Islam sans soumission* (2008/2012) and *Comment sortir de la religion* (2012), Bidar published a book entitled *L'Islam face à la mort de Dieu: actualité de Mohammed Iqbal* (2010) which was dedicated to a close study of the ideas of the Kashmiri Muslim scholar Mohammed Iqbal (1877–1938) and his work on themes such as spirituality in the absence of God, spiritual Darwinism and moving beyond notions of human finitude, brought together notably in a 1955 text entitled *Reconstruire la pensée religieuse de l'islam*, prefaced by the Orientalist scholar Louis Massignon, which is based on seven lectures given by Iqbal between 1928 and 1932. Since Bidar's focus in *L'Islam face à la mort de Dieu* is primarily a critical summary and evaluation of Iqbal's thought and its relationship to other major thinkers such as Henri Bergson and Friedrich Nietzsche, I do not include an in-depth analysis of this text here, except to highlight that Iqbal can be regarded as having a major influence on Bidar with respect to two main issues: first, Iqbal's reflections on the nature of modernity and, second, his discussion of sort of a crisis of universalism and the potential articulation of a new vision of humanity which would be truly universal. Iqbal's interest in the individual, the universal and the possibility of carving out a third way between religion on the one hand and atheism on the other can be regarded as the main areas Bidar seeks to develop within his own thinking in *Comment sortir de la religion*: 'L'intérêt majeur d'Iqbal à mes yeux est qu'il commence d'élaborer ce que nous appellerions aujourd'hui une philosophie pour le monde' (Bidar 2010a: p. 23) (What is interesting about Iqbal to my mind is that he starts to develop what today we would call a philosophy of the world). This new world philosophy can be understood as what Iqbal called 'une spiritualité postmoderne' (Bidar 2010a: p. 32) (postmodern spirituality) which provides Bidar with a potential solution to his profound dissatisfaction with modern absurdist ethics which are, according to him, limited by the notion of human finitude: 'Il y a chez Mohammed Iqbal les premiers éléments d'une spiritualité de "l'infinitude", d'une spiritualité pour notre temps d'infinitisation de la puissance d'être et d'agir de l'homme' (Bidar 2010a: p. 290) (There are in Mohammed Iqbal the first elements of a spirituality of "infinitude", of a spirituality for our times of the infinitisation of human agency). Bidar claims then to find in Iqbal's work the first steps towards the elaboration of a theory of human infinitude and also argues that it is possible to read him as a thinker who is ultimately (if not always explicitly) concerned with the overcoming of religion. Indeed, Bidar argues that Iqbal's framing of his own ideas in terms of the reconstruction of Islamic thought logically leads beyond Islamic thought itself and even beyond religion in general:

> L'islam est ainsi désigné comme 'une sortie de religion' synonyme d'une démythologisation, d'un dévoilement du sens réel des métaphores religieuses et d'une restitution à l'homme de ce qu'il avait prêté auparavant à un Dieu supérieur … ce qui établit une affinité profonde entre 'l'événement Mohammed' et une modernité dont nous avons précisément redéfini le projet comme démythication du sacré. (Bidar 2010a: p. 154)

> (Islam is therefore referred to as an 'exit from religion' synonymous with demythologisation, and an unveiling of the real meaning of religious metaphors and the return to humans of what they had previously attributed to a superior God … which establishes a deep affinity between the 'Mohammed event' and a modernity that we have redefined precisely in terms of a demythication of the sacred.)

However, Bidar talks about Iqbal's work as being 'une pensée inachevée' (Bidar 2010a: p. 203) (an unfinished reflection), suggesting that perhaps Iqbal may have been constrained by the socio-political and historical contexts in which he worked. It is therefore in *Comment sortir de la religion* that Bidar revisits some of the key ideas explored by Iqbal and develops and extends them into a general treatise on the overcoming of religion.

The main themes explored by Bidar in *Comment sortir de la religion?* are the de-westernising of the exit from religion and developing an understanding of religion which can be regarded as a matrix of humanity to come. Bidar's future-oriented concept of humanity can be regarded as part of a broader movement, which he refers to as an existential or ontological revolution or 'un altermondialisme existentiel' (Bidar 2012b: p. 224) (existential anti-globalism). Bidar's main premise is that the exit from religion is already happening and that theses about 'le retour du religieux' (return of the religion) are a red herring. However, his main point is that the Western exit from religion which has until now been the dominant and certainly the pioneering one was badly undertaken: 'Malgré leur intelligence, les théories ont mal enterré le religieux. Elles n'ont jamais réussi à lui donner la sépulture qu'il méritait.' (Bidar 2012b: p. 7) (Despite their intelligence, the theories did a bad job of burying religion. They never managed to give it the burial it deserved.) Bidar's main argument is that the exit from religion needs to be disconnected from its Western origins:

> Il est temps de 'désoccidentaliser' la sortie de la religion … Il est temps, ce faisant de donner au religieux l'opportunité d'accepter sa propre mort et d'y accéder en acceptant que son office soit achevé. Comment? En apprenant à considérer la religion de façon tout à fait nouvelle: comme la matrice spirituelle de l'humanité, dont le rôle ne s'achèvera qu'au moment où l'homme saura concevoir cette sortie de la religion comme émergence hors de cette matrice … C'est en développant ce paradigme ou ce symbole de la religion comme matrice que je souhaite lui rendre enfin justice. (Bidar 2012b: p. 8)

> (It is time to 'de-westernise' the exit from religion … In doing so, it is time to give religion the opportunity to accept its own demise and to reach that juncture by accepting that its function has come to an end. How? By learning to consider religion in a completely novel way: as the spiritual matrix of humanity, whose role will only come to an end when humanity knows how to conceive of this exit from religion as the emergence from this matrix … It is in developing this paradigm or this symbol of religion as a matrix that I wish to finally do it justice.)

So Bidar picks up again the trope of religion as a matrix or maternal (womb-like) figure which 'gives birth' to a new humanity as introduced in *L'Islam sans soumission* (2008/2012a). But he also returns to the theme of Western modernity's post-theological narrative as being defined essentially by the notion of being-towards-death and '"le désenchantement du monde"' (Bidar 2012b: p. 19 in reference to Gauchet 1985) ('disenchantment with the world'). Bidar cites Freud's melancholy, the spleen and ennui of Baudelaire, the despair of Kierkegaard, Camus' philosophy of the absurd and Sartre's concept of existential nausea as being the modern consequences of the Western exit from religion. However, Bidar makes it clear that exit from religion is inevitable but that the Western model has simply failed: 'N'y avait-il pas une "fonction du religieux" qui aurait échappé à la modernité occidentale, qui expliquerait sa faillite existentielle et dont il faudrait aujourd'hui constituer l'équivalent non religieux pour arriver – enfin – à sortir du religieux?' (Bidar 2012b: pp. 25–26 cites Dewey 2011) (Wasn't there a "religious function" that escaped Western modernity, which would explain its existential failure and which would be necessary to establish in its non-religious equivalent, in order to, once and for all, overcome religion?) Bidar's alternative model for an exit from religion is based on a notion of spirituality that develops in the absence of the sacred or divine: 'Nous devons faire du spirituel sans le sacré, du sublime sans le religieux, du transcendant sans aucune croyance en un au-delà' (Bidar 2012b: p. 30) (We need to do spirituality without the sacred, the sublime without the religious, the transcendent without any belief in an after-life). The need for a non-sacred spirituality is, in Bidar's view, a way out of what Liu Xiaobo called the '"philosophie du porc"' ('philosophy of the pig') (Bidar 2012b: p. 18 cites Liu 2011) which has arisen from a current misguided sense of 'la surpuissance humaine' (human superpower) which is self-destructively premised on a logic of capitalist-driven mass consumerism, selfish neo-liberalism or material wealth without existential or ethical wealth. However, Bidar is not trying to maintain any sort of unhelpful binary opposition between the sacred and the profane, hence his emphasis on spirituality. Indeed, he argues that there is a need to move thinking beyond the sacred versus profane dichotomy: 'Choisir entre sacré et profane est périmé ... Croire en un dieu ou en des dieux, croire, au contraire, que l'homme est seul avec sa finitude, tout cela est à ranger au musée des options existentielles.' (Bidar 2012b: p. 39) (The choice between the sacred and the profane is outmoded. Belief in a God or in gods or, on the contrary, that Man is alone with his finitude – all of this should be stored away in the museum of existential options.) The solution that Bidar proposes, the way out of this dichotomy which Iqbal himself tried to break down, is premised on the notion of cultural translation. Bidar thus positions himself as a cultural translator who can mediate a more effective and transcultural exit from religion because of what he calls his 'double culture':

> Sur la base de ma double culture, occidentale et islamique, j'essaie de proposer une universalisation de notre compréhension de la sortie de la religion, fort de la conviction que sur le plan existentiel nous ne sommes plus dans une situation de division fondamentale et plurielle entre les Orients hindou, confucéen, bouddhiste, et les Occidents chrétien, juif, ou sécularisé. Ces frontières historiques sont dépassées. (Bidar 2012b: p. 45).

> (Based on my dual Western and Islamic culture, I try to suggest a universalisation of our understanding of the overcoming of religion, with the firm conviction that in existential terms we are no longer in a context of fundamental and plural division between the Hindu, Confucian or Buddhist East and the Christian, Jewish or secularised West. These historical frontiers are outmoded.)

It is in this book that Bidar takes his thinking the furthest, in that instead of arguing that Islam and the Quran can be read as a religion that places human beings rather than God at the centre of the universe (*l'homme héritier de Dieu* paradigm), he now argues in *Comment sortir de la religion* that all religious discourse should be read as leading towards its own overcoming and that the error of the Western exit from religion was the failure to recognise that 'la totalité du discours religieux est en même temps un discours sur la sortie de la religion, autrement dit que l'univers religieux tout entier est tendu vers sa propre extinction et vers son propre dépassement' (Bidar 2012b: p. 46) (religious discourse in its totality is at the same time a discourse about the overcoming of religion, or in other words, the entire religious realm moves towards its own extinction and its own obsolescence). Bidar's originality, then, is to say that in order to truly overcome religion one needs to operate a turn *towards* religion rather than a turn *away* from it and it is here that his thinking is potentially similar to that outlined by Quentin Meillassoux (Watkin 2011).

The public intellectual in times of crisis

Turning now to consider some more recent developments in Bidar's thought – particularly in the wake of the *Charlie Hebdo*, Paris and Nice terror attacks – it seems that the development of his stance on a number of issues which he has consistently addressed since 2004 invites us to reflect more broadly on the question of the role of the public intellectual in times of crisis. In his essay entitled *Plaidoyer pour la fraternité*, published in February 2015 in the immediate aftermath of the *Charlie Hebdo* terrorist attack (he began writing it on 12 January 2015), Bidar makes a plea for the rehabilitation of fraternity as a universal humanist value. He argues that within the Republican motto *Liberté, égalité, fraternité*, the principle of fraternity has historically been marginalised and, indeed, according to him has never really been realised. Yet after the *Charlie Hebdo* attacks and the ensuing tensions between those who adopted the slogan *Je suis Charlie* and those who did not, or who actively claimed *Je ne suis pas Charlie*, Bidar argues that the notion of fraternity can play a restorative role by bridging the gap between these two camps: 'seule la fraternité, cultivée par les religions mais pas seulement, peut nous rassembler maintenant tous ensemble dans la chaleur humaine d'une société sans barrières.' (Bidar 2015a: p. 90) (only fraternity, cultivated by religions, but not only by religions, can bring us together in the human warmth of a society without barriers.) The fact that Bidar sees fraternity as foundational within religious thought allows him to foreground the links that he sees between fraternity and what he calls 'le sacré' or indeed 'un sacré partageable' (a communal notion of the sacred). He argues that fraternity, which is present in both Eastern and Western thought – in both religious and secular contexts – embodies this shared sense of the sacred or spiritual which can in turn be both a religious and a secular principle which emerges from the notion of transcendence. Bidar's claim that the West brutally cut its ties with the sacred and the notion of transcendence allows him to pursue his cultural mediation agenda in his second essay of 2015, *Lettre ouverte au monde musulman*. Indeed, in this text Bidar seeks to show that Islamic thought can come to the assistance of an ailing Western civilisation – most recently characterised by the alienation of the masses in the face of the totalitarianisms of the twentieth century and their enslavement to the capitalist neo-liberalism of the twenty-first century – by reintroducing the notion of the sacred via a renewed interest in fraternity. Bidar further explores the theme of fraternity in his 2016 book *Quelles valeurs partager aujourd'hui?* by drawing out the links between Western and Islamic ethics of hospitality and 'le partage' (sharing), be it in the literature of Victor Hugo or Lamartine, the work of environmentalist Pierre Rabhi or in the Quran.

By focusing on the principle of fraternity at a time of crisis in a contemporary France deeply affected by a wave of terror attacks and the subsequent state of emergency, Bidar seeks to maintain a consistent focus on a philosophy of humanism as the basis for intercultural mediation between Islamic and Republican intellectual traditions: 'Nous ne pouvons vivre de façon pleinement humaine que dans un système de fraternité. La fraternité est notre écosystème.' (Bidar 2015b: p. 44) (We can only live in a fully human manner in a system of fraternity. Fraternity is our ecosystem.) The metaphor of the civic ecosystem is not coincidental and is arguably part of Bidar's most recent discussions of 'la citoyenneté planétaire', or a fraternal citizenship without borders: 'Qu'est-ce qu'une fraternité citoyenne exige de chacun? De dépasser les conceptions ordinaires de la fraternité: celles du sang, de la communauté ethnique ou de croyance.' (Bidar 2016: p. 166) (What does a civic fraternity require of each of us? To go beyond the ordinary conceptions of fraternity: based on blood, ethnic community and belief.)

Yet despite invocations of world citizenship by Bidar in *Quelles valeurs partager et transmettre aujourd'hui?* (2016), if we think once again in terms of the theme of cultural translation, it would seem that in the last couple of years he has foregrounded a 'nation-building' rather than a 'deconstructionist' understanding of cultural translation whereby he intends to demonstrate how Islamic traditions of *le sacré* and *la fraternité* can be mobilised to 'repair' a crisis of *le vivre ensemble* (living together or community) in a France destabilised by Islamist terrorism. As valuable and important as that endeavour may be, one senses that in Bidar's most recent work he engages in a narrative that – unwittingly perhaps – gives some credence to the notion of a clash of civilisations, even if on the face of it Bidar would deny this. A key example of this is Bidar's text entitled *Lettre ouverte au monde musulman* (published in April 2015) in which he addresses the Muslim world as 'le monde musulman' in the singular, '*tutoie*'s it[6] and calls it 'mon cher ami' (my dear friend). He laments how the Muslim world has become too subservient to the notion of *le sacré* whilst the Occident (his term) has abandoned it altogether and that, as a result, both 'worlds' are in disarray. Here, Bidar seems to be taking up the project of Meddeb (see Chapter 1) by arguing that Islam is affected by a cancer that has emerged from within itself. He claims that the main reason for the sclerosis in the Muslim world is due to the unwillingness of Muslim theologians to fully engage with the notion of 'l'homme héritier de Dieu' (Man as successor to God). He then ends his letter with a plea to the 'Muslim world' to endorse the idea of Bidar speaking on behalf of Islam in order to heal the rift with the West: 'Laisse-moi parler un peu pour toi au lieu de laisser confisquer ta voix par n'importe quel fou terroriste! Laisse-moi être de ceux qui parle un peu en ton nom au lieu de continuer aussi à faire s'exprimer pour toi n'importe quel *savant ignorant*' (Bidar 2015b, p. 51; emphasis in the original) (Let me talk a bit on your behalf instead of having your voice confiscated by some mad terrorist! Let me be one of those who can speak a little in your name instead of letting some *ignorant scholar* make pronouncements on your behalf). In this move that simultaneously claims that Islam is sick (*malade* is the term used) and thus needs a spokesperson to speak on its behalf, it is possible to argue that Bidar's recent work runs the dual risk of both essentialising Islam and silencing the diversity of Muslim voices, whilst reinforcing problematic and hegemonic discourses about Islam.

Is it arguable, then, that in times of political and social upheaval, public intellectuals are abandoning a potentially progressive approach to the question of cultural complexity? Indeed, Bidar's most recent stance has alienated other French Muslims and commentators, as illustrated by the 'Lettre ouverte à Bidar' by Kamel Meziti, published in *Saphir News* (Meziti 2010),[7] an article by Alain Gresh accusing Bidar of cultural essentialisation and reductionism (Gresh 2012) and Pierre Tevanian's piece for the group *Les mots sont importants* pointedly entitled 'Lettre ouverte à mon collègue Abdennour Bidar, marchand de fascisme à visage spirituel' (Tevanian 2015) (Open letter to my colleague Abdennour Bidar, peddler of fascism under the guise of spirituality). The criticism these commentators all make of Bidar is that he essentialises Islam and Muslims and is able to do so because he presents himself as a 'Muslim' scholar (the subtitle of *Lettre ouverte au monde musulman* is 'l'esprit critique du philosophe et le coeur éclairé du musulman' (the critical mind of the philosopher and the enlightened heart of the Muslim), thus escaping accusations of Islamophobia. Whether or not we agree with such negative responses to Bidar, it is surely important to consider why figures like him have been accorded such visibility in the French public sphere. Is someone like Bidar really taking part in a process of cultural translation which is restorative of *fraternité* and cultural complexity, or is his growing ubiquity and popularity due to his status as 'a good Muslim' (Gresh 2012) who repeatedly clamours his gratitude to the French Republic ('Merci ma chère France, et que je sois toujours parmi tes fils reconnaissants!'; Bidar 2015a: p. 30 (Thank you my dear France; may I forever remain one of your grateful sons!)) to reassure a secular French public sphere about what it wants to hear regarding

Islam, namely that it is Islam, rather than a range of actors, including the French state, that needs to move towards 'self-critique'?[8]

Notes

1 *L'Islam sans soumission: pour un existentialisme musulman* was first published in 2008; a second edition was then released in 2012. All quotes from *L'Islam sans soumission* come from the second edition, hence I reference the work as Bidar 2008/2012a throughout.
2 Hashas 2013 uses the translation 'overcoming of religion' for Bidar's term *la sortie de religion*.
3 This formulation is very similar to Babès' stance (see Chapter 3).
4 The OUP 2004 translation does not seem to correspond directly with Bidar's French version of this verse, which would be 'God walks with you wherever you may be' (author translation).
5 Article 18 of the Universal Declaration of Human Rights is cited from www.un.org/en/universal-declaration-human-rights/, accessed 22 January 2019.
6 *Tutoyer*: to use the informal mode of address in French.
7 Kamel Meziti is *Directeur de l'Aumônerie musulmane de la Marine nationale* and has a PhD in history from the Université Paris-Sorbonne. He is also a member of the *Groupe de recherche islamo-chrétien* at the Université catholique de Paris and administrator of *Les amis de la paix*.
8 Following the Paris attacks in November 2015, Bidar published an essay in *Le Figaro* entitled 'Les musulmans doivent passer à la responsabilité de l'auto-critique' (Bidar 2015c). The call for *autocritique* recalls Chebel's stance on autonomy and self-critique as discussed in Chapter 2.

Conclusion

The intellectuals discussed in this book have all enjoyed varying degrees of impact and notoriety in France but if they share one thing in common, it is that their work collectively contributes to a broad narrative of *le vivre ensemble*. They all present Islam as being capable of conforming to Republican *laïcité* and universalism, although they argue that the practices of Muslims do not always facilitate such potential compatibility. These scholars are thus, to varying degrees, critical of certain aspects of contemporary Islam and Muslims for what they regard as a reluctance to fully embrace a secular 'modernity'. Whilst all of the intellectuals discussed in this book do periodically allude to the shortcomings of the Republic in terms of its universalist promise of *liberté*, *égalité* and *fraternité* to all citizens regardless of their origins or religion, on the whole they direct the bulk of their criticism towards Islam, or to be more precise, towards a certain form of Islam, associated with religious conservatism, textual literalism and extremism. As such, these intellectuals feel indebted to the French state and are keen to say so publicly. In a sense, then, they reproduce cultural hegemony in the Gramscian sense, since they cannot be described as subaltern or counter-hegemonic critics of the Republic (Olsaretti 2014). A clear demonstration of such performative indebtedness to the French state can be found in Abdennour Bidar's writings, in which he repeatedly articulates his gratitude to the Republic, such as in *Plaidoyer pour la fraternité* where he states: 'Merci ma chère France, et que je sois toujours parmi tes fils reconnaissants! (Bidar 2015a: p. 30) (Thank you my dear France; may I forever be amongst your grateful sons!). Furthermore, despite Chebel and Meddeb being of a similar generation, i.e. growing up under colonial rule in Algeria and Tunisia, respectively, neither of them make a point of strongly denouncing the colonial subjugation of their countries of origin. If anything, they seem to look back on that period with a certain degree of nostalgia, certainly in the case of Abdelwahab Meddeb. Babès is a fervent supporter of the Republic's stance on the prohibition of the veil, arguing that 'La laïcité s'impose à tous, et c'est ce qui rassemble les citoyens autour des mêmes valeurs, quelles que soient leurs croyances religieuses' (Babès 2004: p. 13) (Secularism applies to everyone; it is what brings citizens together around the same values, regardless of their religious beliefs). A defender of the 2004 ban on religious symbols in public spaces, Bouzar states that 'la France n'a pas à rougir de continuer à défendre cette valeur fondamentale face aux pressions, quelles qu'elles soient, et d'où qu'elles viennent' (Babès 2004: p. 122) (France should not be ashamed to continue to defend this fundamental value in the face of pressure, whatever form it might take and wherever it may come from). As for Bouzar, she has also consistently sought to work with the French state, whether as a researcher at the *Ministère de la Justice* or as a contracted 'expert' on the de-radicalisation of jihadists with the *Ministère de l'Intérieur*.[1] It is perhaps unsurprising, therefore, that all these intellectuals have benefitted from a certain degree of acceptance, promotion or even *consecration* from the political class.

Bidar has certainly become increasingly well-known as a thinker. His work for the *Ministère de l'Éducation nationale* in the drafting of a *pédagogie de la laïcité* is highly symbolic if we consider the fact that this is someone who presents himself as 'un de tes fils éloignés' (one of your estranged sons) of the 'monde musulman' (Bidar 2015b: p. 5). His membership of the *Observatoire de la laïcité* is further evidence of his political mainstreaming. During the 2017 presidential election, he published an open letter to Emmanuel Macron, arguing that since he was 'probably' going to become France's next president, he should consider repairing the social and cultural divisions affecting French society via the creation of a *Ministère de Fraternité*. Given his increased focus on *fraternité* in his latest publications, *Plaidoyer pour la fraternité* (2015) and *Quelles valeurs transmettre aujourd'hui?* (2016), Bidar was perhaps pitching himself to Macron as a possible *Ministre de Fraternité* (Bidar 2017). In the cultural field, his weekly Radio France Culture programme *Cultures d'islam* (presented from 2015 to 2016), aimed at a non-Muslim audience demonstrates that his ideas have been reaching a public that is predominantly middle-class and highly educated. Beyond the political and media bubbles, Bidar is also active in disseminating his ideas to civil society via an association that he recently set up with psychologist Inès Weber called *Sésame*, which is defined as a *centre de culture spirituelle* (spiritual cultural centre). The aims of *Sésame*, as described on its website, are twofold:

1. **un centre d'enseignement** dans lequel seront abordés tous les grands thèmes intemporels de la vie spirituelle, à partir de l'héritage des différentes sagesses philosophiques et religieuses, d'Orient et d'Occident: la connaissance et la réalisation de soi, la qualité du lien avec autrui, la place de l'homme dans l'univers, etc.
2. **un espace d'effervescence créatrice** où chacun, qu'il soit intervenant ou participant, pourra contribuer dans des séances de discussion, de réflexion et

d'imagination collective à l'exploration de cette interrogation majeure de notre temps: quelle vie spirituelle pour aujourd'hui et demain?[2]

1. **An education centre** which will deal with all the major timeless themes of spiritual life, drawing on the different philosophical and religious traditions of the East and West: knowledge of the self, the nature of links with the Other, the role of humans in the universe, etc.
2. **A creative hub** in which everyone, whether speaker or participant, will be able to contribute to imaginative discussion, reflection and collective exploration of one of the major questions of our times: what sort of spirituality is appropriate for today and tomorrow?)

But beyond such high-level activities, what impact has Bidar had amongst Muslims in France? It is difficult to gauge his impact with any scientific accuracy and this is not the premise of this book. However, it is clear that his ideas have not been met with universal acclaim amongst fellow French Muslims, as evidenced by responses to his *Lettre ouverte au monde musulman* (Bidar 2015b) on the Muslim website *Islam et Info*. *Islam et Info* published a letter from one of their bloggers entitled 'Réponse d'une soeur à Abdennour Bidar qui appelle à une réforme de l'Islam' (A sister's response to Abdennour Bidar who has called for the reform of Islam), signed 'Samira B' that makes a pointed reply to Bidar's *Lettre ouverte*:

> A toi qui regarde du dehors et de loin,
> Comment prétendre s'adresser à un monde musulman monolithique et maître de lui-même, à qui l'on exige de rendre des comptes sur son honneur souillé et son temps gaspillé? ... Cher fils éloigné, tu dis que l'Islam engendre des monstres avec la plus folle assurance en la pertinence de ton propos. Mais au combien, ton jugement est partiel, partial et ton indignation sélective. (Samira B 2015)

> (To you who is watching from the outside and from afar,
> How can one claim to address a monolithic, autonomous Muslim world, from which we demand justification for its sullied honour and misuse of time? ... Dear estranged son, you say that Islam engenders monsters with an outlandish sense of certainty in the relevance of your claim. But oh how your judgement is partial and biased and your indignation selective.)

Another Muslim-perspective website, *Saphir News*, has also published articles that are critical of Bidar's position as a self-professed Muslim spokesperson, as demonstrated by Kamel Meziti's piece entitled 'Éloge de l'indignation' (In praise of indignation) in which he responds to a *Le Monde* article written by Bidar in August 2010 (Meziti 2010). Bidar's article was ostensibly written to condemn the Islamic Republic of Iran's sentencing of Sakineh Mohammadi Ashtiani to lapidation for alleged adultery, but after a cursory consideration of the specific case it effectively leads on to a broader denunciation of what he sees as the 'problem' of violence and communal constraints in Islam, with Bidar claiming that 'Hélas!, la religion islamique entière se nourrit de violence' (Bidar 2010b) (Alas! The entire Islamic religion is based on violence). Meziti vigorously rejects Bidar's claim:

> En mettant l'accent sur '*la logique de violence de l'islam*', vous franchissez un pas supplémentaire dans la surenchère fantasmatique qui nourrit les peurs et alimente un climat de xénophobie et d'islamophobie ambiant, à l'intérieur de l'Hexagone comme sur la scène mondiale … En tant '*intellectuel musulman*', vous vous érigez en procureur. … Mais, de grâce M. Bidar, ne vous érigez pas en un Muhammad Abduh ou autre Jamal ad-Dîn al-Afghânî, ou feu Mohammed Arkoun, qui, contrairement à vous, avaient les outils nécessaires pour mener à bien leur entreprise. En outre, vous y gagneriez beaucoup intellectuellement et au niveau de votre 'intériorité' à découvrir l'œuvre d'une grande figure de la pensée musulmane telle que Ghazali … N'allez surtout pas invoquer le courage en guise de justification. Le courage ne consiste pas à 'salir' un quart de l'humanité, en jetant l'anathème sur une religion, à laquelle vous vous identifiez. (Meziti 2010; emphasis in the original)

> (By emphasising 'the logic of violence in Islam' you go a step too far into the fantastical spiral which feeds fear and stokes the ambient climate of xenophobia and Islamophobia, both within France and on the world stage … As a '*Muslim intellectual*', you turn yourself into a prosecutor … But for goodness sake, Mr. Bidar, don't elevate yourself as a Muhammed Abduh or another Jamal ad-Din al Afghani, or the late Mohammed Arkoun, who, unlike you, had the necessary tools to bring their endeavours to fruition. Furthermore, you would gain a lot, intellectually and in terms of your 'interiority', to discover the works of a great figure of Muslim thought such as Ghazali … Don't invoke courage in the guise of justification. Courage does not involve 'smearing' a quarter of humanity and heaping blame on a religion with which you yourself identify.)

Beyond Meziti's rejection of Bidar's stance, other commentators are similarly dismissive of Bidar, including Pierre Tevanian – Bidar's fellow *normalien* who famously argued on the *Les mots sont importants* website that Bidar was 'un marchand de fascisme à visage spirituel' (Tevanian 2015) (a peddler of fascism with a spiritual face) for suggesting that an entire civilisation was 'malade' in his *Lettre ouverte au monde musulman*. Tevanian's response to Bidar's *Lettre ouverte* is unambiguous:

> Vous ne pouvez pas ignorer, Monsieur le normalien, agrégé de philosophie, le sens et la portée de votre métaphore. Déclarer toute une culture atteinte d'un '*cancer gravissime*', qui '*se généralise à grande vitesse*', au sein de '*toute une civilisation*', c'est ni plus ni moins qu'ériger *toute une population* en *danger mortel* … Vous parlez de cancer mais de quel *scanner* vous servez-vous pour mesurer la propagation de la tumeur maligne?

> Quel *logiciel politique* mobilisez-vous pour avoir recours à ce type de sauts rhétoriques, de registre apocalyptique, de métaphores biologistes?
>
> La réponse, vous la connaissez aussi bien que moi, car nous avons fait les mêmes études et vous l'avez comme moi apprise en histoire et en philosophie politique: c'est le registre de l'extrême droite raciste et fasciste. (Tevanian 2015; emphasis in the original.)

> (But surely you, Mr. *École normale*, Philosophy graduate, cannot be unaware of the significance of your metaphor? By declaring that a whole culture is affected by an '*extremely serious cancer*', which 'is spreading very rapidly', within 'a whole civilisation', is tantamount to claiming that *a whole population is in mortal danger* … You talk about cancer but what *scanner* are you using to measure the spread of the malignant tumour?
>
> What *political framework* are you mobilising in order to have recourse to these types of apocalyptic rhetorical leaps and these biological metaphors?
>
> You know the answer as well as I do, because we studied the same thing and you, like me, learnt in history and political philosophy that this is the register of the racist and fascist extreme right.)

Finally, journalist and former editor-in-chief of *Le Monde Diplomatique* Alain Gresh has been a vocal critic of Bidar, arguing that given his essentialisation of Islam in his discussion of the Mohammed Merah atrocity (Bidar wrote an article for *Le Monde* entitled 'Merah, "un monstre issu de la maladie de l'islam"'; Bidar 2012c (Merah, 'a monster born of the malady of Islam')), Bidar conforms to the figure of the 'native informant', as described by Adam Shatz (2003).

Malek Chebel has also been criticised for his promotion of *un islam des Lumières* (along with Bidar and Meddeb) by the political scientist Vincent Geisser (2008), who argued in an article published on *Oumma.com* that Islam 'light' is akin to a consumer product that is flying off the shelves:

> On les entend, on les voit et on les lit partout: à la radio, à la télévision, dans les journaux et dans les conférences de standing. Leurs livres se vendent à des milliers d'exemplaires dans les rayons des supermarchés. En quelques années, ils sont devenus les 'chouchous musulmans' des médias et des intellectuels français. Le secret de cette fulgurante réussite médiatique et commerciale? Un discours formaté sur la 'déchéance' et la 'maladie de l'islam', religion noble qui aurait été corrompue par la 'populace musulmane' ignorante et obscurantiste. (Geisser 2008)

> (We hear, see, and read them everywhere: on the radio, on the television, in the newspapers and at prestigious lectures. Their books, stacked on supermarket shelves, sell in the thousands. In a few years, they have become the 'Muslim darlings' of the media and French intellectuals. The secret to this dazzling media and commercial success? A well-worn discourse about the 'failure' and 'malady of Islam', a noble religion which has apparently been corrupted by the ignorant and obscurantist 'Muslim populace'.)

In the same vein as the 'native informant' thesis of Gresh, Geisser (2008) argues that thinkers such as Bidar, Chebel and Meddeb exemplify a certain 'complexe du colonisé' (colonised inferiority complex), as analysed by Albert Memmi (1985). Geisser writes:

> Contrairement à une idée reçue, ces 'nouvelles Lumières de l'Islam' n'ont rien inventé: elles reprennent dans ses grandes lignes la critique coloniale de la religion musulmane, telle qu'elle était véhiculée par certaines élites indigènes assimilées qui voulaient à tout prix marquer leur détachement par rapport à leur 'communauté d'origine'. (Geisser 2008)

> (Contrary to received wisdom, these 'new Lights of Islam' have invented nothing: they basically reproduce the colonial critique of the Muslim religion, as it was disseminated by certain assimilated native elites who wanted at all costs to signal their detachment from their 'community of origin'.)

Beyond such sharp critiques aimed at Chebel (and others), one must recognise that Chebel made a lasting impact on the French intellectual and cultural landscape in recent years. This was despite the fact that he never held a conventional academic position but instead travelled across Europe, North America and North Africa giving lectures and seminars on his work and publishing an impressive volume of materials ranging from academic monographs, essays, translations, 'guides de vulgarisation' to his review, *Noor* (meaning 'light' in Arabic, in reference to his *islam des Lumières* project). There were a number of projects that he was still working on at the time of his death and this is reflected in the posthumous publication of a series of interviews that he gave to Tunisian journalist Fawzia Zouari at the end of his life, when he knew he was seriously ill. The book, entitled *J'avais tant de choses à dire encore* was published in March 2017 and covered personal as well as political issues that were important to Chebel. Chebel's son Mikaël has also announced that a *Fondation Malek Chebel* is to be set up in his memory to bring the diversity of his work to a wider audience via conferences and seminars. There have also been plans to revive Chebel's *Noor* review. In an interview with *La Croix,* Mikaël Chebel argues that his father was in fact a reclusive intellectual who spent his time writing rather than promoting his own work; in this sense, we could argue that Chebel is quite distinct from an intellectual like Bidar who is more active in terms of media and political self-promotion:

> Mon père a passé sa vie à écrire, un peu comme un ermite, et ne s'est pas tellement occupé de la diffusion de son œuvre. Il avait le souci de ses lecteurs qu'il adorait rencontrer lors de salons du livre. Mais nous avons un peu l'impression d'être face à un trésor caché à faire découvrir au plus grand nombre. (Hoffner 2017)

> (My father spent his life writing, a bit like a hermit, and he didn't really take much interest in disseminating his work. He was interested in his readers who he loved

meeting at book fairs. But we have the slight impression that we stand before a hidden treasure, still to be made known to a wider public.)

Like Bidar and Chebel, Abdelwahab Meddeb's critical reception was also mixed, with his legacy clearly celebrated in secular and atheist milieus, such that he came to embody the reassuring antithesis of Tariq Ramadan. However, Meddeb was heavily criticised by his fellow Muslims for his silence about the Ben Ali dictatorship and was accused of overlooking the violence of the French colonial project in the Maghreb. Nevertheless, there is a sense that Meddeb was appreciated by middle-class non-Muslims, as demonstrated by the release of a documentary about his life and work in cinemas entitled *Islam pour mémoire* in March 2017 (Pagnot 2018). The film-maker, Bénédicte Pagnot, admits that she did not know much about Islam and that the project with Meddeb was motivated by her desire to educate herself. Film critics have argued that in its well-intentioned attempts to promote a positive image of Islam and Meddeb, Pagnot's film falls short of a critical and complex *engagement* with her subject matter (see Sotinel 2017 or Marest 2017).

Leïla Babès is perhaps the only intellectual in this book not to have been subjected to the type of criticism reserved for Chebel, Bidar, Meddeb and Bouzar. This could perhaps have something to do with her decision to situate herself more clearly within the intellectual parameters of the university rather than the media landscape, although she has been an active blogger and weekly radio show *chroniqueuse* until recently. For example, her extensively researched and original monograph *L'Utopie de l'islam* (2011) did not receive much critical attention. Perhaps such a fine-grained historical analysis of the relationship between the religious and political spheres from the time of the life of the Prophet to the present day frustrates an ambient desire for sound-bite-friendly analyses of Islam.

The intellectual most closely associated with a sound-bite-friendly analysis of radical Islamism is Dounia Bouzar, or as she is scathingly referred to by some journalists, 'Mme Dé-radicalisation' (see, for example, Brabant 2016). Dounia Bouzar has indeed been heavily criticised by sections of the media and the intellectual class. Indeed, whilst the self-proclaimed status of Bouzar as an *experte* and *femme du terrain* (fieldworker) may have served Bouzar well initially, via her *Centre de prévention contre les derives sectaires liées à l'islam* (CPDSI) and the myriad of media invitations to take part in current affairs discussion programmes such as *C dans l'air* or BFMTV's *Grand angle* to discuss de-radicalisation, such a status has also created its own pitfalls. Bouzar's integrity as an expert is frequently called into question by the media, her methods as well as her general 'omnipresence' challenged (see, for example, Brabant 2016 or Perrotin 2015). It is arguable that since Bouzar has withdrawn somewhat from her position as policy interlocutor and changed the status of the CPDSI to an independent research centre, no longer in receipt of funding from the *Ministère de l'Intérieur*, her integrity has been challenged even more pointedly. For example, an article was published in *Le Figaro* (Bastié 2016) linking Bouzar to one of the 'mentors' of the Kouachi brothers – an ex-jihadist – who, Bouzar claims, has been helping her carry out her research on radicalisation and de-radicalisation strategies. Bouzar has complained to *Le Figaro* for publishing what she argues are defamatory items about her work, and has released a statement via the CPDSI website refuting the compromising character of the newspaper's coverage (Bouzar 2017; see also Jouan and Leclerc 2017).

How can we interpret the latterly hostile reception of Bouzar's work? Is it potentially linked to the idea that the positions of Muslim intellectuals and experts are expected to be as exemplary as possible, thus demonstrating a sort of permanent 'oath of allegiance' to the Republic and its values? Are the intellectuals who feature in this book accepted in so far as they can be seen to be confirming their faith in the emancipatory project of the Republic and its secular norms? In their analysis of the 'ills' of Islam, they simultaneously neglect to discuss the 'ills' afflicting French society in terms of a postcolonial legacy of intergenerational discrimination and segregation that disproportionately affect those French citizens of Muslim heritage. Have these public intellectuals been recognised and celebrated because, in a sense, they have been telling the Republican elites what they want to hear? If this is the case, then it would mean that these intellectuals correspond to the Gramscian notion of intellectuals who reproduce cultural hegemony, since they seem to operate within a broader narrative of consensus: consensus about the desirability of *laïcité*, universalism and the legacy of the Enlightenment. However, as Chantal Mouffe (2013) argues, the danger in consensus is that it can produce a sort of 'post-politics' or 'post-democracy' whereby the absence of 'agonistic' or positive conflict between different sections of society can lead to the perpetuation of certain forms of social and political exclusion. So, despite the significant contributions of all the thinkers who feature in this book, perhaps the next step should be to look at those figures of contemporary French society who are motivated by the idea of positive conflict, the production of counter-hegemonic discourse and antagonistic relations with the French state. It may be that those figures are active amongst the millennial generation of French Muslims who, by and large, were born and grew up in France and who came of age politically in the new millennium (see, for example, the work of the Muslim and feminist organisation Lallab,[3] which works to 're-write' public narratives about Muslim women in France, or the work of other authors such as Malika Hamidi (Hamidi 2017) or Zahra Ali (Ali & Dayan-Herzbrun 2017) on Muslim feminism or 'decolonial pluriversalism'. This demographic's unquestionable embeddedness within the French nation state may be the factor which encourages a stronger critique vis-à-vis the mechanisms of cultural exclusion that are still perpetuated today. Perhaps from that point onwards, the notion of the *intellectuel(le) engagé(e)* will once again acquire an antagonistic quality as we move into the future struggles of the twenty-first century.

Notes

1 Bouzar ended the partnership between her *Centre de prevention contre les dérives sectaires liées à l'islam* (CPDSI) and the *Ministère de l'Intérieur* in February 2016, in response to the parliamentary bill on *la déchéance de nationalité* (stripping of nationality for dual nationals convicted of terrorism).
2 See http://centre-sesame.com/projet/; accessed 29 June 2017.
3 See www.lallab.org/; accessed 2 July 2019.

Bibliography

'Abdelwahab Meddeb intellectuel chéri par le régime de Ben Ali' (2011) *Oumma.com*, 24 January. Available at https://oumma.com/abdelwahab-meddeb-intellectuel-cheri-par-le-regime-de-ben-ali/; accessed 27 June 2017.
Adorno, T. and M. Horkheimer (2016) *Dialectic of Enlightenment*. London, New York: Verso.
Ahearne, J. (2006) 'Public intellectuals and cultural policy in France', *International Journal of Cultural Policy*, 12 (3), pp. 323–339.
Alexander, J. (2006) *The Civil Sphere*. Oxford: Oxford University Press.
——— (2013) 'Struggling over the mode of incorporation: backlash against multiculturalism in Europe', *Journal of Ethnic and Migration Studies*, 36 (4), pp. 531–556.
Ali, Z. (ed.) (2012) *Féminismes islamiques*. Paris: Editions de la Fabrique.
Ali, Z. and S. Dayan-Herzbrun (eds) (2017) 'Pluriversalisme décolonial', *Tumultes*, 48.
Althusser, L. (1971) 'Ideology and ideological state apparatuses'. In *Lenin and Philosophy*, trans. B. Brewster. London: Monthly Review Press, pp. 127–186.
Anidjar, G. (2006) 'Secularism', *Critical Inquiry*, 33 (1), pp. 52–77.
Arkoun, M. (1975) *La Pensée arabe*. Paris: Presses Universitaires de France.
——— (1993) *Penser l'islam aujourd'hui*. Algiers: Laphomic Enal.
Arnaldez, R. (1987) *Aspects de la pensée musulmane*. Paris: Vrin.
Asad, T. (2003) *Formations of the Secular: Christianity, Islam, Modernity*. Stanford, CA: Stanford University Press.
Asad, T., J. Butler, S. Mahmood and W. Brown (2013) *Is Critique Secular?* New York: Fordham University Press.
Babès, L. (1997) *L'Islam positif: la religion des jeunes musulmans de France*. Paris: Editions de l'Atelier.
——— (2000) *L'Islam intérieur: passion et désenchantement*. Beirut: Editions Al-Bouraq.
——— (2004) *Le Voile démystifié*. Paris: Bayard.
——— (2008) 'Tariq Ramadan contre Abdelwahab Meddeb' [blog], 12 February. Available at http://leilababes.canalblog.com/archives/2008/02/12/7923019.html; accessed 27 June 2017.
——— (2011) *L'Utopie de l'islam: la religion contre l'État*. Paris: Armand Colin.
Babès, L. (ed.) (1996) *Les Nouvelles Manières de croire: judaïsme, christianisme, islam, nouvelles religiosités*. Paris: Editions de l'Atelier.
Babès, L. and T. Oubrou (2002) *Loi d'Allah, loi des hommes: liberté, égalité et femmes en islam*. Paris: Albin Michel.
Bakhtin, M. (2006) 'The problem of the text in linguistics, philology, and the human sciences: an experiment in philosophical analysis'. In C. Emerson and M. Holquist (eds)

Speech Genres & Other Late Essays, trans. V. W. McGee. Austin, TX: University of Texas Press, pp. 103–131.

Balibar, E. (2011) 'Toward a diasporic citizen? From internationalism to cosmopolitics'. In F. Lionnet and S. M. Shih (eds) *The Creolization of Theory*. Durham, NC: Duke University Press, pp. 207–225.

Balyâni, A. (1982) *Épitre sur l'Unicité absolue*, trans. Michel Chodkiewicz. Paris: Les Deux Océans.

Bancel, N., F. Bernault, P. Blanchard, A. Boubeker, A. Mbembe and F. Vergès (eds) (2010) *Ruptures postcoloniales: nouveaux visages de la société française*. Paris: La Découverte.

Bastié, E. (2016) 'L'ex-mentor des Kouachi, Farid Benyettou travaille avec Dounia Bouzar', *Le Figaro*, 20 October. Available at www.lefigaro.fr/actualite-france/2016/10/20/01016–20161020ARTFIG00104-l-ex-mentor-des-kouachi-farid-benyettou-travaille-avec-dounia-bouzar.php; accessed 26 June 2017.

Baubérot, J. (2012) *La Laïcité falsifiée*. Paris: La Découverte.

Beck, U. (2006) *Cosmopolitan Vision*. Cambridge: Polity Press.

Beck, U. and E. Grande (2007) *Cosmopolitan Europe*. Cambridge: Polity Press.

Benjamin, W. (2004) *Selected Writings: Volume 1, 1913–1926*. Edited by M. Bullock and M. W. Jennings. Cambridge, MA: Belknap Press of Harvard University Press.

Bennoune, K. (2013) *Your Fatwa Does Not Apply Here: Untold Stories from the Fight Against Muslim Fundamentalism*. New York: W.W. Norton and Company, Inc.

Ben Rhouma, H. (2014) 'La voix controversée d'Abdelwahab Meddeb s'est éteinte, retour sur son parcours', *Saphir News*, 7 November. Available at www.saphirnews.com/La-voix-controversee-d-Abdelwahab-Meddeb-s-est-eteinte-retour-sur-son-parcours_a19947.html; accessed 27 June 2017.

Bensoussan, G. (ed.) (2017) *Une France soumise: les voix du refus*. Paris: Albin Michel.

Berger, P. (1999). *The Desecularization of the World: Resurgent Religion and World Politics*. Grand Rapids, MI: Eerdmans.

Berman, P. (2011) *The Flight of the Intellectuals: The Controversy over Islamism and the Press*. New York: Melville House.

Bernheim, N.-L., A. Bruneton, C. Enjeu and J. Savé (1975) *Les Femmes s'entêtent*. Paris: Gallimard.

Bidar, A. (2004) *Un islam pour notre temps*. Paris: Seuil.

——— (2006) *Self islam: histoire d'un islam personnel*. Paris: Seuil.

——— (2010a) *L'Islam face à la mort de Dieu: actualité de Mohammed Iqbal*. Paris: François Bourin.

——— (2010b) 'La lapidation, "preuve extrême de la logique de violence de l'islam"', *Le Monde*, 30 August. Available at www.lemonde.fr/idees/article/2010/08/30/la-lapidation-preuve-extreme-de-la-logique-de-violence-de-l-islam_1404384_3232.html; accessed 29 June 2017.

——— (2012a) *L'Islam sans soumission: pour un existentialisme musulman* (2nd ed.). Paris: Albin Michel. Originally published in 2008.

——— (2012b) *Comment sortir de la religion*. Paris: La Découverte.

——— (2012c), 'Merah, "un monstre issu de la maladie de l'islam"', *Le Monde*, 23 March. Available at www.lemonde.fr/idees/article/2012/03/23/un-monstre-issu-de-la-maladie-de-l-islam_1674747_3232.html; accessed 29 June 2017.

——— (2015a) *Plaidoyer pour la fraternité*. Paris: Albin Michel.

——— (2015b) *Lettre ouverte au monde musulman*. Paris: Éditions Les Liens qui Libèrent.

——— (2015c) 'Les musulmans doivent passer à la responsabilité de l'auto-critique', *Le Figaro*, 19 November. Available at www.lefigaro.fr/vox/societe/2015/11/19/31003-20151119ARTFIG00002-abdennour-bidar-les-musulmans-doivent-passer-a-la-responsabilite-de-l-autocritique.php; accessed 16 January 2017.
——— (2016) *Quelles valeurs partager et transmettre aujourd'hui?* Paris: Albin Michel.
——— (2017) 'Qu'allez-vous faire M. Macron contre les fractures de notre société?', *Le Nouvel Observateur*, 26 April. Available at http://tempsreel.nouvelobs.com/presidentielle-2017/20170425.OBS8518/qu-allez-vous-faire-m-macron-contre-les-fractures-de-notre-societe.html; accessed 29 June 2017.
Bidar, A. and Haut Conseil à l'Intégration (HCI) (2013) *Pour une pédagogie de la laïcité à l'école*. Paris: La Documentation Française.
Birdwell, R. Z. (2017) 'From interpellation to recognition: Althusser, Hegel, Dahlberg', *symplokē*, 25 (1–2), pp. 315–329.
Blanchard, P., N. Bancel and S. Lemaire (eds) (2005) *La Fracture colonial: la société francaise au prisme de l'héritage colonial*. Paris: La Découverte.
Bollack, J., C. Jambet and A. Meddeb (2007) *La Conférence de Ratisbonne: enjeux et controverses*. Paris: Éditions Bayard.
Bowen, J. (2007) *Why the French Don't Like Headscarves: Islam, the State, and Public Space*. Princeton, NJ: Princeton University Press.
Bourdieu, P. (1988) *Homo Academicus*. Cambridge: Polity Press.
——— (1991) *Language and Symbolic Power*, trans. G. Raymond and M. Adamson. Cambridge: Polity Press.
Bourget, C. (2008) '9/11 and the affair of the Muslim headscarf in essays by Tahar Ben Jelloun and Abdelwahab Meddeb', *French Cultural Studies*, 19 (1), pp. 71–84.
Bouzar, D. (2004) *Monsieur Islam n'existe pas: pour une désislamisation des débats*. Paris: Hachette.
——— (2005) *Ça suffit!* Paris: Denoël.
——— (2006) *Quelle éducation face au radicalisme religieux?* Paris: Dunod.
——— (2007) *L'Intégrisme, l'islam et nous: on a tout faux*. Paris: Plon.
——— (2011) *Laïcité mode d'emploi – cadre légal et solutions pratiques: 42 études de cas*. Paris: Éditions Eyrolles.
——— (2014a) *Désamorcer l'islam radical: ces dérives sectaires qui défigurent l'islam*. Paris: Editions de l'Atelier.
——— (2014b) *Ils cherchent le paradis, ils ont trouvé l'enfer*. Paris: Editions de l'Atelier.
——— (2017) 'STOP – Diffamation Dounia Bouzar le FIGARO – Droit de réponse', *CPDSI*. Available at www.cpdsi.fr/actu/stop-diffamation-dounia-bouzar-droit-de-reponse/; accessed 27 June 2017.
Bouzar, D. and L. Bouzar (2009) *Allah a-t-il sa place dans l'entreprise?* Paris: Albin Michel.
Bouzar, D. and S. Kada (2003) *L'une voilée, l'autre pas*. Paris: Albin Michel.
Bracke, S. (2011) 'Subjects of debate: secular and sexual exceptionalism, and Muslim women in the Netherlands'. *Feminist Review*, 98 (1), pp. 28–46.
Bruckner, B. (2017) *Un racisme imaginaire: la querelle de l'islamophobie*. Paris: Grasset-Fasquelle.
Buden, B. (2006) 'Cultural Translation: Why it is important and where to start with it', *EIPCP*. Available at http://eipcp.net/transversal/0606/buden/en; accessed 28 March 2016.
Buden, B., Nowotny, S., Simon, S., Bery, A. and Cronin, M. (2009). 'Cultural translation: an introduction to the problem, and responses', *Translation Studies*, 2 (2), pp. 196–219.

Burgat, F. (2010) *L'Islamisme à l'heure d'Al-Qaida: réislamisation, modernisation, radicalisations*. Paris: La Découverte.
Butler, J. (1997) *Excitable Speech: A Politics of the Performative*. London: Routledge.
Butler, J., E. Mendieta, and J. VanAntwerpen (2011) *The Power of Religion in the Public Sphere*. New York: Columbia University Press.
Brabant, J. (2016) 'Dounia Bouzar: Une "Madame Déradicalisation" très médiatisée mais au bilan incertain', *Arrêt sur images*, 1 February. Available at www.arretsurimages.net/articles/2016-02-01/dounia-bouzar-une-mme-deradicalisation-tres-mediatique-mais-au-bilan-incertain; accessed 29 June 2017.
Bruce, S. (2011) *Secularization: In Defence of Unfashionable Theory*. Oxford: Oxford University Press.
Camus, R. (2011) *Le Grand Remplacement*. Neuilly-sur-Seine: Editions David Reinharc.
Catinchi, P.-J. (2016) 'Mort de l'anthropologue Malek Chebel, défenseur d'un "islam des Lumières"', *Le Monde*, 12 November. Available at www.lemonde.fr/disparitions/article/2016/11/12/deces-de-l-anthropologue-malek-chebel-defenseur-d-un-islam-des-lumieres_5030163_3382.html; accessed 10 March 2017.
Centre de prévention contre les dérives sectaires liées à l'islam (CPDSI) (2016) 'Communiqué de presse', *CPDSI*, 11 February. Available at www.cpdsi.fr/wp-content/uploads/2016/02/CP_CPDSI_1_fevrier2016.pdf; accessed 26 June 2017.
Chabal, E. (2010) 'Writing the French national narrative in the twenty-first century', *The Historical Journal*, 53 (2), pp. 495–516.
Charle, C. (1990) *Naissance des 'intellectuels' 1880–1900*. Paris: Éditions de Minuit.
Chebel, M. (2002) *Le Sujet en islam*. Paris: Seuil.
——— (2004) *Manifeste pour un islam des Lumières*, Paris: Hachette Littératures.
——— (2006) *L'Islam et la raison: le combat des idées*. Paris: Éditions Perrin.
———and C. Godin (2011) *Vivre ensemble: éloge de la différence*. Paris: Éditions First-Gründ.
——— (2013) *Changer l'islam: dictionnaire des réformateurs musulmans des origines à nos jours*. Paris: Albin Michel.
——— (2015a) *L'Inconscient de l'islam: réflexions sur l'interdit, la faute et la transgression*. Paris: CNRS Éditions.
——— (2015b) *L'Islam en 100 questions*. Paris: Tallandier.
——— (2016) *Mohammed, prophète de l'islam*. Paris: Éditions Robert Laffont.
——— (2017) *J'avais tant de choses à dire encore…: entretiens avec Fawzia Zouari*. Paris: Éditions Desclée de Brouwer.
Chebel, M. and M. Clark (2015) *L'Islam pour les nuls*. Paris: First éditions.
Coombes, S. (2014) 'Black postcolonial communities in a globalised world as articulated in the work of Paul Gilroy and Edouard Glissant: a comparative analysis', *Commonwealth*, 36 (2), pp. 11–18.
Derrida, J. (2002) 'Faith and reason: two sources of religion at the limits of reason alone.' In G. Anidjar (ed.), *Acts of Religion*. London: Routledge, pp. 42–101.
Deuleuze, G. and F. Guatarri (2004) *Mille plateaux*. Paris: Éditions de Minuit.
Dewey, J. (2011) *Une foi commune*, trans. P. de Mascio. Paris: La Découverte.
Djavann, C. (2006) *Bas les voiles!* Paris: Folio.
Djitli, L. (2004) *Lettre à ma fille qui veut porter le voile*. Paris: Éditions de la Martinière.
Dupuy, J.-P. (2013). *The Mark of the Sacred*. Stanford, CA: Stanford University Press.
Durkheim, E. (1985) *Les formes élémentaires de la vie religieuse* (7th ed.). Paris: Quadrige/Presses Universitaires de France.

Fairclough, N. (2003) *Analysing Discourse: Textual Analysis for Social Research.* London: Routledge.
Fanon, F. (1952) *Peau noire, masques blancs.* Paris: Seuil.
Faure, O. (2010) '"Le voile intégral est une provocation!"', *L'Express,* 6 July. Available at www.lexpress.fr/actualite/societe/le-voile-integral-est-une-provocation_904457.html; accessed 9 March 2017.
Fernando, M. (2009) 'Exceptional citizens: secular Muslim women and the politics of difference in France', *Social Anthropology,* 17 (4), pp. 379–392.
—— (2014) *The Republic Unsettled: Muslim French and the Contradictions of Secularism.* Durham, NC: Duke University Press.
Finkielkraut, A. (1987) *La Défaite de la pensée.* Paris: Gallimard.
Fitzgerald, T. (ed.) (2007) *The Secular-Religious Dichotomy: Historical and Colonial Contexts.* London: Equinox.
Forsdick, C. and D. Murphy (2003) *Francophone Postcolonial Studies.* London: Arnold.
Forsdick, C. and D. Murphy (eds) (2009) *Postcolonial Thought in the French-speaking World.* Liverpool: Liverpool University Press.
Foucault, M. (1972) *The Archaeology of Knowledge,* trans. A. M. Sheridan. New York: Pantheon Books.
Foucault, M. (1977) *Discipline and punish: the birth of the prison.* New York: Vintage Books.
—— (1980) *Power/Knowledge: Selected Interviews and Other Writings, 1972–1977.* Brighton: Harvester Press.
Fourest, C. (2004) *Frère Tariq: discours, stratégie et méthode de Tariq Ramadan.* Paris: Grasset.
—— (2015) *Éloge du blasphème.* Paris: Grasset.
Frégosi, F. (2008) *Penser l'islam dans la laïcité.* Paris: Fayard.
Gaspard, F. and F. Khosrokhavar (1995) *Le Foulard et la République.* Paris: Seuil.
Gauchet, M. (1985). *Le Désenchantement du monde.* Paris: Gallimard.
Gauchet, M. (1997). *The Disenchantment of the World: A Political History of Religion,* trans. O. Burge. Princeton, NJ: Princeton University Press.
Geisser, V. (2008) 'Islam light: un produit qui se vend bien', *Oumma.com.* Available at https://oumma.com/islam-light-un-produit-qui-se-vend-bien/; accessed 27 June 2017.
Gemie, S. (2010) *French Muslims: New Voices in Contemporary France.* Cardiff: University of Wales Press.
Georgiev, P.K. (2012) *Self-Orientalization in South East Europe.* Wiesbaden: Springer VS.
Goffman, E. (1959) *The Presentation of Self in Everyday Life.* New York: Doubleday.
Göle, N. (2011) *Islam in Europe: The Lure of Fundamentalism and the Allure of Cosmopolitanism.* Princeton, NJ: Markus Wiener Publishers.
Göle, N. (ed.) (2014) *Islam and Public Controversy in Europe.* Farnham: Ashgate.
Gramsci, A. (2007) *Prison Notebooks,* vol 3, trans. J. A. Buttigieg. New York: Columbia University Press.
Gresh, A. (2011) 'La maladie d'Abdelwahab et la révolution tunisienne', *Le Monde Diplomatique,* 27 July. Available at http://blog.mondediplo.net/2011-07-27-La-maladie-d-Abdelwahab-Meddeb-et-la-revolution; accessed 27 June 2017.
—— (2012) 'Bidar, ces musulmans que nous aimons tant', *Le Monde Diplomatique,* 25 March. Available at http://blog.mondediplo.net/2012-03-25-Bidar-ces-musulmans-que-nous-aimons-tant; accessed 11 April 2016.
Grewal, K. (2012) 'Reclaiming the voice of the third world woman', *Interventions,* 14 (4), pp. 569–590.

Guénif Souilamas, N. (2000) *Des 'beurettes' aux descendantes d'immigrants nord-africains*. Paris: Grasset.
Guénif Souilamas, N. (ed.) (2006) *La République mise à nu par son immigration*. Paris: La Fabrique Éditions.
Guénif Souilamas, N. and E. Macé (2004) *Les Féministes et le garçon arabe*. Paris: Éditions de l'Aube.
Habermas, J. (2006) 'Religion in the public sphere', *European Journal of Philosophy*, 14 (1), pp. 1–25.
——— (2008). *Between Naturalism and Religion: Philosophical Essays*. Cambridge: Polity Press.
——— (2010). *An Awareness of What is Missing: Faith and Reason in a Post-Secular Age*. Cambridge: Polity Press.
Hamidi, M. (2017) *Un féminisme musulman, et pourquoi pas?* La Tour d'Aigues: Editions de l'Aube.
Hamel, I. (2007) *La Vérité sur Tariq Ramadan: sa famille, ses réseaux, sa stratégie*. Paris: Favre Sa.
Hannerz, U. (1992) *Cultural Complexity: Studies in the Social Organization of Meaning*. New York: Columbia University Press.
Hashas, M. (2013) 'Reading Abdennour Bidar: new pathways for European Islamic thought', *Journal of Muslims in Europe*, 2, pp. 45–76.
Hoffner, A.-B. (2017) 'Une fondation pour diffuser l'"islam des Lumières" de Malek Chebel, *La Croix*, 19 May. Available at www.la-croix.com/Religion/Islam/fondation-diffuser-islam-Lumieres-Malek-Chebel-2017-05-19-1200848503; accessed 29 June 2017.
Hollande, F. (2015) 'Conférence de presse de M. François Hollande, Président de la République, sur les défis et priorités de la politique gouvernementale, à Paris le 5 février 2015', *Vie Publique*. Available at http://discours.vie-publique.fr/notices/157000289.html; accessed 26 March 2019.
Houllebecq, M. (2015) *Soumission*. Paris: Flammarion.
Huntington, S. (1998) *The Clash of Civilizations and the Remaking of the World Order*. London: Touchstone.
Joppke, C. (2004) 'The Retreat of multiculturalism in the liberal state: theory and policy', *British Journal of Sociology*, 55 (2), pp. 237–257.
——— (2015) *The Secular State Under Siege: Religion and Politics in Europe and America*. Cambridge: Polity Press.
Jouan, A. and J.-M. Leclerc (2017) 'Trois parents de djihadistes français mis en examen pour "financement du terrorisme"', *Le Figaro*, 25 June. Available at www.lefigaro.fr/actualite-france/2017/06/25/01016-20170625ARTFIG00147-terrorisme-trois-parents-de-djihadistes-mis-en-examen.php; accessed 26 June 2017.
Keaton, T.D. (2006) *Muslim Girls and the Other France: Race, Identity, Politics and Social Exclusion*. Bloomington, IN: Indiana University Press.
Kemp, A. (2010) *Voices and Veils: Feminism and Islam in French Women's Writing and Activism*. Oxford: Legenda.
Kepel, G. (2000) *Jihâd, expansion et déclin de l'islamisme*. Paris: Gallimard.
Khosrokhavar, F. (2014) *Radicalisation*. Paris: Maison des Sciences de l'Homme.
Kiwan, N. (2013) 'Muslim and secular: Performing "Muslim" exemplarity and public debates on Islam in France'. *Performing Islam*, 2 (1), pp. 45–66.
——— (2017) 'Transformer les perceptions de l'islam? Le cas de l'intellectuel musulman laïque Abdelwahhab Meddeb'. In M. Boucher, G. Pleyers and P. Rebughini (eds) *Subjectivation et désubjectivation: Penser le sujet dans la globalisation*. Paris: Éditions de la Maison des sciences de l'homme, pp. 263–273.

Laborde, C. (2008) *Critical Republicanism: The Hijab Controversy and Political Philosophy*. Oxford: Oxford University Press.

——— (2012) 'State paternalism and religious dress code', *International Journal of Constitutional Law*, 10 (2), pp. 398–410.

——— (2016) 'Elle a perdu son âme', *Libération*, 22 November. Available at www.liberation.fr/debats/2016/11/22/elle-a-perdu-son-ame_1530196; accessed 26 March 2019.

LaCapra, D. (2004) *History in Transit: Experience, Identity, Critical Theory*. Ithaca, NY: Cornell University Press.

Landau, P. (2005) *Le Sabre et le Coran: Tariq Ramadan et les Frères musulmans à la conquête de l'Europe*. Paris: Editions du Roger.

Laurence, J. (2005) 'From the Elysee salon to the table of the Republic: State-Islam relations and the integration of Muslims in France', *European Yearbook of Minority Issues*, 3 (1), pp. 237–262.

Levey, G. and T. Modood (eds) (2009) *Secularism, Religion, and Multicultural Citizenship*. Cambridge: Cambridge University Press.

Lewis, B. (2002) *What Went Wrong? The Clash between Islam and Modernity in the Middle East*. London: Weidenfeld and Nicolson.

Liu, X. (2011) *La Philosophie du porc et autres essais*, trans. J.-P. Béja. Paris: Gallimard.

Long, I. (2013) *Women Intellectuals in Post-68 France: Petitions and Polemics*. Basingstoke: Palgrave Macmillan.

López-Calvo, I. (2008) *Imaging the Chinese in Cuban Literature and Culture*. Gainesville, FL: University Press of Florida.

Maalouf, A. (1998) *Les Identités meurtrières*. Paris: Grasset.

Marest, P.-J. (2017) 'Islam pour mémoire', *Télérama*. Available at www.telerama.fr/cinema/films/islam-pour-memoire,516440.php; accessed 29 June 2017.

Marranci, G. (2010) 'The sociology and anthropology of Islam'. In B. Turner (ed.) *The New Blackwell Companion to the Sociology of Religion*. Oxford: Blackwell Publishing, pp. 364–386.

Mas, R. (2004) 'Love as difference: the politics of love in the thought of Malek Chebel', *European Review of History*, 11 (2), pp. 273–301.

——— (2006) 'Compelling the Muslim subject: memory and post-colonial violence and the public performativity of "secular and cultural Islam"', *The Muslim World*, 96 (4), pp. 586–616.

Meddeb, A. (1979) *Talismano*. Paris: Christian Bourgois.

——— (1986) *Phantasia*. Paris: Sindbad.

——— (1987) *Tombeau d'Ibn Arabi*. Paris: Noël Blandin.

——— (1999) *Aya dans les villes*. Saint-Clément-la-Rivière: Fata Morgana.

——— (2001) *Matière des oiseaux*. Saint-Clément-la-Rivière: Fata Morgana.

——— (2002) *La Maladie de l'islam*. Paris: Seuil.

——— (2004) *Face à l'islam*. Paris: Textuel.

——— (2005) *L'Exil occidental*. Paris: Albin Michel.

——— (2006) *Contre-prêches*. Paris: Seuil.

——— (2008) *Sortir de la malédiction: l'islam en civilisation et barbarie*. Paris: Seuil.

——— (2009) *Pari de civilisation*. Paris: Seuil.

——— (2011) *Printemps de Tunis: la métamorphose de l'histoire*. Paris: Editions Albin Michel.

——— (2017) *Le Temps des inconciliables: contre-prêches 2*. Paris: Seuil.

Meddeb, A. and B. Stora (2013) *L'Histoire des relations entre juifs et musulmans des origines à nos jours*. Paris: Albin Michel.
Memmi, A. (1985) *Portrait du colonisé, portrait du colonisateur*. Paris: Gallimard.
Meziti, K. (2010) 'Éloge de l'indignation: lettre ouverte à Abdennour Bidar', *Saphir News*, 24 September. Available at www.saphirnews.com/Eloge-de-l-indignation-lettre-ouverte-a-Abdennour-Bidar_a11865.html; accessed 11 April 2016.
Milbank, J. (1990). *Theology and Social Theory, Beyond Secular Reason*. Oxford: Blackwell Publishing.
Mills, S. (2004) *Discourse*. London, New York: Routledge.
Montagu, M. (1991) *L'Islam au peril des femmes*. Paris: La Découverte.
Mouffe, C. (2013) *Agonistics: Thinking the World Politically*. London, New York: Verso.
Olsaretti, A. (2014) 'Beyond class: the many facets of Gramsci's theory of intellectuals', *Classical Sociology*, 14 (4), pp. 363–381.
Ory, P. and J.-F. Sirinelli (2004) *Les Intellectuels en France. De l'affaire Dreyfus à nos jours*. Paris: Perrin.
Pagnot, B. (2018) *Islam pour mémoire* [DVD]. Paris: Éditions Montparnasse.
Perrotin, D. (2015) 'Dounia Bouzar, l'experte des dérives djihadistes, arrangeuse de vérités?', *Nouvel Observateur*, 12 March. Available at http://tempsreel.nouvelobs.com/rue89/rue89-nos-vies-connectees/20150312.RUE8237/dounia-bouzar-l-experte-des-derives-djihadistes-arrangeuse-de-verites.html; accessed 15 April 2015.
Pipes, D. (2003) *Militant Islam Reaches America*. New York: W.W. Norton.
Qadiri, S. (2013) 'Abdelwahab Meddeb: a literary path towards an Islamic atheism?', *Journal of Romance Studies*, 13 (1), pp. 49–64.
The Qur'an: A New Translation by M.A.S. Abdel Haleem (2004). Oxford: Oxford University Press.
Ramadan, T. (2003) *Les Musulmans d'occident et l'avenir de l'islam*. Paris: Sindbad/Actes Sud.
Reader, K. (1987) *Intellectuals and the Left in France since 1968*. Basingstoke: Macmillan.
Renaut, A. and A. Touraine (2005) *Un débat sur la laïcité*. Paris: Stock.
Robins, K. (2014) 'Europe and its complexity: what would like to be said', *Cultural Politics*, 10 (3), pp. 262–274.
Roy, O. (2002) *L'Islam mondialisé*. Paris: Seuil.
——— (2005) *La Laïcité face à l'islam*. Paris: Stock.
——— (2011) *Généalogie de l'islamisme*. Paris: Fayard/Pluriel.
Said, E. (1978) *Orientalism*. London: Penguin Books.
Samira B (2015) 'Réponse d'une soeur à Abdennour Bidar qui appelle à une réforme de l'Islam', Islam et Info. Available at www.islametinfo.fr/2015/02/10/reponse-dune-soeur-a-abdennour-bidar-qui-appelle-a-une-reforme-de-lislam/; accessed 29 June 2017.
Sand, S. (2018) *The End of the French Intellectual: From Zola to Houellebecq*. London: Verso.
Scott, J.W. (2007) *The Politics of the Veil*. Princeton, NJ: Princeton University Press.
Shatz, A. (2003) 'The native informant: Fouad Ajami is the Pentagon's favourite Arab', *The Nation*, 28 April. Available at www.thenation.com/article/native-informant/; accessed 29 June 2017.
Sifaoui, M. (2015) *Pourquoi l'islamisme séduit-il? Éléments de réponse*. Paris: Armand Colin.
Silverstein, P.A. (2004) *Algeria in France: Transpolitics, Race and Nation*. Bloomington, IN: Indiana University Press.

Skinner, Q. (1969) 'Meaning and Understanding in the History of Ideas', *History and Theory*, 8 (1), pp. 3–53.

Smith, S. (2004) 'Louis Althusser (1918–90)'. In J. Simons (ed.) *Contemporary Critical Theorists: From Lacan to Said*. Edinburgh: Edinburgh University Press, pp. 51–67.

Sotinel, T. (2017) '"Islam pour mémoire": un voyage inachevé dans la culture musulmane', *Le Monde*, 21 March. Available at www.lemonde.fr/cinema/article/2017/03/21/islam-pour-memoire-un-voyage-inacheve-dans-la-culture-musulmane_5098019_3476.html; accessed 29 June 2017.

Staudigl, M. and J.W. Alvis (2016) 'Phenomenology and the post-secular turn: reconsidering the "return of the religious"', *International Journal of Philosophical Studies*, 24 (5), pp. 589–599.

Syrotinski, M. (2007) *Deconstruction and the Postcolonial at the Limits of Theory*. Liverpool: Liverpool University Press.

Taylor, C. (2007) *A Secular Age*. Cambridge, MA: Belknap Press of Harvard University Press.

Teilhard de Chardin, P. (1969) *Comment je crois*. Paris: Seuil.

Teti, A. (2014) 'Orientalism as a form of Confession', *Foucault Studies*, 17, pp. 193–212.

Tevanian, P. (2015) 'Le ver et le fruit: lettre ouverte à mon collègue Abdennour Bidar, marchand de fascisme à visage spirituel', *LMSI: Les Mots sont importants*, 20 November. Available at http://lmsi.net/Le-ver-et-le-fruit; accessed 11 April 2016.

Tissot, S. (2014) 'Réflexions critiques sur le "vivre ensemble"' [blog], *Mediapart*, 17 January. Available at https://blogs.mediapart.fr/eniloc-mariposa/blog/170114/sylvie-tissot-reflexions-critiques-sur-le-vivre-ensemble; accessed 26 March 2019.

Todorov, T. (2010) *The Fear of Barbarians: Beyond the Clash of Civilizations*. Cambridge: Polity Press.

Touraine, A. and F. Khosrokhavar (2000) *La Recherche de soi: dialogue sur le sujet*. Paris: Fayard.

Triandafyllidou, A., T. Modood and N. Meer (eds) (2011) *European Multiculturalisms: Cultural, Religious and Ethnic challenges*. Edinburgh: Edinburgh University Press.

Turner, B. (ed.) (2010) *The New Blackwell Companion to the Sociology of Religion*. Oxford: Blackwell Publishing.

van Houtum, H. (2010) 'Human Blacklisting: The Global Apartheid of the EU's External Border Regime' *Environment and Planning D: Society and Space*, 28 (6), pp. 957–976.

Vécrin, A. (2016) 'Malek Chebel, l'amoureux de l'islam', *Libération*, 13 November. Available at www.liberation.fr/debats/2016/11/13/malek-chebel-l-amoureux-de-l-islam_1528098; accessed 09 March 2017.

de Vries, H. and L.E. Sullivan. (2006) *Political Theologies: Public Religions in a Post-Secular World*. New York: Fordham University Press.

Watkin, C. (2011) *Difficult Atheism: Post-Theological Thinking in Alain Badiou, Jean-Luc Nancy and Quentin Meillassoux*. Edinburgh: Edinburgh University Press.

Watt, W.M. (1957) *Muhammad at Mecca*. Oxford: Oxford University Press.

Watt, W.M. (1958) *Muhammad at Medina*. Oxford: Oxford University Press.

Winter, B. (2008) *Hijab and the Republic: Uncovering the French Headscarf Debate*. Syracuse, NY: Syracuse University Press.

Wodak, R. (ed.) (2013) *Critical Discourse Analysis*. London: Sage.

Zemmour, E. (2014) *Le Suicide français*. Paris: Albin Michel.

Zemouri, A. (2005) *Faut-il faire taire Tariq Ramadan?* Paris: Editions Archipel.

Internet sources

Abdelwahab Meddeb's personal webpage: www.abdelwahab-meddeb.com/biographie-abdelwahab-meddeb/
Abdennour Bidar's personal webpage: http://abdennourbidar.fr/
Centre de prévention contre les dérives sectaires liées à l'islam (CPDSI): www.cpdsi.fr/
Centre Sésame – Centre de Culture Spirituelle: http://centre-sesame.com/projet/
Dounia Bouzar's personal webpage: www.bouzar-expertises.fr/
Lallab webpage: www.lallab.org/
Malek Chebel's Noor Review webpage: www.noorrevue.fr/
UN Universal Declaration of Human Rights: www.un.org/en/universal-declaration-human-rights/

French government websites

Legislation Database (Legifrance): www.legifrance.gouv.fr/
Observatoire de la laïcité: www.gouvernement.fr/missions-de-l-observatoire-de-la-laicite
Ministère de l'Intérieur: www.interieur.gouv.fr/

Television programmes

Ce soir ou jamais (2008) 'L'islam a-t-il besoin d'etre guéri?', France 3 Télévision, 30 January.

Index

alterity 29, 48, 54
Althusser, Louis 15–17, 89, 115, 118
anti-racism (anti-racist struggle) 107, 126, 128
  see also racism
apostasy 94–96
Arab Spring 34, 147
Arkoun, Mohammed 10, 65, 88, 117, 132, 165
atheism 139, 141–142, 146, 154, 155
  atheist (Muslim, thought) 9–10, 17, 21–23, 30, 46, 48–49, 62, 109, 136, 139, 141, 143, 168

Bakhtin, Mikhail 16–17, 19n.11, 22, 47, 128n.2, 142, 146
banlieues 76, 84n.3, 110, 118
blasphemy 58, 95, 96
Bourdieu, Pierre 12–13, 20–22, 36, 46, 49, 54, 102, 125
burqa 2, 8, 42, 53, 74, 126

Catholicism (Catholic Church) 4, 84n.2, 119
CFCM *see* Conseil français du culte musulman
Charlie Hebdo (attack) 2–3, 5, 17, 47, 158
Christianity 61, 81, 86, 90
clash of civilisations 4, 33, 36, 38, 45, 59, 62, 76, 132, 143, 159
colonialism 17, 25, 32, 33, 35
  see also postcolonialism
communautarisme 4, 91, 98, 136
Conseil français du culte musulman (CFCM) 48, 51n.14, 97, 98, 110, 116, 119, 120–121, 124–125, 146

democracy 5, 7, 24, 34–35, 37, 40, 91, 96, 119
de-radicalisation 8, 9, 126, 163, 168, 169
discrimination 73, 77, 96, 99, 100, 109, 122, 125, 136, 169
Durkheim, Émile 61, 90

education 15, 16, 21, 25, 52, 60, 63, 109, 112, 113, 137, 144, 164
equality 5, 10, 15, 38, 45, 59, 62, 69, 85, 94, 100, 104, 107, 111–113, 115, 117, 123, 125, 133, 135, 136, 137, 143, 146–148
exclusion 7, 25, 77, 96, 169
existentialism 11, 12, 129, 130, 147

feminism 44, 100, 101, 107, 109, 126–128, 169
finitude 132, 137, 141, 145, 147, 151–152, 154–155, 157
Foucault, Michel 13, 15, 17, 21, 145
fraternity 133, 136–137, 143, 146–147, 158–159
Front National 4, 5, 18n.5, 45, 48, 98
  see also Rassemblement National

gender 5, 15, 45, 90, 113, 115, 117, 121, 123, 137
Gramsci, Antonio 9, 162, 169

hadith 69, 72, 85, 104, 113–114
headscarf 1–3, 10, 70, 74, 85, 97, 99, 107, 108, 113
hijab 31, 42
Hollande, François 3

Index

humanism 12, 52, 59, 66, 69, 73, 76, 100, 130–134, 137, 140, 144–145, 147, 148, 153, 159
human rights 41, 69, 75, 95, 100, 133, 147, 161

ijtihad 59, 63–65, 72–73, 101
Ikhwan as-Safa 68, 71, 72
imam(s) 49, 59, 65–66, 94, 96, 117, 127, 135–136, 146
immigration 3, 5, 18n.5, 92, 143
inequality 43, 45, 99, 112
Islamophobia 25, 45, 100, 122, 126, 160, 165

jihad 24, 63, 66, 77, 78, 103, 138–140, 163
Judaism 61, 81

khalifat 59, 76, 95, 101, 148, 149, 153

Lamrabet, Asma 127
liberty 4, 95, 100–101, 108, 133, 135, 136, 137, 143, 146–148

Macron, Emmanuel 98, 163
Maghreb 32, 44, 87, 91, 92, 110, 122, 124, 168
Marche pour l'égalité et contre le racisme 110, 116, 119
Mernissi, Fatima 113, 127
Mohammed (Prophet) 10, 55, 57, 71, 80–84, 97, 140
mosque(s) 4, 10, 49, 64, 66, 110, 117, 141–142
Mutazilite(s) 58–59, 68, 71, 136, 148

niqab 2, 42, 126

Observatoire de la laïcité 8, 11, 18n.8, 107, 129, 163
Orientalism 13–14, 20, 49, 50, 64, 145, 153

pluralism 7, 28–29, 31, 34, 38, 72, 74, 90, 95

postcolonialism 25
  postcolonial legacies 122, 136, 169
  postcolonial women 124

racism 122, 126
  see also anti-racism
radicalisation 8, 11, 121–122, 125, 126, 169
  see also de-radicalisation
Rassemblement National 18n.5
rationality 67–68, 70
reform (reformist movements, Islamic) 10, 32, 49, 54, 63–73, 76, 87, 91–94, 96, 101, 104, 130–137, 147, 164
religiosity 8, 30, 61, 71, 73, 87, 89, 90–91, 93, 102, 135, 144

Said, Edward 4, 13, 25, 33, 37, 46, 49, 153
saints 28–29, 42–43, 87
Sarkozy, Nicolas 3, 4, 53, 119, 124
subjectivity 10, 52–61, 64, 68, 73, 75–76, 101
submission 11–12, 15, 44, 59–62, 73, 116, 129, 146–149
Stasi, Bernard (Stasi Commission) 2, 97, 116, 123–124
Sufi Islam 23, 29, 38, 46, 71, 73, 87
Sufism 28, 29, 51n.8
  see also Sufi Islam

translation (cultural) 12, 19n.11, 36, 52, 67, 130–131, 140, 146, 149, 153, 157, 159, 160
Tunisian Revolution 29, 34–36, 41

Ummah 54, 59, 61–63, 100–101, 112
Union des organisations islamiques de France (UOIF) 48, 97, 98
universalism 15, 37, 75, 100, 105, 130, 141, 150, 154, 162, 169
UOIF *see* Union des organisations islamiques de France

Wadud, Amina 101, 127–128

EU authorised representative for GPSR:
Easy Access System Europe, Mustamäe tee 50,
10621 Tallinn, Estonia
gpsr.requests@easproject.com